Elizabeth Rundle Charles

Tales and Sketches of Christian Life in Different Lands and Ages

Elizabeth Rundle Charles

Tales and Sketches of Christian Life in Different Lands and Ages

ISBN/EAN: 9783337079208

Printed in Europe, USA, Canada, Australia, Japan

Cover: Foto ©ninafisch / pixelio.de

More available books at **www.hansebooks.com**

MAIA AND CLEON.

Tales and Sketches.

TALES AND SKETCHES

OF

CHRISTIAN LIFE,

IN

Different Lands and Ages.

BY THE AUTHOR OF
"THE CHRONICLE OF THE SCHONBERG-COTTA FAMILY."

NEW YORK:
ROBERT CARTER & BROTHERS,
530 BROADWAY,
1865.

BY THE SAME AUTHOR:

THE CRIPPLE OF ANTIOCH. 16mo
THE MARTYRS OF SPAIN. 16mo.

Henry Beyer, Stereotyper, 19 Chatham St., N. Y.

PREFACE.

In writing this little book, I have not felt as if addressing strangers, much less that grave tribunal conjured up by the phrase, "the public;" but simply as if speaking to my friends, and the members of my own family, one by one, of the things we love best. To them I now offer it.

I have not sought to give an outline of the corruptions and controversies of the Church, but of the Life which has at all times pierced through the snows of un-Christian and anti-Christian systems;—of those trees planted by the Rivers of Waters whose leaf has never withered, and with which the hardest and driest times were always "due seasons" for "bringing forth fruit."

Some of the Sketches are historical as to persons and incidents, and some are not. In the "Italian Reformers," only the conversations are imaginary; in the first and third parts of the "Sketches of the Moravians," only the first conversation. The other Tales are merely *founded* on the facts of general history.

In looking over these pages, and thinking of the exceeding grandeur of the realities on which they so feebly touch, I almost shrink from what I have attempted; yet, are not these high truths the very atmosphere of the renewed life—the daily bread of God's "little children?" and is it not as unwise to forget that we are each given a lamp to carry, as to imagine that the light is in us?

Should these Sketches be the means of pointing out to any the inexhaustible Treasure of Truth contained in the Bible—of leading one unsettled heart to the rest of the "single eye," the "straight path," and the "lowest place"—of bringing one, still in bondage, into the peace and freedom of the "child"—of arousing one languid child to the blessed ministrations of discipleship—of reminding any who are "cumbered about much serving," to seek the calm strength given to those who sit at His feet, and hear His words—my most earnest wishes will be fulfilled.

We serve One who rewardeth the cup of cold water, and "upbraideth not."

At His feet I lay the unworthy offering. May that touch and that Holy Spirit who dwelleth with us for ever paralyze every error contained in it, and give life to every truth! With Him I leave it. Let Him do with it what seemeth Him good.

CONTENTS.

MAIA AND CLEON. A TALE OF THE EGYPTIAN CHURCH IN THE THIRD CENTURY.

SKETCHES FROM THE HISTORY OF THE REFORMATION IN ITALY.

EXTRACTS FROM THE DIARY OF BROTHER BARTHOLOMEW, A MONK OF THE ABBEY OF MARIENTHAL, IN THE ODENWALD, IN THE TWELFTH CENTURY.

SKETCHES OF THE UNITED BRETHREN OF BOHEMIA AND MORAVIA.

MAIA AND CLEON.

CHAPTER I.

It was summer, and mid-day. In the swarming city of Alexandria, the rich were resting in their inner chambers, the craftsmen were laboring drowsily in the shade of their open workshops, and the hum of the great city came faint in the quiet of noon to the villa of the old Roman general, Caius Sertorius. The veteran lay asleep on a couch in the portico after his mid-day meal, while two children played in the garden at his feet.

It was a stiff old Roman garden, arranged with a precision as military as the taste of a veteran grown gray in the exercise of Roman discipline could make it; ranks of cypresses, and files of palms, and cohorts of flowering shrubs, marshaled around a marble fountain, and flanked at regular intervals by obelisks and statues —the whole surrounded by a terraced wall, to which one of the mouths of the Nile served as a fosse. But nature did all she could to spoil the plan; not our plodding northern nature, with slow industry weaving out her designs from year to year, but the impetuous nature of the south, doing the work of a season in a day, working fairy wonders in a night, garlanding the stone gods and heroes with living wreaths of glory, festooning the tall trunks with vine leaves, calling forth, unbidden, sweet flowers to drink the sparkling drops which fell from the fountain, and making everywhere fantastic tracery of light and shade.

The children were soon tired with play. The boy leaned against the pedestal of a statue of Diana; the little girl sat on the ground to weave a crown of flowers—her white dress, with its wide purple border, shining in the shade of the cypresses, and her sunny eyes sparkling, as from time to time she flung the long hair back from her forehead, and looked up in her companion's face.

They were not brother and sister: their forms were cast in a different mould. He was Greek, and she was Italian. The first impression of his form, in repose—the long, soft, dark eye, the slight frame—might have been that of languor; but the firmly-set lips contradicted the languid calm of the eye; the slight, muscular frame when in action seemed merely a condensation of strength; and even in the eye itself, if you watched its expression, there was more of the slumber of power than of the lack of it—more of the dreaming of unawakened energy than of the indolence of weakness. She was still a child, the flower of the old Roman's heart—the music of his life—bright and joyous—without a care for to-morrow, or a tear for yesterday. The boy was telling her old Greek stories of the gods and heroes—how in the old times the gods walked amongst men—how they set their love on some, and took them up into heaven to be stars.

"I hope they will never love you or me, Cleon," said the little girl, in a low voice.

"Why, Maia?" he asked.

"Because I would much rather be children like we are, than stars, all alone in the cold sky, away from every one."

"But they give light, Maia, and every one sees and worships them, and they are amongst the gods."

"I would like much better to hear you tell stories," said Maia, "and play with you, and sit on my father's knee, than to be amongst the strange great gods whom we have never seen."

"That is because you are a woman, Maia, and have no ambition."

Maia sat rebuked, and wondered what ambition meant.

Then Cleon told her of the wars of the gods and the Titans—how the rebellious, vanquished giants lay writhing under the mountains; sometimes, in still nights, people had heard their groans echoing through the hollow hills, or quivering mournfully through the trees when no air was stirring—and on summer noons, when everything was quiet, had felt the ground heave with their struggles to get free.

"Poor giants!" sighed the soft-hearted Maia, "I am so sorry for them, Cleon; will they never be let out of prison?"

"I do not know," said Cleon.

"What did they do," asked Maia, "to be so punished?"

"They rebeled against the gods, and wanted to sit upon their thrones; but the gods were the stronger, and so they lost the battle."

"Were they very wicked?"

"I have heard that they were kind to men, and that it is for trying to steal some gift from heaven for men, that one of them suffers so."

"Oh, Cleon! how could the gods do so!" exclaimed Maia, indignantly; "I love the poor giants!—can we not help them?"

Cleon was silent. "There are men too, Maia, that suffer unjustly," he said at length. "My father's family was great in Greece when your people came one day to the city where we lived. I never heard of them before. We had done them no wrong. I remember that night now, though I was a very little child. My mother had just laid me to sleep. My father was resting in the hall, for he had been hunting, and was tired. My only sister, who was many years older than I was, was singing sweet songs to him—I never heard any like them since. A great noise awoke me—screams, and threats, and cries: I hear them now. My mother caught me up in her arms, but rough hands seized me and tore me from her. I was too frightened to see much more; but I think I heard my father's voice, and saw my mother bending over him; I think his hands were bound, and he was bleeding. And I remember my sister Alce's look as they dragged her away—I remember it now, how she kissed me! She did not cry nor struggle, but let them quietly bind her hands, and told me not to be afraid. Then I remember no more until I came here with you."

Maia let her wreath fall, and her bright eyes filled with tears. She rose and laid her little coaxing hands in his—

"Cleon, dear Cleon, I am your little sister now."

He took her in his arms, and seated her on the pedestal against which he was leaning.

"But have you heard of them since, Cleon?" she asked.

"Never, Maia."

"And you do not know at all where they are —or what is become of them?"

"Some people say there is a happy world for the good when they die—but I do not know," he said, gloomily.

"But I do, Cleon," interposed the little girl, undoubtingly. "Nurse says there are green fields and flowergardens where my mother is, whom I never saw."

"And every one glides about pale and cold and restless, and talks of what has been, and can not be brought back again. Oh, do not let us talk of it, Maia! It is not home—it is not life—they can not love, and work, and fight as we do; what joy can there be for the dead?"

Maia was silent for a moment; then she said—"No, do not let us talk of that. Tell me about the sun-god, and the happy nymphs in the streams and the woods, and under the sea—and the dear, kind moon—those are the gods I love, Cleon; talk to me of them, and I will finish this crown and give it to Apollo to-morrow. Perhaps, as a reward, he will send a warm sunbeam down to your mother in the fields of the dead."

Cleon smiled incredulously, but he complied with her request, until Caius Sertorius awoke and came down to join his darling.

"O father!" she exclaimed, "Cleon has been telling me such wonderful stories about the gods and goddesses!"

"It is time Cleon should be doing something better than telling stories to children," remarked Sertorius gravely.

Cleon bit his lip, and Maia colored and pleaded—"But he has been so busy all day at the school in Alexandria—and the masters, you know, told you the other day he might be a philosopher if he liked."

The old Roman had no great respect for school-masters, and no very clear distinction in his mind between thinking and dreaming—intellectual labor being to him little better than a kind of busy idleness, very well for Greeks and slaves, but totally beneath men who might rise to distinction in the state.

"There is no philosophy worth having," he said gruffly, "but the philosophy which will make a man bear pain and meet death bravely; and that is soon learnt by a stout heart. Bear nothing you can avoid, murmur at nothing you can not—that is a soldier's philosophy. Cleon must do something better than split hairs with the Jews and Platonists of Alexandria."

Maia was silenced for the time; but when her father sat at his light meal of honey and bread and fruit that evening, with his little girl beside him, to amuse him with her prattle, she recurred to the conversation of the afternoon, and propounded to him Cleon's theological difficulty about the relative merits of the quarrel between the gods and Titans.

The old Roman was no theologian, but he was a devout believer in his country's gods—or, at least, a devout believer in the expediency of upholding them—and he was proportionately horrified at the presumption of the inquiry.

"The gods of Rome are strong and wise," he said, "and do what they think right. They are the friends of the brave; they help those who help themselves." Then a pause ensued, after which Maia was despatched to bed, with an injunction to make an offering on the morrow in the Temple of Jupiter.

But the question she had started hastened the settlement of Cleon's fate. "Those Greeks can never be quiet; they can not even let the gods alone. If care is not taken, that boy will be turning Christian, like his sister Alce. But that shall never be—by all the gods of the Capitol!—the lad is too noble for that. He shall go off to the wars in the North to-morrow."

Cleon was summoned, and, in a laconic conference, told of his destination. The old man gave the accustomed kiss to his child in her little bed—for she had no mother; and at an early hour the family retired to rest.

"Maia!" exclaimed Cleon the next morning, bursting joyfully into the hall, where she sat spinning her daily task—Nurse Julia having left her for a few minutes alone—"Maia! I am to be a man next March; I am going off to the army to-morrow!"

Maia let her distaff fall on her knees, but she said nothing.

"I am going to the army of the North," he continued, "where the great Decius commands; they say he is the bravest general Rome has: and I am going to fight against the barbarians, whom my people hate as much as yours; and, Maia, I will bring you home such presents—bracelets of gold, and necklaces such as we see the Gothic captives wear; think of your wearing my spoils, dear Maia, when we meet again!"

Maia had resumed her distaff, and had been

working with unusual diligence whilst he spoke, but now she hid her face in her hands, and burst into tears. He tried to comfort her—he talked of his great hopes and projects—the glory he might gain—the trophies he would bring to her; but Maia refused to be comforted, and at length she dashed away her distaff, and ran from the room.

"What has made my pet cry?" asked Nurse, as she sat sobbing passionately on her little bed.

"Cleon, Cleon is going to be a soldier!" she murmured, hiding her face in Nurse's shoulder. Nurse applied her usual nursery medicines;—he would not be killed—he would come back on a beautiful horse—a great lord, with slaves and treasures, and she should be a great lady.

"It is not that!" said Maia, indignantly, suddenly stopping her tears; "I do not want his necklaces and bracelets; I do not care for his going away—if he only would not be so glad about it!"

"Well, I would be glad about it too, if I were you," said Nurse.

Maia thought she would try; and, thanks to her indignant heroism, and a game of play, the last evening with Cleon passed merrily.

But the next morning, when she stole out alone into the garden, and found the little ship Cleon had made for her lying on the steps where he had played with her, and her doll beside it, she felt as if the doll was the only friend she had left in the world, and hugged it, and began to cry bitterly. Her father found her there, and taking her on his knee—

"Now, be a brave little Roman maiden," he said: "the little girls of old Rome used to cheer their brothers, and sing them war-songs when they went to join the armies."

Maia felt rather angry with the little girls of ancient Rome, and the sobs did not stop. Then Sertorius spoke of the glory and greatness Cleon was to achieve. The sobs only came faster. The old soldier was puzzled sorely what line of consolation to adopt. At length he said: "And you shall make crowns of flowers and garlands, and offer them to the gods for Cleon's safe return."

"Will that help Cleon?" she asked.

"The old Romans did it," said the Stoic, evasively, for his faith in the hearing of the gods was not very strong.

"Then I will do it," said Maia, drying her tears. And between the idea of being like an old Roman matron, and the thought of helping Cleon with the gods, and the fact of Cleon himself being rather cast down when the time of parting came, the child contrived to take leave of her old playfellow, in a way that might not altogether have disgraced a playfellow of Brutus.

CHAPTER II.

Had all the to-morrows which were to intervene before they met again risen before Maia as she parted from her playfellow, her philosophy would have sunk beneath the burden; but happily, life only presents us with a series of to-days; and to Maia, with her healthy household occupations and her happy household cares, the days tripped lightly on, making music as they went; each, as it passed, opening for her some fresh flower.

So she sat in the shade of her quiet home, ministering to her father and her household, and looked out thence into the boundless, unknown world, and listened and learned, pondering many things in her heart—and grew silently into womanhood.

With Cleon, the training and the result had been different. The world, which was such an unexplored territory to Maia, had been his home and his teacher. Northern climates, and the rough discipline of the camp, had moulded his frame to manly strength; the battles, and toils, and tumults, and sudden dangers, and perplexing hazards of continued warfare, had braced his will and nerved his mind to master them. Placed in a sphere where command involved peril and required talent, his clear foresight and ready self-possession had early earned for him the toils and glories of military rank.

At length, however, a pause in the war set him at liberty to return to Alexandria.

What the history of his soul had been meanwhile, the following fragments may show:—

EXTRACTS FROM CLEON'S DIARY.

I am once more in my old childish home! I write in the portico where old Caius Sertorius used to rest in the summer evenings. Before me is the garden where Maia and I used to play together.

The trees are grown—Maia must be grown. I am changed. I seem to have lived ages since then. I wonder if she has changed as much! She will return from Italy in a month.

How strange it is to come back to old places, and find nature still treading the same quiet round as when we left, still bringing back her old round of seasons and flowers, and days and stars—and never getting tired of them—ever the same, and ever new; whilst we have passed through seasons which never return;—we always advancing—she always revolving; and yet we, with all our progress, never getting beyond her unvarying circle. She is very great.

Is she, then, the mirror of the Infinite, or only

the veil hemming in our spirits from the Infinite beyond? *What* Infinite beyond? If a veil—if this outward world, and this mortal life, be but a veil—are they a glittering ice-crust thrown in pity over the abyss of darkness, or a shroud of light hiding from us the eternal day of the stars and the heavens?

From us! And what are we? Stars in the night of eternity, or bubbles on the sea of time! Are *we*, or is nature, nearest the Supreme?

These guessing, doubting, trembling, daring spirits of ours—we, who embrace the universe like gods, and perish in the dust like beasts—we, whose thoughts soar to infinity, and whose hands can not make a flower!—we, who can kill thousands of our fellow-men, yet can not restore a dead insect to life—*what are we?* We are not the source of life—it is elsewhere. Where? In nature? Life is teeming, overflowing, flooding around us everywhere; myriads of new living beings are born every day; where, then, is the spring of all this life which flows around us everywhere, and which we can nowhere touch? O to find it, and bathe in it! But what is life?—what is death? Are they not forms of the same idea—phases of the same existence—the clothing and unclothing of God? Life, death, sorrow, joy, love, pain,—are they, then, all shows and phantoms, dreams of a summer day or a winter night? Are we ourselves drops fallen at random from "the abyss of life," destined, after filtering a while through this lower

2*

earth, one day to be absorbed into it again? If this be so, then why thus fall? Is everything thus without aim and without meaning—a mere chaos of confusion? And what is the difference between this chaos and the abyss of life? I, loving, struggling, fearing, hoping, *shall die!* and all my struggles, love, joy, fear, and hope, die with me—then I perish too: for what am I apart from them? Where is the distinction between being nothing, and a fragment of *something not myself?* What is such immortality better than annihilation?

And virtue, crime, the conflicts and victories of noble hearts, the crimes of base natures, the failures of weak ones—have they all no end, no meaning? are they all the transitory phases of some fragment of the Godhead? The Godhead subject to suffering and crime! how can this be?—how can weakness flow from strength, and death from life?

Are there, then, as they say in the East, *two sources* of being?—two forces at work in the universe—good and evil? If so, which is the stronger?

And if there are two sources, there must be two ends. To which does nature belong?—to which do we tend? Is this earth, and are our hearts, the battle-field of the evil and the good? Are we, like nature, a mere battle-field—or are we ourselves *combatants?* If so, we must take our part in the conflict, in which there may be triumph or defeat. Of the two ends, and the two powers, we may choose one. But what is our armor—what our plan of war?

The Stoics say, "Renounce!" Renounce what? —Joy, nature, all the heart delights in! What is that but death before the time?

O for light! O for some one whom to ask for light? I have sought school after school of philosophy, but none of them can satisfy. Some say the desire of satisfaction is childish curiosity, impatience, crime; that the end of life is to endure. I could endure much for an end; but to live to endure, and endure to live!—is there no answer to the soul's question but this?—no employment for all the quick and restless faculties of body and soul but this—*to do no harm?*

Then, I have sought to drown this inward strife in outward tumult—in society, battle, adventure, and daring deeds. There is excitement and content for all the faculties, for a time in these. But in the after-silence, the old questions come back louder than ever—*To what end is all this?* What matters it to me, or to the world, whether the Goths or the Romans tread down the nations— whether the crimes of barbarism, or of corrupt civilization, gain the upper hand—whether Philip the Arabian, or Decius, be the slave of the Pretorians and the master of the world? *To what end is my life?* I ask—and the answer never comes!

The project of Caius Sertorius had not succeeded; the old question of the origin of evil—

the quarrel between the gods and Titans—was not yet settled, nor was it forgotten.

Cleon had fought many battles, and gained many honors—was high in the army for so young a man; but one conflict remained undecided: one thing—*the* one thing—he had not gained.

"I had half forgotten my promise," exclaimed Marcellinus, a young military friend of Cleon's as they were idling, one day, on one of the quays of Alexandria, " to be present at a feast, at the house of the rich merchant Papias. We must separate. Or, stay, he asked me the other day about you, and begged me to bring you to his house. Will you come?—the guests will not be numerous."

"I do not know him; and strangers are always intruders in small companies."

"Well—do as you like; the man is a Christian, but he is no fanatic, and he gives admirable entertainments."

Cleon hesitated; but curiosity at length prevailed, and he accompanied his friend. He had heard much of the Christians during his former studies at Alexandria, as a Jewish sect whose opinions bore some resemblance to those of the new Platonists, with an admixture of some new and strange superstition. He had heard of their sacred books, as containing, amid much incomprehensible mysticism, many excellent precepts. He had met them in the army, and on journeys, and had, on two or three occasions, been struck with their calm endurance of taunts, and their steadfast submission to any suffering rather than pay certain honors to the imperial ensigns. He knew, also, that they had a firm assurance of immortality, and spoke of their life in this world as merely a pilgrim's journey; and he was curious to see if this belief was real—how men lived who were assured of an endless life of joy or sorrow hereafter.

"Do you know many of these Christians, Marcellinus?" he asked, on the way.

"No. They used to shun the society of those who do not hold their peculiar opinions: and besides, they are, you know, for the most part, a poor and illiterate set. But the late emperors have been so tolerant, that they are able to traffic, and feast, and serve in the armies now, like other men, and some of them can enjoy life like reasonable beings."

"They believe they have had immortality revealed to them, do they not?" asked Cleon.

"I am no philosopher," was the reply, "and have not entered into their peculiar tenets; Papias never obtrudes them on his guests, and he gathers interesting people around him, and entertains well; the rest is his concern, not mine. They say our brave emperor, Decius, hates the Christians cordially, and intends to suppress them; if that is the case, either I shall have to give up Papias, or Papias his peculiarities. I know little of them, except that they call one another *brother*, and believe they are sure of some Elysium when they die."

They had now reached the house. Over the inner door was a Greek inscription in gold letters—"*Here we have no continuing city; we seek one to come, whose builder and maker is God.*" And below—"*Our citizenship is in heaven.*" The sublime words arrested Cleon's eye. "What manner of men," he thought, "must these be? how calmly raised above all the storms of time, and the petty perplexities of life, assured of an endless life of joy!"

The merchant met them at the entrance of the hall, and greeted Cleon with marked courtesy. On issuing from the bath, the guests were provided with splendid robes, and conducted to the dining-hall.

Everything was arranged as customary in great Roman houses. The couches, placed round a semicircular table, were richly carved and adorned with gold, silver, gems, and fragrant woods, and cushioned with silks, and fine linen of rich Syrian dyes. Fair Spanish slaves crowned the guests with garlands, and sprinkled them with costly perfumes; all kinds of Roman delicacies succeeded each other at the table; and in the intervals of conversation, slaves danced to the sound of soft music. The air was fragrant with aromatic scents from India, and cooled by the play of fountains in the court, in the centre of the house, which was divided from the hall by a silken curtain. The walls were covered with frescoes by Greek artists.

Some few peculiarities Cleon observed, but did not object to. No libations were offered before the feast, which simply implied an absence of respect to the popular gods—nothing being substituted for them, out of consideration to the religious differences of the company. There were no statues to the gods or heroes. The cups and vases were engraven with doves, palm-branches, and monograms, instead of the usual heathen fables, and the subjects of the frescoes were either from recent Roman history, or groups of symbolic figures, which Cleon did not comprehend, but which, as a resident in mystic Egypt, exited in him no astonishment.

The conversation was animated and intelligent—political changes were touched on lightly—commercial prospects were discussed eagerly—while the rising inundation of the Nile (the "weather" of Egypt) was the subject of much speculation. The theatres and public games were avoided—out of compliment to the supposed prejudices of the host—until he introduced the subject by mentioning a favorite actor. The object of Papias' seemed to be to avoid all suspicion of peculiarity, and he succeeded admirably,—the whole entertainment being as easy and luxurious as in the best heathen families. Only, from time to time, the words rang strangely in Cleon's ears

—" Our citizenship is in heaven." At any rate, the naturalization of the host seemed very complete; there was nothing in his mode of speaking or living to betray his fatherland.

When, however, the slaves withdrew, Cleon expected more intimate subjects would have been introduced. The conversation did indeed take a more philosophical turn. The guests were of many shades of opinion—a Jewish Platonist, a Platonic Jew, a Gnostic, an Eastern merchant, and Marcellinus, who was of the "getting on" religion, quite tolerant alike of truth and error; but all being men of great liberality, who wore their opinions as ornaments rather than girded them on as armor, these differences only served to give a refreshing stir and coolness to the atmosphere.

Of course, in such an assembly, earnest words of Christian faith would have been altogether discordant, as deep organ-tones in a concert of flutes. Papias was far too polished a man to have obtruded them; besides, his faith was hereditary. He spoke much in praise of Plato, and compared his writings with the Christian Plato, John of Galilee—occasionally alluding to some of the Christian doctrines, but in such a veil of philosophical terms as could neither offend nor instruct any one. He spoke of the Reason or Word of God, of the human soul as an emanation from the Highest, destined to return to it; and Cleon listened, and, concluding Christianity to be a kind of modified Platonism, wondered why it should be persecuted as a *religio illicita*, and not rather left to itself as a philosophical sect. As he sat in the place of honor, at the centre of the table, on the right hand of the host, he once, when the conversation had swelled into a chorus, expressed something of this wonder to Papias.

"You see the government does not understand us," was the reply. "They judge from certain ignorant fanatics, and act accordingly; but they are learning to know us better, and for many years they have left us in peace."

"There are, then, still these fanatics amongst you?"

"There will always be men of exaggerated and distorted piety in every sect. Spiritualism and asceticism are matters of natural constitution: such conformations of soul are the natural curiosities of the spiritual world, peculiar to no sect, and characteristic of no faith."

"But, may I ask, are those words I saw inscribed in gold in your portico from your sacred books—'*Our citizenship is in heaven*'?"

"They are; but colonists may make themselves at home."

"True," thought Cleon, "if they are not patriots!" But he said, "You have, then, among you, men who keep to the letter of this rule?"

"Yes, as there are mere literalists among the Jews—men of exaggerated enthusiasm, or men of mere *faith*, who have not attained to the wisdom of the perfect."

Cleon looked surprised: "I had been told your sacred doctrines were common to all. You have, then, an initiated class."

"There are certain doctrines common to all, but the poor and illiterate can not be expected to attain to the heights of ecstatic contemplation. We have what we call the clergy and the laity, the philosopher and the child. For myself, I am a man of business, but I intend one day to devote myself to these things."

"Where do your philosophers live?"

"Dionysius, our bishop, teaches the catechumens frequently at his own house; we have the catechetical school where Clement and Origen once lectured; and in the porticoes and on the quays, you may occasionally meet with some of our teachers, clad and surrounded like Socrates of old."

The conversation again became general, and ere long the guests arose and departed.

Papias reflected complacently when the feast was over,—"At all events, that young Greek officer will not henceforth conclude that we of the Christian Church are a set of bigots and fools."

Cleon reflected mournfully as he went home— "After all, there does not seem so much distinction between Christianity and other philosophical systems; it is not, then, to it that I must look for any solution to the riddle of life."

Is it not ever thus? The Church loses her power of attraction when she relinquishes her atmosphere of repulsion. The profession which will not offend the careless, can not teach the earnest. If the salt have lost its savor, it can not heal the bitter waters.

On the steps of the house, as Cleon descended them, a lame old man was sitting, as if in expectation of something. The young Greek asked what he waited for. "The master of the house," he replied, "gives me food from time to time, for I am disabled from working, and my family are many and young." A servant came out as they spoke, bringing with him a basket of fragments, the relics of the sumptuous feast. "Have you any claim on the rich merchant, then?" asked Cleon; "are you a client or a relation?" "No claim," replied the old man, "but that we are brethren in the Church of God."

"The ties of brotherhood can not be very strong in a family in which one brother is content with throwing the crumbs of his superfluity to another," thought Cleon. "I suppose, like other things, it is only a name."

CHAPTER III.

THE return of Caius Sertorius and his child was delayed, and Cleon resolved to set forth on a tour to some of the recesses of Egypt—the solitudes then beginning to be peopled with anomalous societies of solitaries, the ruins of religions as obsolete to him as to us—the beautiful, quiet places of the valley of the Nile. He lingered some days with the strange Jewish colony on the banks of the lake Mœris, the Therapeutic mystics—the models, probably, of the monks who afterwards thronged the Thebaid.

He conversed with them in their lonely huts; he partook of their evening meal of bread and salt and water, taken in darkness and silence, lest the sun should be polluted by witnessing the nourishment of the despised body, the slave of matter, and the enemy of heaven and the soul.

And on the Sabbath he saw the lonely devotees, men and women, leave their solitary cells, and join in the twilight in a solemn mystic dance, to the sound of wild music.

It was a strange scene, when the large Eastern moon came out shining in dim streaks on the dewy plain, and mirrored in long wavy lines of the lake, when the birds were hushed and all the stir of day was over, to see the white-robed devotees steal out one by one from the shadow of their low huts, until the solitary shore was covered with hundreds of them. Then the silence was broken by the slow swell of a monotonous chant from the men, answered from time to time by the clash of timbrels and other Eastern instruments from the women, rising at length, like the wind in a sudden storm, to a burst of wild and triumphant song. They were echoing, after the lapse of two thousand years, the song of triumph their fathers had sung on the borders of the Red Sea—"Sing ye to Jehovah! for he hath triumphed gloriously; the horse and his rider hath he thrown into the sea."

But to the Theraputæ this song had a deep symbolic meaning. The old national faith in the living God, the God of Abraham, Isaac, and Jacob, was gone, and with it the expectation of a personal Messiah; to them Egypt probably signified the enslaving power of sense and material things, the deliverance from which they sought by this life of renunciation and ascetic solitude.

It will easily be understood how a faith like this might be a stepping-stone to Christianity—to faith in Him who has delivered us from the bondage of corruption, and borne us safely through the Red Sea of death by His resurrection; but, unhappily, devotees such as these were not always content only to *receive;* and in the false spiritualism of such imperfect converts, lay the germ of more than one of the corruptions which subsequently prevailed in Christendom.

The scene and the symbols, however, made a deep impression on the young Platonist. What could this voluntary abandonment of all the joys of life mean, if the beings who practiced it were not immortal—if the world in which it was practiced was *all good?*

Thus musing and speculating, he rambled on through the broad valley of the Nile, now floating up the stream in some boat bound for the quarries of Upper Egypt, now falling in with some caravan of "Ishmaelitish merchants" from the East, or some stray party of Arab horsemen; and at times pursuing his way alone along the tangled banks of the river.

It was a wild and wonderful journey then as now; the old contest between the river and the desert resulting in the same singular contact of luxuriance and desolation, the same marvellous conquest of man over nature, and of time over man. Cities, whose shadows were like those of mountains, silent as the quarries from which they were hewn; gigantic single columns, which seemed as if they could only have been upheaved by an earthquake, left the sole relics of cities; temples, whose worship was as extinct as the worshipers; homes and busy haunts of men, whose domestic music now was the scream of wild birds, and the cry of the jackal and hyena. When had this transition come which converted the populous place into a waste? Had a sudden destruction come upon them, emptying hall and temple in some day of anguish? or had the curse of slow blight fallen on them, withering them away, and leaving some "last man" the sole inheritor of a thousand desolate homes, the sole priest of a dying religion in empty temples?

One day he had risen early to finish his day's journey in the cool of the morning. Saddling his horse, he bounded swiftly over the plain, his heart leaping with a delicious sense of freedom and strength. The startled birds flew whizzing and wheeling around him; flocks of the purple Nile-goose plunged, splashing and beathing their wings into the river; and where the deep drifts of silvery sand encroached on the living verdure, a bright gazelle would ever and anon start from the tangled underwood, and bound away into the desert. Or when he slackened his pace, birds of paradise would perch on the myrtles by his path, and he could hear the contented cooing of turtle-doves in the groves of flowering acacia, and see the bright eyes of green lizards gleam amongst the countless flowers on the banks; while the aromatic perfume of lemons, citrons, and oranges, floated through the clear air, and here and there the shafts of architectural-looking palm-trees shot up from the lower vegetation, with their capitals of leaves. Everything around him spoke of unwearied and salutary power, every faculty of every creature exercised to the full, in the fulness of life and enjoyment. Cleon himself felt free and strong as any amongst them, —a living power in the midst of life, a rejoicing being in the midst of myriads of rejoicing beings and he the king and the crown of them all. All perplexities and cares seemed blown away like unhealthy exhalations of night in the fragrant freshness of the morning. It was one of those moments when the soul seems to soar above the clouds, and on the clear and sunny height all earth-born mists float beneath it like silvery veils, and the thunder-storms of life are borne up to it in tones of music.

Was not nature, this glorious frame of outward things, this exulting chorus of rejoicing creatures, the *holy thing;* and man, with his low traffic and fierce strife, the spot on her unsullied vesture, the *unholy thing?* Was not this material world, after all, nearer God than we?

The shadow of a gigantic column fell upon his path, and, looking up, he found himself at the entrance of a ruined city. He passed silently by the silent portals, and leaping from his horse, left it to graze in the court of a deserted temple.

As he lay resting on the grass, he saw a dark robe moving in and out amongst a distant avenue of columns. In the desert the ties of common humanity are drawn tight, and Cleon hastened to greet the stranger. He was an old man, and returned his greeting with a prayer—"God be with thee, my son, and His peace!"

Cleon concluded him to be one of the mystic solitaries, who were no new phenomenon to him; but the wan yet dignified face of the old man, and the contrast between his keen eye and his subdued mien, interested him.

"Age needs care and comfort," he said; "you can not find these here."

"I came hither to avoid them," was the reply.

"Has life, then, no charms for you?"

"Too many. I dashed the cup from me when it was sweetest, and because it was sweet. I am a follower of Him who died upon the cross: only through crucifixion can we follow Him."

"You believe, then, that nature is only beautiful to seduce?"

"No, the world is good—God made it—but we are evil."

"You believe, then, that the body is the enemy of the soul?"

"We are our own enemies—body, soul, mind, all are corrupt."

"Then what escape is there for us?"

"In renunciation of the world, and contemplation of the Supreme. In looking on Him, we learn to love Him: in loving Him, we lose ourselves."

"But *what* must we renounce?"

"*All*—love, joy, hope, fear—all that makes life, life; always bearing about in the body the dying of the Lord Jesus, that hereafter His life may be manifested in our body."

"Did God, then, make us evil?"

"No; man fell from the image of God in which he was made. God is holy, man is sinful. Only by renouncing self can we be reunited to God."

Cleon paused. "This is terrible!"

"True. Flesh and blood can not endure it."

"But how fly self? I am as much myself in the desert as in the Forum: nay more, self expands like air to fill the vacuum."

"In the desert we are alone with God. Here amidst the ruins of men's works, and the desolation of men's homes, I learn, in the littleness of humanity, to trample on myself—in the ruins of time to trace the footsteps of eternity, and to adore the majesty of the Eternal."

"But it is awful," said Cleon, shuddering inwardly, "for the evil thing to be alone with the Holy One—for the dust to be face to face with the Almighty! The throng of men were surely better than such solitude?"

"The multitude of men," replied the solitary, "are but dust and sin like myself; one breath from the furnace of Heaven could melt them all to ashes; but there is One between me and God."

"Who is He?" asked Cleon, in a low voice.

"It is He who is the Son of God and the Son

of man, holy as the Holy One, yet made of one nature with us."

Two or three days Cleon remained in that ruined city, hearing and questioning the hermit. He left it then full of new and wonderful thoughts. Light had entered into his soul—a veiled light, indeed, still struggling with thick darkness—but nevertheless it was a gleam of the light which giveth life.

The hermit could not teach him Christianity as St. Paul or St. Peter taught it; he knew little of the *grace* of God, very little of the reconciliation it has made for man; yet Cleon returned through the valley of the Nile with other thoughts than those with which he had traversed it before, for he had learned to believe in a living, personal, *speaking*, and *hearing* God—whose image is to be found most truly in no "abyss of life," or vague sea of existence, but in the loving heart and the seeing intellect of man. He believed in the existence of evil as no mere attribute of matter, no transitory stain on the creation, no necessary eclipse in the phases of the light of heaven; but as *sin*—the plague of the heart of man, and of his own responsible nature. He believed man to be fallen from the holy image in which he was made, tempted by one who had fallen before from a greater height; alienate from God, and having in him the thing God can not tolerate. And dimly, as it were through a confused chaos of sights and sounds, he saw something of One standing between the sinner and the Holy One, who, in some mysterious manner, was to be the Way of restoration to him,—a painful way it must be, full of terror and conflict, and pain and peril—a way of sorrow and death, to be trodden with weary feet, bowed beneath heavy burdens; but still, for one bewildered and lost as he had been, it was much—we can scarcely conceive how much—to know that there was a living, personal God, and a way by which man might reach Him.

CHAPTER IV.

THE time at length came when Cleon could settle the question whether Maia were as much changed as himself.

She met him in the old garden, as joyous and fresh and beautiful as ever. She sang him the old songs, they laughed together over their old quarrels, and chatted over their old confidences—and many new ones. She seemed in all respects what she had been—a stranger might have marked no difference in their intercourse; but a reverence had sprung up between them, which, added to the old brotherly affection of their childhood, grew naturally into a deep and sacred love. She was his childish playmate with a sacred halo around her. Had Maia indeed met with the fate she dreaded—been loved by the gods, and made a star in the heavens—he could not have looked on her with a deeper reverence; but now his happiness was, that she was no divine star at all, but a bright and gentle girl, leaning on his love, and depending on his care.

And old Caius Sertorius had speculated on something of the kind, and seemed to find his youth renewed in theirs. And nurse Julia was satisfied.

So Cleon and Maia were betrothed.

And for a time the world became for him a temple dedicated to her—a heaven illuminated by her—holy with her presence—warm with her smile—musical with her voice.

Had his inward conflicts been mere unhealthy exhalations of night, they must have vanished in such a sunshine. But they did not. At times the presence of an awful power would overshadow him even as he listened to her, and chill his heart; but as men always will do with any faith which gives more shadow than light, he sought to fly from the chilling consciousness. He wondered whether Maia ever felt anything of the kind. If her soul was like his—if God was the same to her as to him—she must. But was she the same? Could there be a stain on a heart open and pure as hers—a heart which poured out all its depths to him, and in all its overflowings never overflowed with anything but love and goodness?

The summer and the inundation of the Nile had just passed their climax. Alexandria was converted for the time into a city of the ocean—Egypt into an archipelago of luxuriant islands. Everywhere the flood of light met and glowed in the flood of waters. Earth was azure as heaven; and for her stars, green islands, clothed with acacias and palms, and white temples, gleamed forth from the blue depths. The streets of palaces were mirrored in the smooth waters, which plashed idly against the marble steps; and in and out of the streets, and through triumphal arches of flowers, and close to the doors of houses, glided garlanded boats, full of people keeping holiday: for the Nile had been propitious this year. The gods of Egypt had blessed her fields abundantly, and the people were thronging into their temples to give them thanks and pay them homage.

The day's work of busy Alexandria was at an end. The murmur of recreation had succeeded to the hum of business; and in wooded islands, in temple courts, and on palace steps, the various inhabitants were gathered, amusing themselves with luxurious indolence or energetic vivacity, as national or individual temper might dictate.

The porch of one of the temples was thronged with idlers of all descriptions. At one end, a Stoic philosopher lectured on apathy, to an audience sufficiently apathetic; at another, a knot of young Syrian dandies stood amusing themselves with comments on the passers-by; Asiatic merchants lay on benches, indolently surveying the world with half-closed eyes; Greeks paced up and down, discussing novelties in art or literature, in the language and with the vehemence of Homer's heroes—their eager, classical faces and white dresses glancing in and out of the shadow of the columns; Romans stood in groups

of twos and threes, discoursing on the politics of
the empire, with the gravity of men whose business
it was to govern the world. All nations were
there, all costumes, all languages—an index to
the contents of the swarming city, the smelting-
furnace of that age of fusion.

Cleon stood alone, leaning against a pillar, his
eyes fixed on the water, which had for the time
converted the street leading to the temple into a
canal. He was waiting for the approach of a
religious procession, in which Maia was to take a
part. At length the first boat turned the corner
of the next street. The procession glided on, to
the sound of soft music, and reached the steps of
the temple.

Then the troop of boys and maidens disembarked,
bearing baskets of fruits and flowers on
their heads and in their arms, with priests leading
white oxen for the sacrifice. They entered the
temple chanting hymns of thanksgiving, their
rich southern voices now rising in clear jets of
melody, then bursting into exulting choruses,
whilst the surrounding crowd, from time to time,
enthusiastically echoed the refrain. It was the
natural overflow of hearts full of joy at the abundance
of the earth.

Cleon was borne away by the tide of enthusiasm.
Was not this, he thought, the ideal of the
old Greek religion—childhood the priesthood of
humanity—beauty and art ministering between
man and God? Was not this, after all, the true

religion—this fresh, grateful joy in life? Did not the true wisdom dwell with childlike hearts like Maia's, and with the hearts of all men when emotion had opened them and made them childlike? And was not that terrible sense of discord and sin and judgment under which he had writhed, the mere phantom of a diseased imagination, the disturbed dream of an overworked and overtired reason?

Life, not death—enjoyment, not renunciation—were not these the true offerings for the Living and Rejoicing One?

Was there no alternative but life without God, or God without life? Was not the joyous instinct of the child's heart true, spiritual health—the self-torture of the ascetic, the disease?

With thoughts and feelings like these, he seated himself beside Maia in the little boat which was to bear them to her father's house.

The whole procession reunited at the villa of Sertorius, and the dance and the feasting lasted beyond midnight. Colored lamps were suspended amongst the vine-leaves, and the whole festival was joyous and beautiful as glorious moonlight, and an Eastern garden, and nurse Julia's choicest fruits and confects arranged by Maia's taste, and the happy voices of children, could make it.

At length the guests separated, to return to their several homes, and Cleon and Maia stood on the terrace watching the boats with their lamps glide away like fire-flies amongst the illuminated groves, and listening to the sound of soft laughter as it floated over the water.

The last boat had passed out of sight, the last voice died away, the large lustrous moon was filling the depths of heaven with her glory, and coming down with silvery feet over the waters to where they stood. With snowy fingers she touched the temples, and changed them into the softest alabaster, silvering the feathery crowns of the palm-trees. It was a second day, but day with the repose and the unbroken stillness of night—such a light as might have harmonized with the songs of angels as once they transpierced the silence, and sang—"Glory to God in the highest, and on earth peace."

"How good it all is, Cleon!" murmured Maia; "how the gods must love the world and us!"

"The next feast will be our marriage-feast, Maia—a festival to last through all our lives."

His boat struck against the steps as he spoke, and hastily taking leave of her, he sprang into it, and was soon out of sight.

On the morrow she was to accompany her father on a government embassy into Upper Egypt, and on their return they were to be married.

"And everything *shall* be good to her," he thought, "for ever. I will stand between her and every sorrow. The conflict and evil that have reached my heart I will bear alone; they shall never come near that pure and happy soul."

In the strength of his love, he felt so strong to defend her.

The moon had set; and, real and solemn as the armies of stars which day hides, came upon him the voice which day had hushed—the voice of an uncalmed conscience and the awful consciousness of God. Everywhere throughout the Infinity he felt surrounded with the presence of the All-holy and the Almighty—and he a sinful creature.

Once more he was in the moral universe, a responsible being before the all-searching Eye, a guilty being before the Judge. For, in the night, again the shadow fell upon his soul.

Dreams cast no such shadows—

What cast them?—

Himself! His own shadow dimmed the world to him, for his face was turned from the Sun.*

The part of the city in which he lived was on high ground, raised above the flood, and he was glad to land and try to lull the restlessness of his heart by bodily activity. On his way he had to pass through some of the poorest and worst streets, whence sounds of riotous mirth, interspersed with angry voices and passionate threats, reached him from time to time, polluting the still night-air. And in these voices he must recognize the voice of his kindred—the echo of that corrupt nature within him, from which he could not fly.

* „Was lehr' ich dich vor allen Dingen?"
  Möchte über meinen eignen Schatten springen. —Göthe's *Gedichte*, 240. II.

As he passed on, the sound of a low, distinct voice, as if in earnest pleading, arrested him. It came from a wretched hut, run up against the corner house of an alley, apparently the last refuge of the lowest poverty. But the voice was gentle and sweet as that of Maia; there was something in it which compelled him to pause; it was so strange, and yet so familiar, and the words were those of his own eloquent, native Greek. The door of the hut had no fastening, and was half open. He stood concealed in the shadow of the projection of the next house, and listened. The calm voice was interrupted by another, weak and broken as that of a dying person, but full of passionate earnestness.

"It is of no avail. You do not know me; you never can know the depth to which I am fallen. Blessings on you for your words of pity; but the same heaven could never hold you and me!"

Then the calm voice spoke again:—

"'And there was a woman in the city, which was a sinner; and when she heard that Jesus sat at meat in the Pharisee's house, she came and stood at his feet behind him weeping, and began to wash his feet with tears, and to wipe them with the hairs of her head, and kissed his feet, and anointed them with the ointment.' That was Jesus, the Holy One of God."

"Did He suffer it?"

The voice continued—"'Now when the Pharisee which had bidden him saw it, he spake within himself, saying, If this man were a prophet, he would know who and what manner of woman this is that toucheth him: for she is a sinner.' The Pharisee was not the Holy One."

"But did He rebuke her?" it was asked, faintly.

"He rebuked the *Pharisee*. 'Jesus answering, said, Simon, I have something to say unto thee. And he saith, Master, say on. There was a certain creditor which had two debtors: the one owed him five hundred pence, and the other fifty. And when they had nothing to pay'—*(they had both nothing to pay)*—'he frankly forgave them both. Tell me, therefore, which of them will love him most. Simon answered, I suppose he to whom he forgave most. And he said unto him, Thou hast rightly judged. And he *turned unto the woman*, and said unto Simon, Seest thou this woman? I entered into thine house, thou gavest me no water for my feet: but she hath washed my feet with tears, and wiped them with the hairs of her head. Thou gavest me no kiss: but this woman from the time I came in hath not ceased to kiss my feet. My head with oil thou didst not anoint, but she hath anointed my feet with ointment. Wherefore I say unto thee, Her sins, *which are many*, are forgiven; for she loved much: but unto whom little is forgiven, the same loveth little. And he said unto her, Thy sins are forgiven thee. And they that sat at meat with him began to say within themselves, Who is this that forgiveth sins also?'—But He did not heed them; there was but one *who understood Him* there, and to her He said, 'Thy faith hath saved thee: go in peace.'"

"Forgiven!—forgiven!—peace!" echoed the voice of the dying woman, now broken with sobs; "but I can not come to Him as she did; if I dared, I can not anoint His feet, and bathe them with tears. There is nothing that I can do for Him."

"It is true," replied the other voice, in the tenderest accents of pity—"*you have nothing to pay.*"

"Oh, if He were here! if He were near! If I could hear His voice, and know He would not cast me out!"

"He is here—He is near," it was whispered; "and He has done more to show *you* His willingness to forgive, than ever He had done for her. He has taken on Himself all you deserved. He has not only forgiven, but *paid* the debt. He has let them mock Him, and put Him to shame, and crucify Him. *He has died for you.* He lives to hear you, to forgive, to give you His peace. *Will you reject Him?*"

There was no reply but broken words and low sobs, as of a penitent child, weary with passion, on the bosom of its mother. The weary child of sin had found rest on the breast of her Father.

There was a long silence. Then the calm voice rose once more in prayer and thanksgiving; and as the speaker rose to leave the hut, Cleon heard from within, again and again, the words, "Peace—peace—thy sins are forgiven."

At length the door opened, and a lady stepped softly out into the street. When she had left the hut, Cleon followed her at a little distance, to watch that no harm befell her, until she entered the door of a large plain house, and closed it after her. He marked the house, and resolved to visit it on the morrow, for he felt that, if anywhere, the power of God and the secret of peace were there. He had heard something that night which seemed to make an opening for him out of the labyrinth in which he was lost. The daylight gleamed on him in the distance, like the faint star which it seems, at first, to one emerging from the recesses of a cavern.

The Holy One, because holy, able to touch, and love, and forgive the sinner! What did this mean? What wondrous news was this? Was it, then, meant for him? Could this be the doctrine men hated so? Surely all must fall at the feet of such a Son of such a God! Why, then, was He thus opposed and hated? Then the words recurred to him, "The Pharisee despised the sinner, and did not welcome the Holy One. The Pharisee, shut out from God by his self-imagined righteousness, and from men by his narrow selfishness." The wonderful truth seized his heart; it is He who knows what sin is, and who can not tolerate it, who alone can pity and receive and forgive the sinner.

When he reached his own rooms, he sank on his knees before the Compassionate One, Jesus the Holy One of God, and prayed—

"O God, I am not the Pharisee; I am the sinner. Wilt Thou receive and forgive me—even me?"

And a strange peace came down on his heart as he prayed, from the place of peace where the Son of God, having put away our sins, pleads for the sinner—He whose blood has made the holy of holies the throne of grace.

CHAPTER V.

Early on the next day, Cleon retraced his steps to the house which he had seen the lady enter on the previous night. The owner of it, the people told him, was a presbyter of the church of Alexandria.

They ushered him into the atrium. The mistress of the house rose from amidst her maidens to receive him, and ask his pleasure. Two little children clung to her dress, and, in a further corner of the room, a boy of about fourteen sat at a table, with his back to them, reading so intently that he did not notice the interruption.

The lady was not young; her face had a calm, motherly look, and her whole bearing was, like her voice, very gentle and lowly, but dignified from its simplicity. Cleon begged her to pardon this abrupt intrusion of a stranger. He asked if the master of the house was not a teacher of the Christians.

"You would see my husband?" she replied; "I will take you to him."

As she led the way, he said, "My errand is a simple one, yet to you it may seem strange. I heard your words at the hut last night, and tracked you home."

The lady started slightly, and surveyed him rather anxiously; there had been rumors of a coming persecution—could she be betraying her husband to some emissary of the government? She hesitated for an instant—but Cleon's frank countenance seemed to reassure her, and she proceeded.

They entered a small inner room, where her husband was writing.

"Isidore," said his wife, "I bring you a stranger who has a message for you."

"Nay," said Cleon, returning his courteous greeting, "I have no message for you. I come to know if you have none for me." Then turning to the lady, he said, "To me my errand is one of life or death. If you or your husband can teach me as you taught that poor dying creature yesterday, do so, and I will learn like a child."

The lady seemed touched by his earnest tone. She looked at him long, and with a strange interest, and, whispering something in her husband's ear, she hastily left the room.

Cleon was now left alone with his host. The room was plainly, but not barely, furnished, and opened on a pleasant court, through which a stream was flowing.

Isidore had passed the middle age, his face

was furrowed, and his hair gray; but there was a kind and happy light in his eyes, which drew the heart to him.

Cleon, with his arms folded, stood before Isidore, while he gradually elicited from him the history of his spiritual inquiries and conflicts.

"The Stoics," Cleon said, "preached endurance as a fragment of the great All; the Platonists counseled me to lose self in mystic contemplation of the moveless, passionless Source of being; but how can I contemplate or love the inconceivable?—the effort must end in madness, or spiritual paralysis. Then, from the East, I heard of the double nature of all things—of God and Evil the forming Spirit and formless Matter, and, perhaps, a deforming Spirit, marring the creation, and the soul. Some of the Jews of Alexandria, and the Therapuæ, spoke of a holy God, and of certain things to be done and endured, in order to propitiate Him."

"All that, the Jews could teach without a temple and without sacrifices," observed Isidore.

Then Cleon spoke of his interview with the hermit on the banks of the Nile. "He called himself a follower of the Crucified," he said, "but the substance of his lessons was much the same as those of the philosophers and the Jews: 'Renounce, toil, struggle, seek to regain the lost presence and love of God'—save that he taught His living personality, showing me, as I had never seen it before, the terrible truth, that the evil which mars and corrupts the creation is bound up with every fibre of our complex being—that our hearts and minds, that *we ourselves*, are corrupt. This thought has weighed me in the dust. To be myself a stain and a defilement on the creation of God, a thing on which His eyes can not bear to rest;—gladly would I have sought the shades of death, could they have hidden me—but I know they can not. And, last night, I heard words which seem like the dawning of a hope. The hermit spoke of One who has opened a way back to God—your wife spoke of Him as forgiving sin, and making the sinner holy. I come to ask if you know this way, and if you will show it me. I do not care what torture, and strife, and weariness there may be in treading it, if only you can show me a way which will make me holy in the end, and such as God can love. If you know this, tell it me."

He had uttered these words with passionate rapidity, and now stood motionless, his dark penetrating eyes fixed on Isidore, awaiting his reply.

The Christian paused for a few moments, shading his forehead with his hand; then looking up, and meeting Cleon's gaze with a cordial smile, he said, slowly and calmly—

"You have all begun at the wrong end. You do not want *death*, but *life*. You have not to begin with *renouncing*, but with *receiving*."

"But must we not renounce evil; and is there not evil in me?"

"You will probably find enough to renounce by and by," replied Isidore, quietly—"we all find it so; but that is not what you have to begin with. Before you can renounce, you must receive. You want forgiveness, you want holiness, you want life. Your renunciation, to be complete, must stop short of nothing but the grave; for your whole nature is corrupted and estranged from the Source of life. You do not want *death*, but *life*."

"And who," exclaimed Cleon, bitterly, "can *present me* with a second life?"

"God is the *giver*," replied Isidore, solemnly; "hitherto you have only thought of Him as the *claimer*."

"Nay," interrupted Cleon, "I have known Him as the giver long. Has He not given us this glorious world? Has He not given us reason, light, and eyes, our hearts, and our beloved ones? And have I not lately heard that He has given us His Son, to win back our wandering hearts? But the greatest gift of His goodness is the bitterest drop in my sorrow. For, for all His gifts, I have returned Him worse than nothing—a sinful nature, a selfish life, a heart which turns with joy from the thought of Him, to worship His creatures or His gifts!"

"Pardon me, but you have *never* yet looked on Him simply as the giver," continued Isidore; "you have looked on Him as the *creditor*, and therefore in each new gift of His you only see an addition to the immeasurable list of His claims."

"Is it not true that we owe Him all?" said Cleon.

"Undoubtedly. And it is also true that we have nothing to pay. Now, I ask you to forget yourself for a time entirely, and listen to the few words I have to say to you about God. Our religion is not so much a philosophy as a history. That is, it answers the perplexities of the intellect and the heart—the actual perplexities, arising, not from a diseased organ of sight, but from actual contradictions and discords in the nature of things—by revealing to us certain actual occurrences. Now, we may guess at abstract truths, but we can never know anything of facts, except by seeing them or being told of them. The truths of our religion are facts—facts about God, His character, His acts, His relations with men. You must see that none but God can write such a history. He *has* written it. Our faith, then, rests simply on God's history of a wonderful series of facts. Some of these facts you know already, but of one you know nothing. It is quite true that you are sinful, and that God is holy; it is quite true that He has claims on you which you can never meet: but you have not yet learned that He is love; you have yet to learn that He comes to you, not as the creditor, claiming his just due—not as the proprietor, requiring fruit from the vineyard which he has dressed—

but as the king, making a feast for his son, of which he invites you, a rebel and a beggar, freely to partake. You have been thinking about yourself and your poverty—God is thinking of honoring His Son, and of the joy of filling His heaven with holy and happy beings. I want you now simply to fix your eyes on Him in whom God has delighted from everlasting—on Him through whom He can look on you and be satisfied."

So saying, he rose and took a roll of manuscript from a cabinet, and Cleon listened with close attention as he read:—

"*'In the beginning was the* WORD, *and the Word was with God, and the Word was God. The same was in the beginning with God. All things were made by him'*—made perfectly good, made in His image. *'In him was life, and the life was the light of men. And the light shineth in darkness.'* The light in which men were created they had darkened—so darkened, by sin and unbelief, that when the light shone amongst them, they *comprehended it not.* You see the contrast. In the world, nothing but darkness and death—in Him, light and life. But still He did not give up His gracious purpose of enlightening man. The time came when this Eternal Life would manifest itself. *'The Word became flesh, and dwelt among us (and we beheld his glory, the glory as of the Only Begotten of the Father), full of grace and truth.'* The light was manifested, not as *fire,* but as the light-giver; the Sun of righteousness arose, not to scorch, but to heal. He came to declare the glory of God, and in Him the glory of God shone as '*grace and truth.*' They beheld Him day by day—for He dwelt among them many years, teaching in their streets and talking with them in their homes. The Eternal Wisdom—the living Son of God—took upon Him our nature, and came into the world, which He had made, as a little child. For thirty years they knew Him only as the lowly and gracious son of Mary; for He took on Him the form of a servant, and lived in dependence on God, and in subjection to his parents, showing simply all that man should have been, and was not. Men loved Him, and God was pleased with Him. But the time came for the light to manifest itself, and, by shining, to manifest also the darkness. He arose and taught the people. He told them of the claims of their Creator and their Lord. He unveiled to them their lost and sinful state, but only that He might unveil to the sinner the heart of the Father—the depths of pity and love which there are in Him who had send His Son to seek and to save the lost. He proved the truth of His message, chiefly by the power which came with His words and His holy life, to the hearts of men; but also by many wonderful works, by healing the sick, giving sight to the blind, and raising the dead. '*The light shineth in darkness, and the darkness comprehended it not. He came unto his own, and his own received him not; but to as many as received him, to them gave he power to become the sons of God, even to them that believe in his name.'* Here is the lost link supplied between the dead and the living. Those who receive Jesus receive life, and live—*'which were born, not of blood, nor of the will of man, nor of the will of the flesh, but of God.'*"

"Truly," said Cleon, "this history must be divine."

"Some believed it so," continued Isidore, "and believed Him to be the Son of God. These were His disciples, and followed Him whithersoever He went."

"I would have received Him—I would have believed Him," said Cleon.

"I have more to tell you yet," replied Isidore, his face lighting up with a serious joy. "Some received Him, but the greater part received Him not; and some hated Him, and tried many times to put Him to death."

"Why?" interrupted Cleon, abruptly.

"Is He the only one," replied Isidore, gravely, "whom men have put to death because He was holier than they? *'This is the condemnation, that light is come into the world, and men loved darkness rather than light, because their deeds were evil.'* They tried many times to put Him to death, and failed."

"How should they succeed?" said Cleon; "was not He the Life?"

"At length they did succeed," Isidore rejoined. "The chief priests and rulers sent an armed band, who took Him, and led Him before the High Priest and the Roman Governor. They found no fault in Him, either of them, though they sought hard for some pretext—yet they sentenced Him to die the death of a criminal."

Cleon seemed for a moment lost in thought; then his eye brightened, and he said, "I think I comprehend it. What is death to the sinless? His death—if indeed He died—must have been but a triumphant entry into the presence of God —the joyful crown of His spotless life!"

"He was crucified between two thieves. The thought of death was agony to Him. He shrank from it, so that the sweat of His agonized expectation was as great drops of blood. The scourging and the nails, and the long agony of the cross, drew not one murmur from Him; but there was one thing which wrung from Him on the cross an irrepressible cry of anguish. Just before He died, '*He cried with a loud voice, My God, My God, why hast thou forsaken me?*'"

Cleon fixed his eyes earnestly on Isidore.

"What does this mean?" he said. "Is not God just?"

"God is just," replied Isidore, solemnly, "and because He is just, the Son of God died. *He bore our sins. The Lord hath laid on Him the iniquities of us all.*"

Cleon's eyes fell. He leaned on the desk before

him, and covered his face with his hands. He could not speak. At length, with a firm, deep voice, he said—

"Could the grave hold the Deliverer?"

"It could not," was Isidore's reply. "The Lord is risen—the sacrifice is accepted, and our sins are taken away—buried in His grave. During forty days, He appeared at intervals to hundreds of His disciples—the witnesses of His resurrection. Now, for a time, the heavens have received and hide Him; and we, dead unto sin and alive unto God through Him, are waiting for Him to return and restore all things."

He who alone can reveal the Saviour to the sinner, the Teacher and the Comforter, had spoken with power through the feeble words of Isidore. After a pause, Cleon arose, and grasping the hand of the Christian, said slowly, though with a low and broken voice—"*I believe.* I too receive the Crucified for my Lord."

"It is well," said Isidore. "His strength shall sustain you. He also will receive you as His redeemed disciple, and present you to His Father as His reconciled and ransomed child."

And kneeling down, he prayed aloud. As he called on God as the Father, and gave thanks, he earnestly besought strength, and the anointing of the Holy Ghost, for the recovered wanderer, in the conflict which must ensue. Cleon wept silently, like a child; but they were all tears of joy. He had no fear of any conflict now: he thought only of the joy of being beloved and blessed unceasingly by God; and if the idea of sacrifice crossed his mind, it was only as the eucharistic offering which he might lay at the feet of Him who had redeemed him with His blood.—But he had yet much to learn.

When he left, Isidore pressed his hand affectionately, and presented him with a copy of St. John's Gospel.

"It has been my light in many dark days," he said, in a tone of earnest tenderness; "may it be such to you!"

Cleon returned to his solitary home, and read the divine history again and again with absorbing interest, and as he read, the light steadily increased.

In a few days he came again to Isidore. After some time spent in conversation on the deep truths which now possessed Cleon's mind, the presbyter said—

"The Lord Jesus, when He ascended into heaven, left two tokens to mark His disciples from other men. The first of these is Christian baptism. Will you keep this His commandment, and thus enlist yourself as His soldier?"

"Let me receive the seal of my allegiance as soon as I may."

"It is a sign of reproach to the world," said Isidore. "It may require from you many sacrifices; it must bring on you much shame."

A glimpse of one possible sacrifice, which

seemed *im*possible, flashed before Cleon, and for a moment he paused; then he said calmly—

"Am I not already His—and should I shrink from saying so?"

"You will need a surer strength than the mere ardor of youthful purpose," observed Isidore, gravely; "wait a few days before you resolve—*and pray.*"

CHAPTER VI.

Those whom God has taught the meaning of conversion—what it is to be delivered from self-righteousness, and self-searchings, and fruitless toils, and baseless speculations, into the happy and lowly liberty of the children of God, may know what new aspects life now wore to Cleon.

The web of doubt and guesses—the chrysalis web which he had grown so weary in weaving, which every struggle had only coiled tighter around him, hiding him from heaven and entombing him from his kind—was burst, smitten by a breath from above; whilst now, heaven was bright in its own sunshine, and around him were happy voices, and hearts open as his own.

His heart was opening as a flower in a spring morning, and heavenly dews and sweet winds and sunbeams fell upon it; and the heavens also were opened, and the angels of God came forth from the pearly gates to minister to him. The eye which had so long been wearying itself with looking inwards, straining itself in the darkness, until nothing but the hot eye-balls met it everywhere, was now lifted up. The scales had fallen from it, and at the same moment the clouds were parted from the sky, and wherever he looked, he met the eye of a Father resting on him in love.

He had sat, like some gray alchymist, poring over the furnace of his heart, growing old in vain efforts to manufacture the elixir of life; and now God himself had drawn near and held to his parched lips the cup of eternal youth. All that it is to be a "new man" in Christ Jesus, and through Him a beloved and dependent child of the Almighty God—to be endued with all the energies of new life—to be spent in the service of One so worthy, Cleon felt. As yet, he knew little of the conflict, but it came upon him very soon. The light broke on him at once, like a sudden Egyptian dawn, and the day's work began almost with the daylight.

Maia was not yet returned from her journey with her father, so that time was given him for deliberation. He did not question for an instant the necessity of confessing his Master before men, nor hesitate as to doing so at once, although in these hours of sober thought the whole array of consequences ranged themselves vividly before him. No sacrifice could be so terrible or so repugnant to him as to have to live a lie.

He knew he must encounter much derision from his old associates; that, without any peculiar hard-heartedness or illiberality, they must —not comprehending the facts which had been revealed to him—look on him as a hot-brained enthusiast, or as a morbid dreamer, the weak victim of a superstitious delusion. This he knew, and did not shrink from enduring; but there was one thing from which his whole nature, the pure human feelings of which his new faith had so strengthened and deepened, recoiled and sickened. Again and again he met, in imagination, the frown, the scorn, the bitter denial of Caius Sertorius; and again and again he sought to meet Maia, and could not. He knew she would not scorn, nor distrust, nor blame him, but he knew she would suffer. And every fresh attempt to endure the conflict before it came, only brought the dreaded reality more vividly before him, and left him weaker, until, at length, he resolutely banished the thought, or sought to meet it with some words of Jesus, or with prayer. He read much in the Gospel of St. John, and the other Christian Scriptures, and on the "first day of the week" he attended for the first time a Christian assembly, to which Isidore had invited him.

It was held in a hall in Isidore's house—the fear of threatened persecution, and the terror occasioned by a recent popular outbreak, having made the Christians more cautious in their movements. Cleon stood amongst the catechumens. The service began with the early morning, and was evidently a service of thanksgiving—a festival for all. Isidore, from a raised platform, read aloud to the people from the New Testament—

whilst an interpreter translated sentence by sentence into Coptic, for the benefit of the native Egyptians. When he had finished reading, he explained the words in familiar and earnest language, comparing them with others from the same source, and pressing them on the hearts of his hearers, to be carried home, he said, and lived on.

The whole assembly responded from time to time to the prayers. They prayed, and sang, and listened, standing, because it was the resurrection-day, and they were disciples of Him who had raised the fallen; and the whole service, the sacred day itself, the very lives of the believers, were to be a eucharistic resurrection-feast—a living witness to His resurrection.

But what struck Cleon most was the singing; the low chant rising, he could scarcely tell whence, and swelling from different parts of the room, until all joined in a joyful chorus—not tumultuous, like the heathen songs of triumph, but calm and thrilling as a hymn of rest after toil, sung by a family reunited in their father's house. To Cleon, too, the sounds came with overpowering sweetness; for, besides his own new and deep sympathy in the words, they seemed to bring back to him the songs his sister Alce had sung in his own home in Greece.

After the last hymn had been sung, many brought offerings of bread and wine, and money, for the poor of the flock, to Isidore, who laid them on the table before him, offering them to God in the name of the whole Church—the royal priesthood consecrated to offer spiritual sacrifices.

Before the communion, according to the custom which crept so early into the Church, and gave occasion for so many scandals amongst the heathen about the "Christian mysteries," the listeners and candidates for baptism withdrew. Cleon waited in the garden-court until the assembly should disperse, and give him an opportunity of speaking to Isidore.

As he paced the court, two little children came bounding into it, chasing each other. They paused suddenly on seeing the stranger, and were making their escape, when Cleon caught the foremost and detained her. He was one of those people whom children seem intuitively to love, and the little creature let him seat her on his knee, and soon she began to prattle quite confidentially. Her brother, who seemed a year older, stood silently beside them, mounting guard over her.

"There were three of them," she said, "Dioscoros, and Philip, and herself. She was very fond of Philip, but Dioscoros was the dearest of all; he made playthings for her, and was so gentle and so good."

"Where is he now?" Cleon asked.

"He is gone to the feast," she replied.

"What feast?" said Cleon.

The little girl looked wonderingly at him.

"The feast of the blessed Jesus," she replied, with childish reverence.

"Do *you* not go, then?" Cleon asked.

"No," interposed Philip; "my mother says we are too little."

"But we know about Jesus," continued the little girl; "my mother and Dioscoros have told us, and we love Him indeed very much, although we may not go to His feast yet. Do *you* love Him?"

"I do," he replied, stroking her hair.

A question seemed on her lips, but she stopped, and colored.

He answered her look: "I shall join that feast too, before long." And, after a short pause, he added, "But what can you know about the Lord Jesus, my child?"

"He came from heaven that He might make us happy," she said; "He is the good shepherd, and little children are His lambs, and He carries them in His bosom, and loves them; and when we sleep, He watches over us and blesses us."

"You are not afraid, then, of the darkness?"

"Oh no!" she said, smiling, "for, you know, He can see."

Cleon did not answer, but he took the child's lesson to his heart.

"What do they call you, my child?" he asked at length.

"Alce," she said; "it is my mother's name."

A suspicion flashed across Cleon: the strangely-familiar voice—the earnest, inquiring look of the wife of Isidore—the half-remembered hymns—and now the child's name!—the electric chain seemed complete—and yet he hardly dared trust that it was so.

Just then Isidore joined them, followed by his wife. They both greeted him affectionately.

"Have you decided?" Isidore asked.

"I have," was the reply.' "I am a Christian, and desire to seem so."

Isidore embraced him cordially, and his wife gave him her hand—and again her soft, earnest eyes rested on him, with the look of wistful questioning he had before remarked.

"Are you a Greek?" Cleon asked abruptly.

"I am," she said.

"Was your home ruined by the Romans."

"It was," she replied.

"And you yourself bound, and carried into captivity?—forgive the question."

"I was," she answered; "they carried me to Egypt"—and seeing how eagerly he hung upon her words, she continued—"Bishop Dionysius and the church of Alexandria ransomed me, from love to our common Lord, and soon after, I married. My husband and I lived many years in Syria, and we only returned to Alexandria a few months since."

"Had you a brother?" asked Cleon, anxiously.

"I had—I had!" she exclaimed.

"And you loved and tended him like a mother, and sang Christian hymns beside his cradle?"

"Cleon!" she cried, all her calmness giving way in a burst of tears, and the brother and sister were clasped in each other's arms!

Doubly brother and sister now, by a tie how doubly strong!

"Ye shall receive in this life houses, and brethren, and sisters, *with persecutions.*"

CHAPTER VII.

Before Cleon would take another step, he hastened to inform Caius Sertorius of his convictions and his purpose.

He was prepared to endure many bitter and harsh words; he knew the old man's heart—he knew the tenderness which lay hidden under all his outward roughness—he knew how all this deep hoard of love was "garnered up" in Maia—and he knew that it was in this very point he had to wound him—he whom, a captive and a stranger, Sertorius had cherished and guided as a son. And he knew that the reason he had to give must seem to him a mere flimsy cloak for deliberate and base ingratitude. Gently, therefore, though with a calm decision which left no room for remonstrance, he confessed and explained his faith.

The old man heard him in stern silence, not replying for many minutes, but at length he said, with bitter emphasis—"Choose between your new gods and Maia—both you can not have."

Cleon's purpose could not waver—but how make the old Roman soldier understand that there was One whose claims to obedience and loyalty were beyond those of benefactor, liberator, father, and betrothed bride? He attempted no retort, but suffered himself to be turned contemptuously from the house, for he felt that the old man, believing as he did, was just; and in his pity for his old and generous friend—his father—the father of his Maia—he almost forgot his own still harder lot. Yet not harder—agonizing as it was—for could he not *pray*, and pray for Maia?"

But another conflict still remained for him.

It involves something, in a world estranged from God—nay, more, at enmity with Him—to take His Word as the rule of every day's conduct —not only to draw from it a general plan of life, but, day by day, as perplexities arise, to seek guidance there with a single eye, resolved in all things to do, not what self-will, or expediency, or human authority, although divinely authorized, may dictate, but what God directs—to have nothing between the soul and His direct command, but in all things to obey Him rather than man. It *involves much*—far too much for any amongst us, did it not imply *more*—did it not imply that God our Father is on our side, ready to give more grace for the increasing need—were not the command, "Walk before me, and be thou sincere,"* preceded by the sustaining assurance, "I am the *Almighty God*."

* Gen. xvii. 1, margin.

On this strait track, this narrow way of obedience and of *peace*—for they are one—Cleon entered, and God gave him a single heart.

As he read the Gospels and Epistles, he became convinced that his calling as a soldier was not of God; that it became not a follower of Him who resisted not evil, to gain his livelihood by strife. To bear the sword even in a just cause appeared to Cleon contrary to the mind of Him who rebuked the disciple who sought to defend Him with the sword; and the wars of the empire, which he had been engaged in, were often wars in the cause of disorder and injustice—wars of conquest, or plunder, or selfish contests between rival generals.

"We," he thought, "are called to be perfect, *even as* our Father in heaven is perfect, and He sendeth rain on the just and the unjust. Endurance and trust are our only weapons. Even as He has dealt with us—as He acts towards the world—must we act—with patient forbearance. For the Lord Jesus, in reading His commission from the prophet Isaiah, closed the book abruptly before the concluding clause. The 'day of vengeance' is not yet come."*

He, as a young man and a novice, consulted many of the elders and wise men of the Church on the subject, but they could not agree. Isidore said that some true disciples had fought in the imperial armies, and some had refused, and

* Luke iv. 18, 19, *compare* with Isaiah lx. 1, 2.

suffered; but he declined to give him any counsel, referring him to the revealed will of God, and remarking, that convictions derived from man had not basis enough to stand the tempest.

The Roman soldiers were frequently required to attend and assist at ceremonies which no Christian could tolerate—and some advised him at least to wait until some such requisition were made, and not to invite persecution. His old acquaintance Papias strenuously urged him to this course, warning him with many prudent axioms against the enthusiasm of youth and fresh convictions.

Cleon resolved to wait until his baptism; not that his purpose was weak, but because he felt it would keep. At length the period of his probation was over; his catechetical course was finished; and at the approaching Easter festival, the pious and judicious Bishop Dionysius was to baptize him with the other catechumens.

It was an exulting spring morning, the Eve of Easter day. The Christians of Alexandria repaired in groups of twos and threes to the tomb of one of their martyrs, situated in a quiet spot on the banks of one of the mouths of the Nile. It was his *birthday*, as they called the anniversary of the martyr's death, and they met at his grave to sing their Easter hymns of hope and thanksgiving.

There was also to be a baptism that day, for the early Christians delighted in celebrating the blessed type of their death and resurrection with Christ, at the season when He "burst the bonds of death, and opened the gates of everlasting life to all believers." It was a joyous and impressive festival. A deep solemnity seemed to pervade the little band, and a peculiar tenderness of brotherly affection, for they knew that a tempest of persecution was impending over them, and they nestled together under the wings of the Almighty. The powers of the earth threatened them; but the power of the Highest overshadowed them, and they were at peace.

It was a quiet place; the dew was not yet off the grass; the low sun glittered in the drops, and glowed in the river, shooting oblique golden rays up through the palm-trees which grew around the martyr's tomb.

One by one the catechumens made open renunciation of the world, the flesh, and the Evil One —a profession that to many of them might soon have a serious significance. One by one they went down into the river, "buried with Christ" —one by one they rose again, typifying their having passed unharmed through the deluge of death—death, the curse of sin—by His resurrection.

Then the presbyters and deacons clothed them in the white robes of purity—as one day they hoped to stand before the throne in robes washed and made white in the blood of the Lamb; and all kneeling before the Bishop Dionysius, he signed them with the sign of the cross, as the badge of their warfare, anointing them with the consecrating oil, in sign of their being a holy priesthood set apart to offer spiritual sacrifices, acceptable to God through Jesus Christ, the atoning sacrifice and the great High Priest.

The whole assembly then joined in singing a hymn of the Resurrection; and when the last note of the joyful chorus died away on the fresh morning air, birds and waters, and young leaves rustling in the wind, all seemed to Cleon to take up the response, "The Lord is risen indeed."

On the next day, the Alexandrian Christians met again at Isidore's house; and after the Agapé, or common meal of love, for the first time Cleon with gladness and singleness of heart sat at what little Alce had called the sacramental "feast of the blessed Jesus."

Cleon passed the week after his baptism—the week in which the newly-baptized remained clothed in their white garments—in the house of his sister. It was a resting time, and such he sorely needed. The right hand, which it had been imposed on him to cut off, could never be replaced, and the wound did not heal. His whole nature had been so identified with Maia's, that on earth he had literally not a hope nor a project left. Every day taught him this the more, and at times, in the happy family circle of his sister, he could not bear it. At such times, he found it wiser to give up the struggle, feeling less lonely when alone; for then God, in all His blessed relationships to the regenerate soul, came near to him, and in His ear he could pour out his whole soul in prayer for her of whom he could not speak to any other. That week was a season of refreshment and bracing for the conflict which was coming; for before the end of it, an edict was issued in Alexandria for a festival in honor of the Emperor's birthday; his statue was to be borne in triumph, and the soldiers were to pay it homage, and offer sacrifice on his behalf to the gods of Rome.

Now, therefore, there remained no alternative for Cleon. He knew what lay before him, but he felt thankful that the requisition was such as left no possibility of doubt or compromise.

The day of the festival at length arrived, such another day of cloudless Egyptian sunshine as that on which he had met Maia on the temple-steps, with her thank-offering for the inundation. The first peal of the trumpets, and the hurry of joyful preparation in the city, brought a thousand recollections thronging over his heart. The tempest of doubt, which that sunny day had only hushed for a while, was now stilled for ever by the only voice which can still such storms, and in his soul there was a great calm. But who could say what tempest might this day shatter his life? He saw it lower already; in every tumultuous burst of acclamation, in every eager glance or gesture of the crowd, he saw it drawing slowly nearer;—but strong in the strength of obedience, he went calmly forth on his ordinary duties to encounter it.

The procession formed and moved with joyous pomp through the streets; priests, with garlands and white robes, leading the white oxen for the sacrifice—children, with flowers and mimic standards, looking up proudly to catch the eyes of their mothers and sisters in the crowd—soldiers, with their plumes and shining armor and their impassive faces, marching to the wild monotonous clang of Eastern music;—Cleon rode amongst his comrades, and the people greeted them with shouts, and threw wreaths in their path as they passed.

At length the procession reached the elevated open space appointed for the sacrifice. One after another the soldiers advanced to strew incense before the imperial statue, and to swear the customary oath, "By the genius of the Emperor." Cleon alone refused the idolatrous homage. The crowd, not understanding the reason, grew impatient of the interruption; but when the cause was known, their impatience was instantaneously converted into rage—those who could not ascertain the occasion catching the contagion of the common feeling. A thousand eyes glared fiercely on him—a thousand voices burst forth in cries of contempt and fury—a thousand arms were raised to menace one who dared so inauspiciously to arrest the tide of festivity. But he stood in the midst, his face lighted up with a serene enthusiasm.

"I can not swear by your gods," he said firmly, "for they are no gods. There is but one God, even the Father, and one Lord Jesus Christ, whom we serve: I am a Christian."

Many reasoned with him earnestly, pitying his early manhood; and from the group nearest him one voice whispered—

"What harm is there in scattering a little perfume to please the people, or in swearing an oath which can injure no one?"

Was it the voice of the tempter? Cleon turned hastily, and ere he was lost in the crowd, he caught a glimpse of the sharp, restless eyes of Papias, the rich merchant.

One friendly old man would have forced the censer into his hand, but Cleon gently repelled him; and to all seductions and menaces he replied simply—

"I can do no otherwise—I am a Christian."

The rage of the multitude at length grew ungovernable—they would have pulled him in pieces, crying, "Death to the godless!" "To the cross with the worshiper of the Crucified!" but the officers of justice, having bound his arms, bore him forcibly through the throng to the prison. One stone, however, aimed at his temple, made a deep cut in his forehead—his lip curled, and his eye for a moment flashed scornfully at the yell of triumph with which the unmanly act was greeted.

Yet amongst that crowd were women who would have died to save those they loved, and men who would have wept to see their little children suffer. How, then, could these things be? Cleon remembered the *Cross*, and ceased to wonder or to be impatient.

None of his friends were allowed access to him during the three days of his imprisonment. They were days of solemn communion, passed alone, in the innermost sanctuary, with God. When the officers returned to take him before the tribunal, he was calm and collected as one acting under authority. Like Hezekiah, he had already encountered the enemy in the temple, and vanquished him there.

"We have given you time," said the chief magistrate, courteously, "to retract your purpose; doubtless you have used it wisely."

"I have, I trust, used it wisely," replied Cleon, calmly: "my purpose is confirmed; I dare not break my oath of allegiance to the King of kings."

"Are you prepared, then, to share the fate of your King?" asked one of the magistrates, sarcastically.

"I believe that He who died for me will strengthen me to die for Him, if needful," said Cleon, quietly, "and will raise me again where He is risen."

"He is like the rest of them," muttered one of the magistrates; and having consulted together for a few minutes amongst themselves, one of them, who seemed the most bitter against the Christian faith, said, "There is but one way in which a Roman soldier can evade his duty—and that is by being degraded to the condition of a slave, and branded as a criminal. We can offer you this means of escape, if you desire it."

Cleon's color mounted high. "I have deserved something better than this from the armies of Rome," he said, bitterly.

"Doubtless the Emperor will consider your claims," replied the magistrate, coolly, "if you choose to remain in his service."

Cleon pressed his hand for a moment to his forehead; in that moment the hopes and love of years—Maia—honor—all that made it life to live—rushed in a torrent over his heart; but on its bosom a still small voice was borne to him, whose music pierced the roar: and it said, "Him that confesseth me before men, I will also confess before my Father."

And looking steadfastly in the judge's face, at length he said—

"If it must be so, I am ready; I can neither sacrifice nor fight, for I am a Christian."

Then, pale as death, and as motionless, save for one heavenward glance, and one quiver of the compressed lip, he stood whilst the sentence was pronounced.

He was young, and his nature was proud and impetuous; the "glory" had by no means "passed away from earth" for him, nor was his keen relish for it dimmed. The path of faithful obedience for him lay straight athwart that he would have chosen, but One had trodden it before, and trod it with him now.

They deprived him of the rights of a Roman citizen—of his freedom; but he knew that God had prepared for him a city, and now he realized the truth of the golden words—" Our citizenship is in heaven." They declared him a slave, but he remembered Him who " took on Him the form of a slave" for our sakes. And when, in the garments of slavery, they led him forth before the troops, and with a hot iron branded his forehead with the indelible mark of infamy and crime, he looked unto " Him who endured the cross, despising the shame, and is now set on the right hand of God." " And this," he thought, " is not the cross."

He was not borne above the trial in any ecstasy of unconsciousness; he passed through the midst of it, feeling it keenly; but He who is persecuted in His people passed through it with him. Bitterly as he felt the shame, and heavy as this affliction seemed, in the depths of his soul he felt that it was light in comparison with the exceeding weight of the glory which should be revealed.

The sentence was carried out to the full. They sold him into slavery, and put his price into the public treasury.

He knew not who had purchased him, nor

whither they would lead him, nor what master he would have to serve—already he had suffered too much to care; and, besides, he trusted implicitly in the guidance of the Hand into which he had given up his all. At length, however, as they led him through the city, when he looked up, arrested by some scornful words, he thought he recognized the street—it seemed familiar to him. In another moment he was at his sister's door. She led him into the hall. The Church of Alexandria had ransomed him.

"Nay, my sister," he said, withdrawing from her speechless embrace, "I can not stay here. It has been the will of my God to bow me very low, but I will not sink you with me."

She did not reply, but taking his burning hand in hers, she led him to a couch, and knelt beside him. And as he sat there in silence, his head bowed down, the little Alee crept softly towards him, and climbing on his knee as she was wont to do, and clinging round his neck, she kissed his forehead. The kisses of the child came where they had branded the mark of shame, and laying her soft hands on the wound, she said, wonderingly, "Mother—they have hurt him!"

Cleon did not seek to repel her; he pressed her close to his heart. The fever within him was cooled, and his tears fell on the forehead of the child.

But such furnaces can not be passed through unscathed. The spirit indeed was willing, but the flesh, although it had been sustained, was weak. Before the end of the week, a virulent fever laid Cleon low.

For many days he was delirious. At times he would start up vehemently, and conjure them not to let Maia know. And then he would plead like a child, that they would let him see her, and explain it all to her; he was sure she would understand. Often visions of glory seemed to float before his eyes, and he would exclaim, "Tell her that I do not repent; that it is worth the sacrifice." Then he would press his hand to his forehead, and say, "Do not shudder, do not turn from me, Maia; it is only the cross they signed on my forehead at my baptism. It burns, but it is light. Will you be baptized with the baptism that I am baptized with?"

Alce sat by his bedside night and day, watching every movement and every change. And he seemed, at times, to confuse her strangely with Maia, and heaven with his old Greek home. "Did they say it was ruined?" he would say; "that can not be, it is incorruptible—neither moth nor rust, nor thief can enter there, nor sorrow, nor sin. It is a city which hath foundations—and God is its builder and its light."

When the healing sleep was given him at last, and he awoke and looked around him again collectedly, Alce still was watching beside him. The light of her calm eyes seemed to compose his half-awakened spirit. "I have had a long dream, Alce," he said; "was it *all* a dream?"

By slow degrees consciousness and strength returned. One day, when he seemed stronger than usual, Alce ventured to ask him about Maia, and then the long-restrained confidence flowed forth freely; he told her all he had lost. It was a comfort to Cleon to think that Alce's prayers would now be joined to his own on her behalf, and that she perhaps might watch over Maia, as he could never hope now to do.

Besides, he had much to learn: so many of God's most blessed words seem as if written with invisible ink, to be brought out and made legible only by fire. There were treasuries of truth and hope, of which he had but just crossed the threshold. The heavenly citizenship, the actual reconciliation of the Church, and her expectation of her future purchased but unredeemed possession—which make it so well worth while to be a stranger on earth for the "little while;" the "Great Mystery" of the Bride and her Lord—the Church given by the Father to the Son to be His companion throughout eternity, purchased with blood, and raised from the dust, to manifest the glory of Him who had loved her to angels, to share His joy and minister His grace to all creation, and in the Father's house to be loved for ever with His unutterable love—that love, which now, through the wilderness, it was such peace to lean on;—these, and many of the other great realities which make the glory of earth so flimsy and pitiful, and the meanest service for God so glorious, came with overwhelming power upon his mind, and made it calm and strong—brought to his remembrance by the Comforter, who abideth with the orphaned Church for ever.

For the reproach of men who knew not what they did, the acknowledgment before God and angels and men that He has loved us; for the inward desolation now, the white stone with the new name, known only to him that receiveth it—was not the exchange good?

And meanwhile the gentle, peaceful character of his sister, the quiet smile that often shone in her eyes as if she had a hidden store of happy thoughts; the earnest, holy life of Isidore, so rigid to himself, so tender to others, so open to all good influences from without; the honest, though somewhat hard-won affection of Philip; the watchful kindness of Dioscoros, whom his father used to call his young *Parabolanus*,* because he so loved to help and watch the sick; the caresses of his little pet Alce;—these, and the thousand other wholesome influences of a Christian home, were like the breath of healthy sea breezes to the invalid, healing and bracing him insensibly.

The air of the morning seemed always to pervade the whole family, as those just risen in health and fresh hopefulness, to the work of a short and busy day. They were emphatically

---

* An office amongst the early Christians, something similar to which seems to have been revived amongst the United Brethren of Bohemia, under the name of *Garde-malade*.

"children of the *day*." One fact seemed the centre of their thoughts and lives, and that was the resurrection. As in the paintings and sculptures of the old Roman catacombs, the cross, for them, was garlanded with wreaths of victory from the opened sepulchre. Yesterday was to them the day of the resurrection of their Lord; to-day, the day of service, with all the energies of the new life; to-morrow, the morning of the resurrection of the just, when the dead in Christ shall be raised, and the living changed. Such an atmosphere could not be around Cleon continually, and leave him desolate as it found him.

The Church of Alexandria, too, loved to honor one who had so honored her Lord. It was no golden age for the Church then, any more than in the days when that of Corinth gave such trouble to St. Paul, or that where Gaius lived, led away by Diotrephes, refused to receive the beloved disciple. She was not then broken up into many contending sections, nor had she yet identified herself with the Gentile nations. There was still one visible Catholic Church on earth, manifest to all, and the early Christians yet shone as the light in the darkness throughout the world, manifesting that they were the disciples of Jesus, by the love which they had one for another.

But Cleon could not always bear the honor they would have done him, and it was settled by Isidore and Alce that it would be better for him to leave Alexandria for a while, and fulfil the desire which had been given him of proclaiming the grace and truth of God amongst the Eastern nations.

He was therefore ordained by Bishop Dionisius and his presbyters, and sent forth, with the prayers and blessings of the Church of Alexandria, to labor amongst the churches which St. Thomas had first planted in southern India.

"You will remember Maia?" he said to Alce, at parting.—She did not forget.

CHAPTER VIII.

Nor did Maia forget Cleon. When first her father told her that Cleon was a Christian, and that they were never more to meet, the blow seemed to prostrate her and she wept passionately for days. But the very excess of her grief brought healing with it. Hope was so natural and unchecked with her, and sorrow was so new, that she felt sure it could not last. She knew more of her father's heart than of his will, and was persuaded he would soon relent. To her it made not the slightest difference what Cleon's religion might be—would he not still be Cleon? Under these influences her spirits gradually returned, and Caius Sertorius began to hope that she would fulfil his notion of young maidens in general, and soon be ready to flutter off to some new flower. To make this the easier, he provided her with every amusement in his power, to make her home bright, and he was becoming very easy about the result—not knowing the tears she shed at night. But at length the rumor of Cleon's disgrace and suffering reached Maia. Every one had been strictly charged not to tell her, but having heard the rumor, she would not rest until she had extracted all. Then, in her indignant sympathy, she would have flown at once to share his reproach, but they concealed from her the place of his abode, and ere she could ascertain it, Cleon had left Alexandria—left without a word, or a sign of remembrance for her—left, they said, for ever! She was sure she knew his inmost heart—sure he could not have changed; still this new religion, which every one spoke of as infamous—how could she tell what magical power it might have exercised over a mind earnest as his? And beneath the cold shadow of doubt, all her joyous nature was chilled and benumbed. Her spirits failed, her interest in everything ceased; the beautiful earth became but as a dead floor for her weary feet, the arch of heaven as the vault of a tomb—for Maia had nothing besides Cleon to lean on. Whilst the staff was there, she scarcely knew that she leaned on it; but when it was removed, she fell helpless and powerless. She did not struggle, nor give way to passionate lamentings, she simply sank powerless and crushed! Her world was empty—her heart was blank; but it is often on the blank heart that God writes His best messages.

Her father saw it all, and tried in vain amusements, society, traveling; she listened, and saw, and smiled, but enjoyed nothing; she seemed to

have become a mere spectator of others' lives—
her own concluded. She could not but be sensible that his tenderness increased with her need;
but though she felt it deeply, it could not cheer
her; it only wounded her the more. The tide of
his love flowed over her heart as over a channel
the heat had quite dried up—and left it dry.

But one day, when she was sitting on the old
garden steps, where she had so often sat with
Cleon, gazing into the river, not expecting her
father home so soon, chancing to glance up suddenly, she saw him looking wistfully at her.
How long he had been standing there she did not
know, but when he met her eye, he brushed the
tears from his rough cheeks and turned sadly
away. The sense of her injustice came over her;
she felt that he needed her; and rising, she went
quietly to him, and, hiding her head on his shoulder, wept there silently. The other side of her
woman's nature was touched; she felt that one
depended on her, and the sense of having to support him made her strong. In sustaining him, she
was sustained herself. And so she learnt to endure.
But she was much changed—all the child had
passed away from her, and in the gentle, serious
girl, who waited on her father at his meals, anticipating his wishes, or sat quietly spinning at
his side, listening to his old stories of the wars
and the barbarians, few would have recognized
Maia. But Cleon's name was never uttered.

At length the spring came round—it was the

second after Cleon had left—and Sertorius began to observe a change in his child. Something of the old light came back to her eye, and the old spring to her step. A new life seemed to animate her, and her face would often beam with a natural though quiet smile. He could not comprehend it, but it rejoiced his heart.

Would it have rejoiced him as much had he known the cause? It was indeed a new life which animated Maia. A desire to know what this new religion could be that had robbed her of Cleon induced her to buy a copy of St. Luke's Gospel and St. Peter's Epistles from a Christian pedlar; and, enchained by the irresistible truthfulness of the narrative, simply, without doubt or questioning, she had believed it. She was weary and heavy laden, and she came to Jesus and found rest. The light came to Maia before the darkness; and from the atonement made for it she first learnt her sin.

The light had naturally manifested the darkness to her; on the knowledge of the love of God, and what it has given, followed the sense of responsibility and obligation. She longed to tell every one of the treasure she had found; but fear, and all the prudent reasons fear can always suggest, withheld her. She would show her faith by the joy and peace it brought into her life; and then, when her father noticed this, she would tell him the blessed secret, and lead him to embrace it too. Besides, she was yet very young in the faith, and very imperfectly taught; and, if she were hasty and incautious in her confession, she might be deprived of all opportunity of further growth. Thus, as it always is when we look to circumstances, and not straight to God, Maia's eye was bewildered, and her conscience clouded, until at length she was losing even the peaceful temper which was to work such wonders on her father.

At length, however, an accident aroused her to decision.

Persecution broke out in Alexandria. One evening Sertorius came home with the tidings that the Christians were flocking to the temples to sacrifice in obedience to the imperial mandate, and amongst them a rich merchant, called Papias. "They seemed," he said, "alike afraid to sacrifice, and afraid to refuse."

"Did any refuse?" asked Maia, trembling.

"Yes," he said; "some persisted in their madness; some were scourged, some racked, and some thrown into the flames: their obstinacy is marvellous. One boy, called Dioscoros, the son of one of their priests, was tortured, so that the sight of it made me, old soldier as I am, and used to sights of blood and suffering, shudder; and yet the child never uttered a murmur."

"Did he endure to the end?" asked Maia, her heart sickening.

"He persisted in his refusal, but the governor had compassion on his youth, and his life was spared. His companions were burned. Their madness is incredible. If it were not for their superstition, one could not help admiring their patience; but the man whom they worship as their God has promised them some wonderful felicity after death, and they believe His words as implicitly as if they saw the things."

Maia rose abruptly, and standing before him, pale and trembling, with a strength of resolution not her own, exclaimed, "Father! O, do not say a word against Him—I believe in Him—I am a Christian!"

She was not prepared for the burst of passion which her confession excited. At first, he sat mute with amazement; but when, though half fainting with fear, she persisted in her assertion, the old man seemed beside himself with grief and anger. "The curse of the gods has lighted on my house!" he exclaimed; "Cleon is fallen; and now my child!"

He buried his face in his hands. Weeping silently, she watched him for some minutes, until at length she ventured to lay her hand on his arm, and whisper, "Father!"

But he rose, and, sternly repulsing her, said, "No Christian is a child of mine! This house can no longer be your home. Go where you will, serpent that I have cherished in my bosom! share Cleon's shame, if you will, and leave me in my old age alone."

But Maia did not leave. For a little while she kept to her own apartments, only watching that all her father's comforts were attended to, and at length she ventured to wait on him as she was wont at his meals. At first he scarcely spoke, and tried to keep up his stern manner, but his eyes would follow her when she left the room; and one evening he said to her abruptly, "Why do you not sit down, child?—you look tired." Her eyes glistened, as she brought her spinning-wheel, and sat down beside him in silence.

By degrees she crept into all her old ways and places; the old man forgot his stoical purpose altogether; and when he was a little querulous with growing infirmities, she was so gentle, and cheered him so with her pleasant words, that he grew to depend on her like a child, and could not bear her to be out of his sight.

She never spoke to him of her faith, but she spoke much to God for him, which was, perhaps, the more direct way. One day, however, after many weeks, she ventured to say that she should like to attend the Christian assemblies. Sertorius did not reply, and she sat, casting her care on Him who careth for us, yet trembling for the result. But when she kissed him, and wished him good-night, he murmured, "Do not stay long, child, if you must go." From that time, he never interfered with her movements, suffering her to visit the sick, and assist the widows and orphans of the martyrs, whilst she, on her part, cheerfully resigned all that fidelity to a higher authority did not require.

He used always to send a slave to fetch her when she returned from the place of prayer, until one day, when the civil war was raging in the city, and she was later than usual, he grew anxious about her and went to meet her himself, and from that time he constantly guarded her home. Once or twice she fancied he had been listening at the door, but he never said so. And about this time she missed her copy of St. Luke's Gospel; she did not search for it; but prayed earnestly that, into whosesoever hands it fell, it might penetrate the heart.

In the Christian assemblies, and in her quiet ministries amongst the sick and bereaved, Alce watched her with motherly care, often encouraging her with words of faith and sympathy; but of Alce's history and family Maia knew nothing.

CHAPTER IX.

Meanwhile the Church of Alexandria had rest, and was reaping the peaceable fruit of the persecution—those who were not of it being sifted out of it, whilst the true disciples were bound together with redoubled affection. Divisions were healed, and, walking more simply in the light, they had fellowship one with another. As the good Bishop Dionysius wrote, "All are rejoicing everywhere at the unanimity and brotherly-love now prevailing, and are glorifying God for the same."

There had been much disputing about the thousand years' reign of the Lord Jesus—some contending for an earthly paradise, whilst others, in their zeal to preserve intact the heavenly destinies of the Church, perhaps lost sight of the promised redemption of creation at the manifestation of the sons of God, and the earthly destinies of the Jewish nation; although, probably, none amongst them doubted that the Lord would return in like manner as He had ascended, to judge the nations, and gather His redeemed, quick, and dead, to Himself.

After the persecution came a pestilence. Alexandria, long wasted by famine, and by riot and civil war, which had made it at times a perilous thing to pass from one street to another, was now laid waste by the direct scourge of God.

Pestilence, with all its awful accompaniments of helpless panic and reckless lawlessness, raged in the city. The fearful poison seemed to lurk everywhere—in the people's food, in the air they breathed, and in the clothes they wore. Men were afraid to breathe, afraid to eat, afraid to touch one another, afraid even to fly! The icy touch of death fell upon every home in Alexandria; and Alexandria, with her wealth and luxury, and subtle philosophy, and open sin, was without God in the world! In their despair the people thronged the temples and made vows of self-immolation assaulting the Christians as the enemies of the gods and the authors of these calamities.

It is a joyful thing, amidst all the failure and grivous lukewarmness of the Church of God before the world, to know how clearly her light shone before men in that day of thick darkness —how manifest it was that He who was in her was greater than he who was in the world.

Peril made the heathen desperate; it made the Christians calm. "The heathen," Eusebius says, "repelled those who began to be sick, and avoided their dearest friends. They would cast them out into the streets half dead, or throw them out, when dead, without burial, striving to shun any communication and participation with death..... Many of our brethren," he continued, "through their exceeding great love and brotherly affection, neglecting themselves and befriending one another, constantly superintending the sick, ministering to their wants, without fear and without cessation, and healing them in Christ, have died most willingly with them. Filled with disease from others, catching disorders from their neighbors, they drew the pain from others, and infused it into themselves. They took up the bodies of the saints with their own hands, and on their bosoms, closed their mouths, carried them on their shoulders, and composed their hands, embraced them, clung to them, and prepared them decently, washing them, and wrapping them up; and ere long, they themselves received the same offices—those that survived always following those before them."

In the house of Sertorius one of the slaves died; then old nurse Julia was taken. Maia closed her eyes, and she had reason to hope that their opening gaze would rest joyfully on Him who was pierced for her.

At length, Caius Sertorius himself began to betray symptoms of the fatal disease; and no sooner had these been manifested than all the household fled, leaving the old man alone with his child.

He entreated her to fly, but she would not listen, and at last he ceased to desire it, suffering her to do what she would for him.

The disease advanced with fearful rapidity.

One evening, when it had grown dusk, whilst Maia watched beside her father's bed, praying—

"My child!" the old man gasped, "take that book from the niche beside my bed, and read to me about Him in whom you trust."

Maia eagerly took down the roll—*it was her lost Gospel of St. Luke.* She knelt down by the bed, and sobbed out her thanks to God.

"Maia," he asked, fixing his hollow, bright eyes, with a look of intense earnestness on her, "do you think there can be pardon for me?"

"Father," she said, "when you believed me an ungrateful and rebellious child, *you* could not find it in your heart to cast me from you. Our Lord Jesus teaches us to call God *Father*."

The old man was silent for some moments: then he said, "What you say is wonderful; but I believe it is true. Read to me, Maia."

She read of the prodigal son. As she read, a man's footstep echoed through the empty house. The doors were open; she thought it might be one of the bandits who used to plunder the deserted palaces. Her heart grew chill, but she read on in faith—

"And when his father saw him, he was moved with compassion, and ran, and fell on his neck, and kissed him, saying, This my son was dead, and is alive again; was lost, and is found."

The footsteps paused at the door—

"It is Cleon!" gasped the dying man.

Maia started—her senses grew dizzy—she had not thought the old feeling was so strong—but the presence of death, and of God, soon restored her calmness.

Cleon came forward to the bedside. Maia saw the scar in his forehead, and she held out her hand. He took it in both his. They could neither of them speak.

At length the old man gathered up his remaining strength, and said, "Maia, will you shrink from sharing his reproach?"

She could not answer, but she laid her other hand on Cleon's.

"Cleon," said the dying man, "I have sinned grievously, but I trust God will receive me, even as I welcome you. Forgive me, and guard *her* well."

They knelt silently beside him and joined their hands in his: he laid them on his breast, and whispered, "Our Father." And so saying, he fell asleep.

Cleon took her to his sister's house. There, too, death had been busy, carrying the youngest and the eldest to their rest. Isidore had finished his fight, dying at his post; and little Alce had been bidden up higher, to the "feast of the blessed Jesus" above.

At length the pestilence subsided—and once more the Church of Alexandria was gathered together in the hall of the house of Isidore.

There were many widows and orphans there; but still, amidst their tears, the little assembly raised their voices in heartfelt thanksgiving, praising God for those whom He had taken to Himself, and also for those whom He had yet left in the world to serve Him a little longer amongst men. They chanted the 107th Psalm—

> O give thanks unto the Lord, for he is good,
> For his mercy endureth for ever.
> Let the redeemed of the Lord say so,
> Whom he hath redeemed from the hand of the enemy."

On that day two lives were to be joined together before the Church of God; Cleon and Maia were to be married.

Maia was led forth by the deaconesses, in a long white linen veil—they then plighted their faith to each other; and the bishops and the presbyters blessed them, the whole assembly responding with supplications of blessing on their union. Then, together, they laid a gift on the table of the Lord, and, with the whole Church, they partook of the sacred memorials of His love in whom they were one.

Henceforth all their lives were to flow together in one holy stream of blessing—their table was to be their Lord's table—their house His temple; so, with a subdued yet trustful joy, they went on their journey of life together.

What the ideal of a Christian union was in those early days, we may learn from one who lived in them:—

"What an union," says Tertullian, "is that between two believers, who have one hope, one desire, one rule of life, one service of one Lord, in common! Both, as brother and sister, one in body and spirit, yea, in the true sense, two in one flesh, kneel together—together fast and pray; they teach, exhort, and bear with one another: they sit together in the Church of God, together at the table of the Lord. They share distresses, persecutions, joys, hiding nothing from one another; freely do they visit the sick and assist the needy; psalms and hymns resound in their home; and they emulate one another which shall sing the praises of their God the best. Christ rejoices, seeing and hearing such things; to such He sends His peace; where two are, there is He; and where He is, there the Evil One is not."

Thus did our brethren, in those days, understand the distinction between the labors of the ascetic and the free service of thanksgiving—what it means to be like Him who is perfect man, as well as perfect God.

Thus holy, and blessed, and blessing, was the home-life of Cleon and Maia.

The two families were to take a final leave of Alexandria in a few days after the marriage of Cleon and Maia, to settle together amongst the

Indian churches, where Cleon had labored successfully.

On the day before their departure, the widowed Alce and her children, with Cleon and Maia, met at a quiet place without the city, where many bodies of the saints of Alexandria slept, to take a last farewell of the resting-place of their beloved. They were not clad in mourning, for the early Christians feared this might seem like murmuring against Him who they knew does all things well.

They knelt on the graves, and Cleon prayed. Insensibly his prayer took the form of thanksgiving. When they rose they all felt—even Cleon and Maia, to whom so much had been given on earth—that much of their treasure was already laid up in heaven—that they had much "precious seed" laid in the ground, until the time when he who "sowed in tears" shall doubtless "come again with joy, bearing his sheaves with him."

"Alce," said Cleon, "it is but a little while for all of us."

She bowed her head, and murmured, "It is well."

"For we," he added, "'sorrow not without hope.'"

"No," said Maia, smiling brightly through her tears; "He will bring them with Him."

"We on earth, and they in the better place 'for ever with the Lord,' we wait alike for the day when He with whom our life is hid shall appear, and we with Him."

And so, patiently laboring from day to day, before God—sent into the world as their Master was sent—ministering to all, even as He ministered—doing their Father's will, and resting on His grace,—they looked on through the night to the cloudless morning of the resurrection.

SKETCHES FROM THE HISTORY

OF THE

REFORMATION IN ITALY.

I.

SEED SOWN BY THE WAYSIDE.

If you had chanced to be at Ferrara, one summer's evening, some three hundred years ago, you might have seen a number of men, of all classes and ages, issuing from the door of a building apparently connected with the Ducal Palace. There must have been an assembly of some kind within. It did not seem to be altogether a public meeting, for the people did not throng out of the doors, and disperse openly through the streets, but came quietly in groups of twos and threes, and either kept together in earnest conversation, or separated silently, each to his home. Nor was it, apparently, the resort of mere idlers, called together by one of the brilliant spectacles so frequent at the gay and classical court of Ferrara; these men had nothing of the mien of mere idlers; you might trace them through the streets, thronged as they were, at this holiday hour of the south, by gay and eager multitude—by their earnest, absorbed looks—their low, serious converse—the silent pressure of the hand at parting. Yet there was nothing stealthy or timid in their bearing—nothing of the suspicious glance of conspirators: they moved on like men engaged in some great common undertaking—unobtrusive, but unfearing.

"The Duchess has been holding one of her Lutheran prayer-meetings again," said a soldier at the corner of one of the streets, as one of these groups passed by, to the prosperous-looking landlord of the inn, at the door of which he stood.

"Every one his own way," was the somewhat latitudinarian reply of mine host; "the sun shines and the vines grow; let each man thank God in his own language."

"Holy Mary! my excellent gentlemen," exclaimed a little shrivelled vender of relics, from behind her stall, "the saints defend us from the Lutheran poison! Father Anselm says the prayers of the heretics are worse than curses. In Germany, they say, the wretches have burnt the holy images as if they had been mere wood; and buried the relics of the saints"——

"As if they had been the bones of honest men!" interrupted the soldier, laughing. "So much the better for your trade, mother Berta: the scarcer the goods the higher the prices."

"If I may be allowed to offer an opinion, worthy sirs," interposed a spruce little barber, with an introductory hem, and in an oratorical and oracular voice, "the powers of Christendom had better look about them. Portentous signs are abroad. At Lucca and Pisa, heresy stalks in open daylight; at Venice, they have had the audacity to petition the Senate for a place of worship. At Naples, (I have it from the highest authority,) the disease has crept into the noblest families. If I were the Pope, I would lay a strong hand on the rebels."

"The Pope is a mere phantom!" retorted the soldier; "no one believes in the Pope who has been at Rome. If you had seen the Lutheran lanzknechts drag the cardinals through the streets, as I have—mock the mass in the church—lay bare the sacred toys and tricks of the monks—parade a rough fellow, like me, through the city on an ass, as Pope, and kneel to receive his benediction before the very eyes of Clement, crying out, 'Life to Pope Luther!' you would know something! Let Heaven defend its own."

At each successive enormity of this narrative, Monna Berta had crossed herself; but at the climax she groaned aloud, and exclaimed, in a tone of unfeigned terror, "All the saints preserve us from Luther and all the devils!"

"Freedom is good, but safety is better!" said the barber; "I am for a general council."

"Your free life has given you some rather lax notions, my friend," said the complaisant landlord.

"The Lutherans are the men for freedom," was the reply. "'Down with priests and beggars!' say they; 'let the Word of God speak for God, and every man for himself!' But what do you say about it, my pretty child?" he continued, turning to a little maiden who was selling fruit—diving meanwhile into her grape basket—"Luther or the Pope? the Duke or the Duchess?"

"O sir," said the child, "if it is of the good Duchess Rénée you are speaking, we can never pray enough for blessings on her. We were starving, and she sent us food; my father was dying in prison because he could not pay his debts, and she paid them with her own purse, and sent Luigi to school, and gave me fruit from her own gardens to sell, until my father could leave his bed. Oh, she has been to us an angel of God!"

"Good!" pronounced the soldier. "Let the heretics live like angels and fight like Germans, and they may pray as they will, for me. A glass of your best wine, Sir Landlord, and here's long life to Pope Luther!"

"Young men like new ways," said an old man, shaking his head over his glass; "trodden paths are surest."

"What news from the kingdom of heaven, Messer Ludovico?" demanded the soldier of a young student, who had just made his exit from the palace.

"There is life in the words of these men!" was

the serious reply. "There were two speakers to-night—one, a Capuchin friar, tall, pale, worn, it seemed, with fastings and inward battles. His soul seemed of fire—it flashed from his eyes, between his hollow cheeks and dark brows—and his words rushed out like a torrent of flame from Vesuvius."

"That was Ochino, the Tuscan, from Sienna, general of the Capuchins," observed the landlord: "no man in Italy can speak like him."

"True," said the little barber, patronizingly, "the man has a very pretty knack of talking."

"While he spoke," continued the young student, "we seemed to forget all but him. We hung on his words as on the sentence of life or death; the hearts of the whole assembly were gathered into one, and heaved to and fro, like a light skiff, in the tempest of his thoughts, while he spoke to us of sin and death, and the unfathomable chasm on the brink of which we stand. We were breathless: it seemed as if a breath might have broken the thread which bound us to this visible world, and sent the soul, naked and shivering, into the presence of the Judge!"

"*Jesu Maria!* it is so!" exclaimed the soldier. "The friars tell us of the saints, and their merits, and we go comfortably to sleep; or if by chance a poor fellow starts up, and begins to tremble and fear it is not all right with him, some soft-spoken monk will come and tap him on the shoulder, and say, 'Don't distress yourself, my good friend; I have a little interest up there; a few dollars from your next forage, and we will soon set all to rights!'—Bah! it is as if the judgment-seat were like the court of the Pope! But these Lutherans, they bring one face to face with hell and heaven, sins and all, just as one is; fly who may, there is no hiding. And then, when they speak of salvation, there is some meaning in it!"

"That was just Ochino's way," the student rejoined. "Then, when he pointed out the Saviour—the cross of our redemption; the Judge himself stretching out His hand between the criminal and executioner—his voice was low and calm; the tempest was hushed; it was as if the axe had been turned aside from our own necks; as if the Lord Christ himself had waked, and come to us in the midst of the storm, and whispered, 'Pease!' A great calm came over us, and strong men wept like children."

There was a pause—then the landlord asked, "And the other preacher, Messer Ludovico?"

"Ah! he was a man of another mould; they say he is a young Frenchman, from Picardy. His accent was foreign, but we soon forgot that. He was tall, with a marvellously grave, firm countenance; straight, chiselled features; eyes that looked not at, but through you; grand level brows; a mouth fit for an emperor—so resolute! I never saw a nobler head. Michael Angelo might have carved it for a god, if the Almighty himself had not chiselled it for a saint! A smile of heavenly calm rested at times on his face; nevertheless, it might chance to be easier for him to command the armies of heaven than to serve the servants of Christ."

"It must have been Charles Heppeville," said the landlord, "although I have heard that is not his true name. He has been long at the palace; they say he is a kind of confessor to the Duchess —only the Lutherans do not confess. How did he speak?—not like our fiery Capuchin, I trow."

"A weapon of another temper altogether," was the answer. "There is fire in him too; but it does not flash out. You only see the strength of the furnace by the temper of the steel it has cast. Every word of his told; each blow fell on the right place. There was no bravado; no display of tricks of fencing. The sharp point pierced through the very knot of the difficulty, and the whole tangled web fell to pieces in an instant."

"Well, every man to his trade," observed the soldier: "the stiletto for the student; Luther's good heavy broadsword for me."

"No foreign religion, German or French, for us," interposed the old man, sharply. "Italy for the Italians."

"You speak truly, old man," said a gentle voice, which had not before joined in the colloquy. "The Lord Jesus Christ is no foreigner."

The party turned to survey the new-comer.

He had joined them a few minutes previously, and had listened with interest to the conversation. His dress was plain—that of an ordinary citizen; his appearance and manner would not have arrested attention, and yet there was something in him to fix it when once aroused—a calm determination, an expression of earnest thought in the large, serious eyes, melancholy when in repose, but at times lighting into enthusiasm.

"God can speak in Italian, as well as in Saxon or Latin," he continued; "would you be pleased to listen a while to some of His own words?"

They acquiesced, and, quietly seating himself on a bench at the door, the stranger drew from his loose sleeve a clasped book, and in a deep, calm voice, began to read.

He read of the last supper, the betrayal, and the crucifixion. As he read, the attention of his auditors grew more and more intense, and their numbers increased. The landlord forgot his customers, the customers their wine, the little barber his orations; old Monna Berta unconsciously upset Madonnas and *Agnus Deis*, as she leant over her stall, in her eagerness to catch every word; Lucia, the little fruitseller, sank down on her knees by her basket at the stranger's feet, the tears coursing one another down her cheeks; the soldier never moved his eyes from the reader, and when he came to the dividing of the garments—"The cowardly thieves!" he muttered, clenching his hands, "if I had only been there!"—then shrinking back, as if ashamed of his impetuosity, he leaned on the shade of the porch, and listened—every now and then brushing the tears from his rough cheeks.

At length the reader paused, and as in plain and direct words he told them how *their* sins had done all this to the Saviour—how for their sakes He bore it all because He loved them—sobs of pity and shame burst from that passionate southern audience; and when he rose and left them, saying, solemnly, "Go home and tell what great things the Lord hath done for you," no one spoke for many minutes.

At length the soldier said, as he moved slowly away, "Every word goes through one like a word of command."

"The saints defend us from heresy!" exclaimed Monna Berta. "The holy images are good, but such words are better; they bring the things themselves before us."

The group separated in silence; even the little barber had no speech for the occasion.

And little Lucia followed the stranger, and timidly pressed into his hand her best bunch of grapes.

"Take them, good sir, for the love of God. Is it, then, indeed true, that the great God loves us even better than the good Duchess?"

"Your name, friend?" said the soldier, laying his hand on the stranger's shoulder. "That was strange news that you told us—the general taking on himself the punishment of the deserter: there is no abandoning one's post after that."

"My name is Faventino Fannio, of Faenza; if you have learned to rejoice in the good tidings, my friend, spread them."

"We shall meet again, Signor Fannio."

"If it pleases God," was the reply, "and when He pleases."

II.

THE PALACE.

Meanwhile, a different group was gathered on the terrace of the Ducal Palace. At one end sat the good Duchess Rénée, of France, daughter of Louis XII., and wife of Ercole of Ferrara, bending over some delicate embroidery. Before her, on a small clawed marble table, lay some books, and a silver basket, the work of Benvenuto Cellini, filled with silken and golden threads. A beautiful child leaned against her knee, her hair falling in rich clusters on her shoulders, as she looked up with her dark, languid eyes, in her mother's face. It was Leonora d'Este. The fair child was ripening into that touching beauty which was to be the worship and the woe of Tasso.

Around the Duchess stood three gentlemen, gesticulating with Italian vehemence. On a stone seat at the other end of the terrace, resting his arm on the balustrade to encircle a book which he was reading, sat a young Frenchman. His dress was severely plain—his lofty brow was slightly knit, and his lips compressed, and every now and then he drew his hand thoughtfully over his moustache and beard. Two little girls were playing near; one of them, a lively child of twelve, tried from time to time to catch his attention; but although the little tempter was no other than the fascinating Lucrezia, afterwards Duchess d'Urbino, all her arts were in vain. John Calvin, better known at Ferrara as Charles Heppeville, was deep in the Epistle to the Romans.

The Duchess had nothing royal in her appearance. You would not have singled her out from her ladies as the one born to command. Her features were plain—her figure homely—her dress as plain as the manners of the time allowed. A velvet train, open in front, displayed the ample folds of a brocaded petticoat; her straight bodice was unadorned; a jewelled necklace rose and fell beneath her transparent stomacher, and her hair was concealed in a tight velvet hood. By the table at which she sat stood a lady of far queenlier bearing. She was young, and simply attired: a black velvet dress fell around her graceful form, confined by a silver girdle; a plain white collar stood up around her throat; the sleeves of her dress fell from the elbow, and at the wrists the snowy lawn was clasped by silver bracelets; these, with the miniature of an old man with gray locks and beard, which rested on her bosom, were her only ornaments. The miniature was a

sketch of her father, a distinguished physician—
by the young Raphael. Her head was slightly
bent, and in her hands she held some of the
Duchess's broidery threads, which she was ar-
ranging; the long lashes shaded her rounded
cheek, and her dark hair,

> "Not over wide dispread,
> Parted Madonna-wise on either side the head,"

was confined in a golden network.

But as from time to time she raised her head
suddenly, when something in the conversation
aroused her—in the expressive, half-parted lips,
the broad forehead, the sunny eyes, you could
see the light of a clear intellect, and the glow of
a warm and generous heart. She was Olympia
Morata, one of the most gifted of the women who,
in the time of that great awakening, gave them-
selves to the cause of Christ and of freedom.

But although the Duchess bore on her brow
no inscription legible to vulgar eyes, "I sit a
queen!" every line of her homely but expressive
features bespoke her the true-hearted woman.

Her brow was not smooth—years and cares
had furrowed it; her eyes were not bright, for
they had shed many tears. Her face did not
glow with Olympia's high enthusiasm, but the
quiet smile that rested on her lips as she looked
down on her little Leonora, or beamed in her kind
eyes as she raised them at some sentiment she
liked, was worth much—it was so chastened, and

yet so cordial—she looked so good and true. You might not have loved the Duchess Renée for her face, but you would soon have loved her face for her sake.

Although poorer than Olympia in natural endowments, the good Duchess was far richer in those fertilizing experiences of love and pain, and joy and tenderness, which are involved in the names of wife and mother. Left an orphan at the age of five years, to struggle alone with life, in the midst of a selfish and intriguing court, Renée had early learned that childlike faith in God as her reconciled Father—in His Word as the guide and staff of her heart, which she afterwards so sorely needed. They had married her, as an article of some treaty, to a prince who never loved her, and who, if he had cared to try, could never have been able to appreciate a nature so delicate and noble as hers. Her judgment ripened, and her character grew in strength and dignity under the pressure of the trial, whilst all the deep tenderness of her nature was developed by the little family which sprang up around her. Renée was singlehearted. The problem of her life had been, not at how little personal inconvenience she could preserve her title to the eternal inheritance; but how she could best encourage every resource —"spend and be spent" in the service of her adored Sovereign; not how little fidelity required, but how much love could do.

She was not, therefore, content with the safe

toleration of her own convictions, or even with their open recognition; she braved patiently all the numberless petty tyrannies of a worldly family, and the more serious annoyances of a despotic and ungenerous husband, in the defence of her brethren in the faith. Thus for many years the court of Ferrara became not only a centre of light for Italy, but a city of refuge for oppressed Protestants of all nations. The Duchess maintained this privilege at no mean cost; but as long as a fragment of power remained to her, she did maintain it. The Italian Reformers loved and revered her as a true mother in Israel; and meanwhile she continued lowly and single-hearted as a child, for she dwelt in the presence of God.

The conversation was abruptly interrupted by the appearance, at the head of a winding staircase which led from one end of the terrace, of a man whose rich doublet seemed to betoken rank, and whose short Spanish cloak bespoke a nativity of which the Reformers were apt to be suspicious.

He advanced towards the group; and as soon as the Duchess perceived him, she smiled, and offered him her hand, over which he bent with a grave, yet easy courtesy.

"The Chevalier Valdes is always welcome," she said. "You bring us tidings from Naples?"

The Spanish knight and minister looked inquiringly around. "We are all friends," said the Duchess, answering his glance; "the Padre Ochino you already know. Allow me to introduce to you the Signor Burlamacchi, pastor of the church at Lucca; and Messer Ludovico Paschali, with whom you may chance to have further intercourse, as he is on his way to visit our brethren in the Waldensian colony in Calabria. He has left the army of the emperor for that of the emperor's Master."

"No chivalry like the army of martyrs," said Valdes, bowing to the strangers, and giving his hand cordially to Paschali; "and from all accounts, the Vaudois valleys have raised large levies for that host."

"The muster-roll is written in heaven," replied Paschali; "they were a small immortal band of the King's own bodyguard, who remained true to his colors when all Europe deserted them. They have their reward."

"My father never would set his seal to the massacres of the Vaudois," said the Duchess; "he commanded the restitution of their stolen and confiscated property. He used to say, whenever any one objected to this, 'Let them alone, they are better Christians than we are.'"

"Honor to his memory!" said Valdes; "surely he would bless your highness's labors, had he lived till now."

"It often comforts me to think so," she replied, raising her sweet, sensible face, with a bright smile.

"The best reward of the Christians of the valleys," observed Burlamacchi, "is to see the dawn for which they have so long watched at length breaking over the nations."

"It is indeed a morning of time," said Valdes; "every moment some new hill-top catches and flashes back the sunrise. In Naples there is scarcely a noble family which does not number some recruits for the good cause; and in Sicily, too, 'light is sown,' and is silently springing up from place to place."

"At Lucca, we have a regularly-organized and recognized church," said Burlamacchi; "and from our city the glorious news has spread to Pisa, where once more the Supper of the Lord has been celebrated in its own touching simplicity, as before the night of Gethsemane."

"We must be prudent," observed the cautious Spaniard, somewhat uneasily; "it is not wise to depart unnecessarily from time-hallowed rites."

"Time can never hallow error," rejoined the Lucchese pastor, vehemently.

"And Florence?" asked the gentle Duchess, interposing.

"Florence will never receive anything from Pisa!" replied Burlamacchi, bitterly.

"Nevertheless, there are true disciples there," said Valdes; "and from Modena, Faenza, Imola, Bologna, Cremona, Milan, Genoa, and even from Rome itself, I have letters full of the richest promise."

"Brucioli's Italian Bible is worth an army of propagandists!" observed Calvin, who could no longer see to read.

"True," responded Valdes, courteously saluting the Picard Reformer; "it finds its way into homes and hearts where no other messenger of God could penetrate. Truer spouses of Christ are nourishing in the depths of many convents than they ever knew before."

"Alas!" sighed the Duchess, "they will have much to suffer."

"The grace of God is sufficient for them," remarked Calvin.

"Yes, God keeps the soul—but I long to save them the fiery trial," said the compassionate Duchess.

"The fragile lamp can but break, signora," said Olympia, in a low voice, "and the Divine light can not be extinguished."

"Do you specifically controvert the Papal errors?" asked Valdes, addressing Paschali.

"I do not," was the reply; "I believe that error is *nothing*, except as attached to sin. I trust, therefore, that the truth of God, simply spoken, will of itself reprove sin and nullify error. Light not only dispels darkness, but annihilates it."

"It has been the method of all our Italian Reformers," said Valdes, "and it certainly has prospered wonderfully."

"I believe," observed Paschali, "that there is not a city throughout the land, nor a village buried amongst the rocky recesses of the Apennines, nor a monastery shadowed beneath the very wall of Rome, where the gospel of the free and liberating grace of Christ has not penetrated, and drawn hearts to the Saviour."

"Never was there such a burst of life!" exclaimed Burlamacchi. "It vivifies all sciences, and glorifies all arts; painters paint and poets sing as never the world saw or heard before; tongues of flame descend on millions—it is a day of Pentecost for all nations! Oh, if Dante could only have lived to see the day which shall make her with the

> * natura malvagia e ria
> Che mai non si empie la bramosa voglia
> E dopo il pasto ha piu fame che pria,
> . . . . . . morin con doglia!'"*

"Everything is in our favor," rejoined Valdes: "all Italy's best and greatest and wisest are with us."

"And God is with us," interposed Calvin, gravely, "which is much more."

The Duchess looked up with her quiet, intelligent smile.

"Is it true," Paschali asked, "that in Venice the adherents of the evangelical faith have petitioned the Senate for liberty of public worship?"

"It is," replied Valdes. "I have just received a letter from that prince of letters and true servant of God, Pietro Carnesecchi—full of the brightest and most confident anticipations."

"The flame can not be stifled much longer!" Burlamacchi exclaimed; "Italy will burst her

---

* "Divina Commedia," c. 1, p. 97—"Inferno."

chains, and once more sit a queen among the nations. God himself is setting free the hearts of her sons, and the freed hearts will create free institutions. The gospel will force a channel for itself. But are they not still somewhat fettered to the mass in Venice?" he continued, addressing Valdes.

"They are Lutherans—no fanatical Anabaptists," was the hasty reply.

Again the soothing voice of the Duchess interposed: "Even in the Sacred College, it is reported we have friends."

"The people that sat in darkness have seen a great light, and to them which sat in the region and the shadow of death, light is sprung up," said Calvin; "but let them come out of Babylon, if they would not be partakers of her plagues."*

"We must have prudence, my friend," replied the courtly Valdes. "Prudence is the virtue of high places. What would be cowardice in a private soldier is but caution in the general."

"We are all privates in the army of the great King, and what would be treason in the peasant is treason in the prince. Christ's witnesses are martyrs, not diplomatists," was the rejoinder of the future founder of the theocratic republic.

"But the Cardinals Contarini, Marone, and Pole, are with us in all essential points," Valdes

---

* I quote what was, I believe, the common interpretation of the Reformers of the sixteenth century.

replied; "and we may well tolerate what our Master can."

"If they are not ashamed to own Him, we will certainly not be ashamed to own them," said Calvin; "but if the day of decision came, and the question lay between burning and being burned, on which side would the Borderers be?"

"The hour will reveal the men," was the reply. "When the danger comes, the invisible armies will manifest themselves."

"Cardinals, popes, literary men; so many wise, so many noble, on our side—even the very nobles of Babylon," observed Calvin, dryly— "we could almost stand alone without supernatural aid; but where is the enemy? If the Church is so universal, where is the world?"

"Who knows," exclaimed Burlamacchi, exultingly, "that the time may not be come when the kingdoms of this world shall become the kingdoms of our God and of His Christ—that this may not be the dawn of the morning without clouds!"

"Who knows!" they all exclaimed. "We who watch shall see."

There was a pause; the long, level streak of sunset light was fast fading from the western marshes of the Ferrarese, and before the party separated for the night, the Duchess requested Olympia Morata to improvise a song.

She took up her guitar, and, after gazing a few

minutes at the eastern towers of the city, behind which the moon was slowly rising, a smile came over her glowing face, and in a rich, touching contralto voice, she sang—

THE SONG OF THE WALDENSES.

" ' Watchman, what of the night?'
   We have waited long for the day—
From time to time came flashes of light,
   But they died in the dark away.

" Some breathings of life have stirr'd,
   But in blood they soon were crush'd;
And we caught the song of an early bird,
   But its voice was quickly hush'd.

" Joy to the patient and brave!
   The dawn is breaking now!
It crisps the crests of the purple wave—
   It crimsons the mountain's brow.

" It gilds the towers with its rays—
   It cheereth the narrow street—
It waketh a tumult of work and praise,
   And a stir of busy feet.

" Joy, joy! it cometh up,
   Wider and brighter and higher;—
It poureth life in the meek flower's cup—
   It tippeth the peaks with fire.

" We have watch'd in the darkness long,
   But the day is come at last,
The world o'erfloweth with light and song—
   The night and the cold are past.

" The light, the light is come!
   Light on the chain of the slave;
The light of God on the laborer's home—
   Light on the martyr's grave!' "

She ceased. The Reformers took leave. Ochino had withdrawn early, wearied with his energetic preaching. The moon had gone some way on her journey, with her one faithful star: her image floated in the river far below. The night breeze rustled the vine-leaves overhead, and shook the clusters of purple grapes. No one spoke until the little Leonora, clinging closer to her mother, whispered—" Mother, how beautiful it is! I think God sings to us in the silence."

The children kissed "good night," and Olympia and the Duchess were left alone.

Olympia sat on a cushion at her lady's feet. The Duchess smoothed back the hair from her forehead, and said, " You are young, and full of hopes, my child."

" I am full of trust, signora!" was the reply; " God rules, and the right must triumph."

" Yes, that is a glorious certainty—the right must triumph, because God is almighty; but He only knows through what conflicts!" she added, mournfully. " I feel, Olympia, as if the evangelical cause had a baptism to pass through in Italy—a baptism of weakness: we must drink of the cup He drank of. We are too strong in our own strength; too wise in our own wisdom: we think too much of the mighty; too little of the Almighty."

"The wisest are indeed as children before Him," rejoined Olympia; "but He does not, surely give strength in vain!"

" Then these melancholy divisions!" continued the Duchess. " The name of Pisa is as a curse to Florence; a Lutheran is a Papist to a Zuinglian, and a Zuinglian little better than a heathen to a Lutheran. I fear, if the pressure were removed from without, our cause would not expand, but fall to pieces. I think we must drink deeper of the Master's bitter cup, before we shall have more of His spirit. Suffering is the school of love."

"But not of *hope*," replied Olympia. "The pinions of love are only bathed in the bitter waters, and she rises refreshed; the delicate wings of hope are weighed down and crushed. Your highness will teach us to love, and we will teach you to hope. Surely," she continued, emphatically, "God does not spread our table with painted food—He does not fill the cup with hope and joy, that He may dash it from the parched lips untasted!"

"He does not tantalize, but He does try," replied Rénée, gently. "If I can not hope as you do, Olympia, it is not that I distrust our Father's tenderness, but our insight. I do not doubt about the result, but the process."

The Signora Morata retired; but long afterwards the Duchess might have been seen pacing the terrace alone; and in the moonlight, perchance the angels saw a pale face, wet with tears, turned trustfully to heaven, and heard the muttered prayer, "Father, Thou lovest Thine own better than Thy child can; the cup which Thou givest, Thou wilt give us strength to drink!"

III.

THE PEASANT.

The golden gleam had faded from the rich chestnut forests, just lingered on the edge of the upper pine-woods, and had melted into a crimson glow on the snowy peaks of the Calabrian Apennines, when the little Lois came tripping down from the upland pastures with her father's goats.

As she passed through the dim aisles of the tall old woods, their shadows fell heavily on her heart; and to make a sunshine for herself, she began carolling one of the old chants of her people, which they used to sing together in winter over the crackling pine-logs.

The song was not in the Calabrese dialect, and it did not tell of love, or war, or knightly prowess; the traditions of Lois' people were of another stamp, and her little heart rose and grew courageous as she sang of the warfare in which death is victory, and the holy land beyond the stars, and God.

Soon she came out of the forest on a wild thicket of myrtle, arbutus, and oleander: the glossy leaves shone in the last gleams of light, the fragrance of the flowers came freely out in the still air, the birds were singing their last songs; at the entrance of the wooded valley the meadows sloped out on a low beach, on which the waves came up quietly; between the cliffs the level line of the purple sea melted into the sky; whilst, above, the crescent of the young moon floated like a silver boat in a golden flood.

There was one point, however, in the valley, on which Lois and the goats were more intent than on all the rest—the little wooden hut, from the windows of which, amidst its orchard of oranges and lemons, and the elms and poplars festooned with vines, gleamed the pine-torch which was Lois' guiding star. Above the hut rose abrupt precipices of gray rock, in the crevices and clefts of which sprang the aloe and flowering cactus; while the wild goat browsed on their edges.

As she came out on the meadow cleared by her father's toil, a stranger met her coming up from the beach, with the wallet of a wayfarer. He leant on his long oaken staff, and looking towards the sea, greeted her kindly.

BRINGING HOME THE GOATS.

Tales and Sketches.

"That was a sweet song you were singing, my child. I heard the air once before, many hundred miles away."

"My grandmother taught it me," she said. "Our fathers brought it with them from the valleys in the north."

"That was long ago," the stranger answered. "Do you live near this?"

She led the way to the hut; her mother stood at the door watching for her.

"You are late this evening, Lois."

"Yes, the goats would browse as they came along, and I went out of my way with Martha. They say the king's troops are abroad, and she was afraid to go home alone."

The stranger was hospitably welcomed. A supper of maize-cakes, olives, and goat's-milk cheese, with a skin of native wine, was quickly spread before him; and as he ate and rested, he had leisure to observe his hosts.

Two children were asleep in a crib by the corner; the mother's attention was divided between her spinning-wheel and her baby's cradle; the old blind grandmother sat knitting in the window. Lois was soon busied preparing her father's supper; whilst a brown-skinned, bright-eyed urchin knelt before the pine-logs on the hearth peeling chestnuts.

Before long the sheep and goats were safely folded, and the father of the family came in with his eldest son. He was a quick-eyed, strongly-built man, with limbs knit and features bronzed by toil. At first he regarded the stranger rather suspiciously: there was something military in his air which he did not like. But his suspicions were quickly disarmed, as the traveler, rising, grasped his hand cordially, and said, in the Vaudois dialect:—

"I bring you the blessing of the Highest, from the valleys of your fathers. The secret of the Lord is with them that fear Him."

The effect of this watchword was electrical. The whole family quickly grouped around their guest; even the old grandmother let fall her threads, and, raising her sightless eyes to heaven, exclaimed, "Blessed be he that cometh in the name of the Lord!"

"Amen!" said the stranger, who was no other than Ludovico Paschali, on a mission from the Vaudois of the Piedmontese valleys to their brethren in Calabria. From that moment the stranger was a brother to the simple Christian peasants.

"You have had a glorious post in the great army," said Paschali, "and you have kept your trust well."

"We were a little, lowly band," the father replied, "when our fathers abandoned their mountain-home in the north to flee from the sword of the persecutor, and were led, by ways that they know not, to the valleys of Calabria. Two hundred years have passed since then; our flocks and herds have increased, and the Lord has given us grace in the sight of our enemies; but we have not been so faithful as we might. We are a poor and unlettered people: our pastors died, and none arose in their places; the way from our ancient dwelling-place was long, and beset with many dangers; and as the years passed on, and troubles came on the Alpine valleys, our brethren forgot us, and we were left without guides in the land of the stranger."

"But you did not abandon the treasure of your fathers?" Paschali said.

"Thank God, no!—we did not put out the light; but we hid it under the bushel, until, I fear, with many of us it has waxed dim. Many of us were led astray to frequent the idolatrous worship of the country;—we had wives and children, and we feared the oppressor. Like Naaman of old, we would bow down in the house of our master's god, and worship Jehovah in our own. But I fear it has not prospered; the fire has smouldered in the close place, and our hearts have grown chill."

"The sun is still in the heavens," answered Paschali, gravely; "you have only to lift your hearts up towards it to feel its warmth. The love of God, you see, still watches over you, and your brethren from the valleys have sent me to bring you the message of peace."

The old grandmother clasped her hands, and exclaimed, in a tone of fervor, "Truly, God is gracious to His people! The Lord hath been mindful of us—He will bless us."

It was soon arranged that a meeting should be held that very evening; the visit of a pastor was too rare a blessing to be neglected.

The father and son, and even little Lois, hastened with pine-torches to cottage after cottage scattered among the hills; and in an hour's time an assembly of eager and attentive hearers were gathered in the peasant's hut, to receive the teaching of Paschali.

Old men, with tottering limbs and thin locks; fathers of families, with their little ones; rough men, hardened by out-door labor, and young muscular mountaineers, gathered around the teacher—a congregation of teachable and simple hearts.

He took a clasped Bible from his breast.

"It is the Book—it is the Book!" they murmured, and every head was bowed in reverence as he read the words of life. Every sound was hushed when he closed the volume, and poured out his heart before Him who was their God, and the God of their fathers.

He took as the text of his simple sermon, "As an eagle stirreth up her nest, fluttereth over her young, spreadeth abroad her wings, taketh them, beareth them on her wings; so the Lord did lead him, and there was no strange god with him." And as he unfolded before them the wonderful love of Him who had given "His Son,

His only Son, whom He loved," as a ransom for them, and had borne with them, and fed them, all the days of old, and then pointed out to them their own coldness and ingratitude, and urged them by His patient faithfulness to be faithful to Him, to stand boldly on the Lord's side, irrepressible sobs of humiliation and gratitude burst from many a manly breast. Then he told them of the dawn that was breaking over the nations; how the blessed tidings of free redemption had thrilled and liberated thousands of fettered hearts; how many had counted not their lives dear unto themselves for the testimony of Jesus and the word of His grace; how, not in Angrogna and Pragela, and the Piedmontese valleys alone, but throughout the world, the heavenly dews were falling, and in the desolate places rich harvests were springing for heaven, and the Word of God had become the dearest treasure of thousands of souls—old men raised their hands to heaven and blessed God that He had visited His people, tears of joy ran down rough cheeks, and young hearts beat high with thankfulness and loyal purposes of fidelity, and devotion, and endurance. The simple service concluded with one of the traditional hymns of the Waldenses. At first many hearts were too full to join; but ere it closed, a chorus of triumphant praise swelled through the valley, such as those hills had never rung back before.

It was late when the assembly broke up.

The next morning, Paschali set out on a tour of the Vaudois villages.

Paschali and his friend Negrino labored long among those simple children of the valleys. They had abundant fruit of their labors. The Spirit of God was poured forth on the people, and the Vaudois villages of Calabria were filled with humble hearts and holy deeds, and the voice of prayer and thanksgiving.

This time their light was not hidden, and many around them learned from them to glorify their Father in heaven. We shall see ere long how sorely this strength was needed.

IV.

REFORMERS IN THE CHURCH.

In a small inner chamber of a Roman palace, fitted up with all the apparatus of luxurious piety, sat Vittoria Colonna, widow of the Marquis of Pescara, the friend of Bembo, Contarini, and Pole, whom Michael Angelo revered as a glorified being.

Everything about her was subdued—toned down, as if to harmonize with her own chastened beauty. The room was full of a faint aromatic perfume; from the court below was borne the languid trickling of many fountains; through the crevices of the Venetian shutters the light fell quietly on her fine, but worn features, on the black folds of her nun's habit, on alabaster Madonnas and bronze crucifixes, and on a "Holy Family" of Raphael's, in his early spiritual Perugino coloring.

She sat, her pale cheek resting on her hand, her eyes fixed on the head before her, with its crown of thorns, and in the other hand a miniature of her husband, her thoughts perhaps divided between the two images of her heart—Him whom not having seen, she loved; and him whom having loved, she had lost.

She could not be much past fifty, yet she had been twenty years a widow. She was a woman of great constancy of purpose and affection. Betrothed at the age of three years, her childish dreams, her enthusiastic girlish visions, the deep love of her womanhood, the passionate agony of her first sorrow, the patient suffering of her long widowhood,—all had flowed from one source, and flowed back to it.

Many years before, she had sung—

"Io sono, io son ben dessa, or vedi come
M' ha cangiato il dolor fiero ed atroce,
Ch' a fatica la voce
Può dar di me conoscenza vera.
Lassa! ch' al tuo partir parti veloce
Dalle guance, dagli occhi, e dalle chiome
Questa a cui davi come
Tu di beltade, ed io n'andare altera
Che me'l credea, perchè in tal pregio t' era
* * * * * *
Com' è ch'io viva quando mi remembra
Ch'empio sepolcro; e invidiosa polve
Contamina e dissolve
Le delicate alabastrine membra."*

Her cheek was indeed hollow and wasted, the few locks that escaped from her snowy linen

---

* The following may serve as a rough translation:—

"Yes, I am she you loved—I still am she,
  Though wasted thus by years of changeless woe—
Knowest thou not her *voice* who loved thee so?
  When thou wast taken, love, all loveliness
  Faded from cheek, and eye, and flowing tress;
The beauty that thou gavest fled with thee."

hood were gray, her eyes were sunken and dimmed; yet in the delicate features, the classical head, the lips which, when they had closed for ever, Michael Angelo longed to press as those of a sculptured saint, there were traces of the noblest beauty.

Vittoria's mind was vigorous as her heart was passionate. Hers had been a life of realities— real love, real joy, real conflicts, real bereavement and desolation; and the reality of twenty years of widowhood was only to be solaced by the reality of piety. Hearty and intelligent sympathy in the visions and labors of the men of genius who loved to throng around her, earnest interest in the cause of religion in this world and its promises in the next;—such were her consolations and occupations.

Her piety was not, indeed, so simple, and therefore not so fruitful, as that of the Duchess of Ferrara. Christ was less its centre, His word less its rule. She rested more in ideas and feelings.

In ascending to heaven, her devotions were apt to be entangled in images—in descending to her fellow-creatures, to be lost in mists of emotion; and although the clouds were often sunlit, and the mists transfused with prismatic colors, the pure daylight which they intercepted was at once more beautiful and better to work by.

Like Contarini and Pole, and the other Reformers within the Church, she united much of the simplicity of evangelical faith with an enthusiastic devotion to her ideal of the Church, embodied in the Papal system. The honor of her Church was to her as the honor of her family; she clung to the traditions of her infancy with all the affectionate tenacity of her nature; she was as scrupulously and enthusiastically loyal to her idea of the Church as to the memory of her husband.

As she sat thus, the door of the room was opened softly; she turned her head, and two visitors were ushered into this sanctuary, where only her most intimate friends were admitted.

One was attired in doublet and hose, the other in a clerical costume. One spoke with a tinge of the soft Venetian dialect, the other with a slightly foreign accent. They were Pietro Carnesecchi and Cardinal Pole.

They had not been there long, when another priest, with peculiarly mild and courteous expression and manners, was announced as Cardinal Contarini. They were all intimate friends of one another and of the Marchioness. During her previous residence at Rome, and whilst she had lived in the convent at Viterbo, where Pole was legate, they had often met and shared in religious exercises, and visions as to the future of the Church.

The conversation was animated and interesting, although perhaps more artistic than edifying. Much of that pleasant gossip was introduced which becomes history when attached to great historical names. There was the last statue of

Michael Angelo, the last fresco of the young Raphael, to be discussed.

"How glorious our old Rome will be!" exclaimed Vittoria; "the heretics almost deserve heaven for the penance they undergo on earth in losing our sublime ceremonial."

"Heaven was earned for us by sufferings of another stamp than the deprivation of the luxuries of the eye and ear," said Contarini, gravely.

"I spoke hastily," said the Marchioness, coloring, but with a sweet humility; "thanks, father, for the rebuke."

"It is little self-denial," observed Pole, sarcastically, "for men to whom the gift of sight is denied, to renounce the pleasures of seeing."

"Many of the Lutherans are men of the finest taste and feeling," answered the candid Contarini. "We must not quarrel much with those who, in remedying the sins and sorrows of the world, have little leisure to revel in its beauty. If we could only meet, all might be well."

"Meantime," said Vittoria Colonna, "never will there have been such a solemn and joyful Easter as this year: the music will be angelic."

"To angelic hearts, signora," observed Cardinal Pole.

"What a miracle of grandeur and beauty St. Peter's will be," she resumed, "when it is finished! it will be fit to transfer entire to the heavenly Jerusalem."

"Our fathers killed the prophets, and we build

their sepulchres," murmured Carnesecchi, who was turning over some architectural designs.

"I trust there are many hearts in Rome," Contarini said, "which are indeed risen with the Saviour—to which the Easter festival is the commemoration of a glorious reality; but for me there is no festival as long as Christendom remains torn with these melancholy schisms."

"Woe to the presumptuous spirits that have dared to rend the seamless vesture!" exclaimed Vittoria; "to point a sword at the breast of their mother!"

"And woe, too," said Carnesecchi, "to the mother who made her own children pass through the fire in honor of golden images!"

"There is need of reformation, truly," conceded Cardinal Pole; "but we must recur to the ancient traditions, not rend ourselves from them; we must retrace our steps, and not rush wildly on the unknown."

"They should have waited for a general council," said Contarini; "but even now the rebels may be won back to the standards, if we can but bring them to a parley; something must be conceded; the Catholic Church is not so frail that a few repairs will make her totter."

"Cardinal Contarini thinks everything can be effected by conferences," observed Carnesecchi— "that any disease can be cured if the physicians will only have a consultation about it; but what if, in the first place, the physicians will not meet

—in the second, they can not agree—and in the third, the disease is past medicine? And, firstly, how will you get the council together?"

"I trust the preliminary negotiations will soon be completed," replied Contarini. "His holiness seems favorable, but Christendom is a heavy body to move."

"And meantime," remarked Carnesecchi, dryly, "to every pious soul that asks counsel of you in perplexities of faith, you must reply, 'Wait a little, until we can collect some six or seven hundred reverend fathers together, and then, if we can agree about it, I will let you know what you must do to be saved.'"

"Salvation is a simpler thing," answered Contarini, seriously; "we have the words of the Saviour and the apostles."

"Will an œcumenical council give us more?" demanded Carnesecchi.

"It is a question of interpretation," interposed Pole. "We must have a standard of faith, and the standard must be fixed by the authorities."

"But supposing the council should be divided, as councils have been before now?" pursued the Venetian.

"Signor Carnesecchi surely forgets the promised aid of the Divine Spirit, to teach us all things," rejoined Cardinal Pole, rather haughtily.

"The Holy Spirit teaches us by bringing the words of the Saviour to remembrance," was Carnesecchi's reply; "not by giving new revelations, but by unsealing the old. The last court of appeal, therefore, the ultimate standard of faith, must be none other than the Sacred Scriptures."

"Undoubtedly," said Contarini; "Scripture is the arsenal of the Church."

"And the Church is the guardian of the arsenal," added Cardinal Pole.

"But supposing," resumed Carnesecchi, "that this council and the Bible differ?"

"The very possibility involves the whole question of the authority of councils," Cardinal Pole replied.

"Reginal Pole," said Carnesecchi, solemnly, "this is no question of dialectics; you believe firmly that the Word of God is above all traditions of men; and you would venture the salvation of your soul on the grace and merits of your Saviour alone. Now suppose, for one instant, that of the six or seven hundred priests collected at this council, the majority should decide in favor of the equal authority of tradition, and against justification by faith, (and you well know that the party in the Church which would decide is large,) which would you then abandon—the decision of the council, or the conviction of your own soul?"

"May I die before such a thing comes to pass!" exclaimed Contarini.

"Convictions are not to be given up at pleasure," said Pole, uneasily; "but," he added, "the thing can not be; the voice of the Church is the voice of God."

"Allow me to pursue my supposition one step further," continued Carnesecchi: "suppose the voice of the Church were thus to contradict the voice of your own soul, and the Church (as you well know she would) were to proceed to chastise and torture those who could not sacrifice their conviction at will to her decision—would you be among the persecutors or the persecuted? Would you light the torch, or be bound to the stake?"

"The Church is the handmaid of the Highest," said Pole, "but I never could persecute for conscience sake: it would go against all my feelings; and, besides, it does not answer."

"And yet," pursued Carnesecchi, in a low, calm tone, "that day may come. On one side or the other we must stand, and then, unless Christ is to us greater than the Church, dearer than all our most sacred traditions and most cherished ideals, I can tell you what we, what you, Cardinal Pole, just and tender-hearted as you are, would do. You would never indeed cast a stone at the martyrs, but you would hold the garments of those who slew them."

There was a pause. Carnesecchi had spoken with such solemn earnestness, that none of them could shake off the impression.

At length Vittoria Colonna arose and said, "The Church is the mother of the martyrs, not the shedder of their blood; the spouse of the

Crucified: she suffers, but can she persecute? Think of the millions of lowly, and holy, and self-devoted men who have been fed at her bosom: and shall she be abandoned of the Highest?"

"Signora," said Carnesecchi, as he took leave, "pardon the roughness of a plain citizen; but, believe me, it is not the Church that nourishes the faithful, but the Saviour. She is not the way to Him, but, through faith in Him, we are truly united to her. He is the door of the fold, as well as the Shepherd of the sheep. Where He is, the Church is; and if our souls are united to Him, neither Pope, nor council, nor stake, can excommunicate us." With these words, he left.

"Carnesecchi goes rather far!" said Cardinal Pole.

"But there is truth in his words," remarked Contarini, thoughtfully.

"Ah!" sighed Vittoria Colonna, "for the rest beyond the storms, with the Friend of the heavy-laden and the weary!"

V.

THE PRISON.

Some years had passed—not many, but eventful. The soft cool of the summer's evening fell again upon Ferrara.

The citizens poured out of their houses in their gay dresses; the street of the Ducal Palace was thronged with eager multitudes keeping holiday. But in the palace much was changed. No groups of earnest men issued from it; the doors were closely guarded, and it was long since the glad tidings had echoed from its walls. Preachers and hearers were scattered far and wide;—some had been exiled—some had suffered—some had denied. The Duchess remained faithful, but she was left almost alone.

As the evening grew dimmer, a side door opened softly, and from it came a lady, tightly muffled in a black dress and hood. She moved quickly along, choosing the quietest streets, until she stopped at the gate of a high, gloomy building, with narrow slits of windows and massive walls. It was the prison of Ferrara. She spoke a few words to the sentinel, and he let her pass in.

Faventino Fannio, the evangelist of the Romagna, sat on a pallet in his cell. His voice was gentler, his eye calmer, than ever; but the sadness had passed from his face—hollow and sallow as two years' imprisonment had made it, it was full of blessed peace.

By his side, against a damp wall, leaned a man in military costume; for people were allowed free access to Fannio's cell, and, like St. Paul, for two whole years he preached Jesus Christ, and "taught those things which concern the kingdom of God, no man forbidding him." And many believed.

That soldier was a changed man since the summer's evening many years before, when he had listened to the Divine message from Fannio's lips. The great change which transforms old, hardened, worldly men into lowly and simple-hearted children of the kingdom of heaven, had come over him. They had been talking very earnestly. The martyr had been counselling the convert to fly from the persecution.

"Fly from my post, father! I can not—I dare not!" was the vehement reply; "it would be to deny my Lord!"

"My son," said the old man, in a trembling voice, rising and laying his hand on the soldier's arm, "Peter would have died with his Master; when others fled, he followed; and yet, in the very presence of his Lord, his courage failed, and he denied. Believe me, death is terrible, when it does not steal over us in slow decay, or rush on us in the excitement of the fight, but is offered to our deliberate choice. It was offered me so once"—and the old man hid his face in his hands—"the cross was offered me, and I put it aside, and denied my Redeemer. He has forgiven it now, I trust, since He deigns to let me—me, traitor that I am!—suffer for His sake; but, oh, the agony and shame of that remembrance! It is not the strength of youth that will serve us in that day, young man. Oh, do not dare to court the trial!"

"Pray for me, father, that my faith fail not."

They were about to kneel, when the lady in the muffled cloak was ushered in, and the door was barred again on the outside.

"Signora Morata!" said the old man; "this is kind!"

"The Duchess made these with her own hands," Olympia said, as she opened her basket, and gave him some warm garments.

"The blessing of Him for whose sake ye both labor rest on her and you!" he said; "your visits and your words are better to me than food or clothing, for they refresh and warm my heart."

"It is the last time!" she said, in a faltering voice. "They have banished me at last. The Duchess will be left alone."

"Like the Saviour!" exclaimed Fannio, with a sad smile. "They who come out of the great tribulation with the white robes, will come from the palace as well as the prison."

They stayed some while in earnest conversation, and ere she left, the martyr, the soldier, and Olympia, knelt and prayed together fervently for all who suffered for the Crucified throughout the world, in convent, palace, or prison; that the tempted might be faithful, the fallen raised, the faithful sufferers strengthened. As she left, he took her hand, and said, "A blessing will go with you everywhere, signora. 'I was sick, and in prison, and ye visited me.' You will hear those words one day from other lips than mine, and these will follow them—'Enter thou into the joy of thy Lord.'"

Not many days after, they strangled him in the prison, and committed his body to the flames. He was the first martyr for the recovered truth in Italy.

At the prison door Olympia met her maid Lucia, once the little fruitseller, who was to accompany her mistress, now become the wife of Dr. Gunthler, into Germany. She was an orphan now. And as they turned away, an old woman accosted them, and placed something in Lucia's hand. It was old Berta, the relic-vender.

"Take this, my child," she said, "with the blessing of an old woman: you were very good to me in my long sickness, and I often think of the words you spoke to me then. It is the choicest relic in my stock; and although I know you do not much value such things, the toe-nail of St. Christopher has saved many travelers' lives, they say, before now; and it is no harm, at any rate, to be armed on both sides."

"I will treasure your blessing, dear Berta, but keep your relics."

But the old woman had slipped round a corner, and was nowhere to be seen. Lucia opened the parcel, and found there, besides the relics, two gold pieces, carefully folded, the savings of old Berta's hard and frugal life.

VI.

THE PARTING.

The court of a princely villa: colonnades of marble, avenues of cypress, dim arches, and deep shadows crossing each other on the marble pavement. Above, the "eternal pearl" floating in an azure sea; below, on the steps leading to the water's edge, two women weeping.

The youngest leant against a stone column and wept passionately; the other took her hand, and said, in tones of such sweet gentleness as sorrow alone can teach, although her voice faltered, "This is only one more of the dark days, Olympia! one more—that is, one less to come."

"But I had such different hopes—everything promised so gloriously. Italy free, the Church purified, science, art, wisdom, wealth, power, all glorified as they had never been before, casting their crowns at the Deliverer's feet."

"My child, the day will surely come yet. Let your hopes but build a little higher. 'The sparrow hath found her an house, and the swallow a nest for herself, where she may lay her young:

even thine altars, O Lord of hosts, my King, and my God.' There the spoiler comes not, nor the storm."

"The band of our brethren was swelling so fast," said Olympia, "and now we are broken and trampled in the dust!"

"We have borne witness, and that is enough," the Duchess replied; "what is the Church now but as the tabernacle of testimony in the wilderness? A tent, you know, is made to be taken down. Ah! could we only see inside the threshold of the Temple!"

"But, oh, it is bitter," said Olympia, "to see our brightest and holiest visions stained, and scorned, and trampled in the dust!"

"Dust to dust!" replied the Duchess, "and the immortal essence to the light; the corruptible is burned, the incorruptible is but glorified in the furnace. Could we see how one by one the living stones are built into the radiant sanctuary, we should not mourn so much that our poor edifices crumble together when they are taken. One less among the wanderers in the desert, one more among the blessed family in the home. We are not scattered, dear Olympia, we are only gathering home."

"But my country, my paradise, our Italy!" exclaimed Olympia; "to leave her for ever, and to have her bound and bleeding in the hand of the oppressor!"

"The sun rises again, Olympia, and the Lord reigns."

"It is not for me to murmur," Olympia said, passionately, "but for you, my princess, my mother, to leave you, and so alone!"—and she fell on her knees and clasped the Duchess's hand's to her lips and breast.

Rénée raised her, and gently laying her head on her shoulder, wept in silence without restraint.

"You have been as a sister and a child to me, Olympia, God knows, and now I have none beside."

For many months she had not been allowed to see her children.

A soft splashing of oars broke the silence, and the Duchess whispered, "Not alone, Olympia, not orphaned. The Saviour may yet have some wounds for me to bind up, and He will not leave me comfortless, nor you."

She had just time to press a little Testament into Olympia's hand, when a boat glided to the steps.

A foreigner sprang on shore—a German physician; and as the Duchess laid Olympia's hand in that of her husband, she said, "You will not let my southern flower die in the cold north!"

"Love is of no climate, signora," he said; "if our suns are cold, our hearts are warm. I take her as the dearest gift my God can give me, to love and cherish for her own sake and for His."

Olympia looked trustfully at him through her tears. They stepped into the boat, the rowers took their seats, and in a few moments they were out of sight.

Olympia left her country for ever. The Duchess returned with slow steps to her desolate palace.

VII.

THE MARTYR.

Another prison and another martyr. Ludovico Paschali, the missionary of the Waldenses, sat at a table in his damp cell.

His head was bare; his limbs wasted with hunger and confinement.

They had already starved his friend Negrino to death. The cords had been removed for a few minutes from his lacerated hands and arms, whilst his brother Bartolomeo was with him.

He spent the time in writing a few words of encouragement and consolation to his beloved brethren and children among the Calabrese Apennines. He wrote thus:—

"My state is this: I feel my joy increase every day as I approach nearer to the hour in which I shall be offered as a sweet-smelling sacrifice to the Lord Jesus Christ, my faithful Saviour; yea, so inexpressible is my joy, that I seem to myself to be free from captivity, and am prepared to die for Christ, not only once, but ten thousand times if it were possible. Nevertheless, I persevere in imploring the Divine assistance by prayer, for I am convinced that man is a miserable creature when left to himself, and not upheld and directed by God."

The letter was written as well as the prisoner's stiff and torn hands would allow. Bartolomeo was summoned, and the cords were again tightly bound around Paschali's arms.

The brother wept, but the sufferer smiled.

" I have been learning something of what *He* suffered," he said, pointing to his lacerated hands, " and of *how He loved.*"

The brothers embraced and were separated, but once again Bartolomeo saw Ludovico.

The court of the castle of St. Angelo was arranged and crowded as if for a festival. Priests and cardinals were there, and the dignitaries of the Holy Office (recently established in Italy on the Spanish model); and the Pope himself was there.

There was, as in the days of old, to be a great sacrifice to the gods of Rome. The victim was led out, not crowned and garlanded like the sacred offerings of old; it was an emaciated man in a sordid dress, with a paper mitre on his head, in mockery. His limbs tottered, so that he could scarcely walk, and he seemed dazzled by the daylight. The face was young, although so haggard, and there was light in the sunken eyes.

They dragged him to a platform, to exhibit him to the derision of the multitude.

Raising his thin hands to heaven, and turning to the Pope and cardinals, he said, in a calm, solemn tone—

"I summon you to appear before the throne of the Lamb, and give an account of your cruelties."

Paschali's brother saw no more.

It is now long since that summons has been answered; the martyr has been dwelling three hundred years in the joy of his Lord.

VIII.

DESOLATION.

AND Paschali's converts, the Waldensian peasants, to whom his words had been the keys of the kingdom of heaven—what had been their fate?

Evening had come down on the mountains around the Calabrese village of Santo Sisto. The woodman came whistling home from the neighboring forest; his little children caught sight of him, and left their play, and ran to cling, laughing, about his knees. His wife met him at the door with the baby in her arms. Over the supper they chatted merrily of the day's work and the morrow's schemes.

The shepherd boys and girls came home from the hills, the flocks were safely penned, and before the little ones were laid to sleep, the whole family listened to the Word of God, and knelt together to pour out their simple wants and praises. And in their prayers the good teacher from the North was not forgotten—they had not heard of his death. Then all voices joined in the hymn, for in Santo Sisto there were many happy Christian homes.

But it was for the last time.

Two monks came into the village that night, emissaries of the Inquisition; they exhausted all their arts of persuasion in enticing the Waldensian peasants to attend the mass—but in vain. They had not much logic, but they had that single-hearted loyalty which is so much surer and stronger. To them the mass was idolatry. It was a question of personal fidelity to an adored Master, who for their sakes had shrunk from no extremity of suffering.

They did not shrink from suffering for His sake. Before the next evening the whole population fled in a body to the forest. They left their old men and little ones behind. They thought the inquisitors would have some pity; but they were mistaken.

The inquisitors passed on to La Guardia, the other large village of the Vaudois colony, situated on the sea-shore. They told the inhabitants that their brethren of Santo Sisto had yielded. The temptation and the terror, with this example, were too strong, and the people of La Guardia attended the mass in the Roman Catholic church. But it was in vain. The inquisitors would not give up their victims, and God did not suffer His own to lose the crown.

Troops were sent after the fugitives of Santo Sisto. They rushed into the forest, crying—"*Amazzi, amazzi!*" ("Kill, kill!") The peasants made a brave resistance, but they were driven to a neighboring mountain. There they made another stand, and entreated the captain of the troops to let them escape from the country. They asked only for their lives. The request was denied. Roused to desperation, the little band made an heroic onset, and repulsed and routed the king's troops. But the force against which they contended was overwhelming. New troops were sent, the Viceroy himself accompanying them, to see that the slaughter was complete. The fugitives were driven to the heights of the mountains. The greater number were slain, and the rest perished with cold and hunger. The village of Santo Sisto was burnt to the ground, and the feeble remnant of its population murdered. Pardon was offered to all the outlaws who would join in hunting down the heretics, and thus they were tracked to their hiding-places among the recesses of the mountains, and murdered one by one.

Yet this was not the worst. When the inhabitants of La Guardia found how they had been deceived, they were almost maddened with indignation. They would have joined their brethren in the forest, but it was too late. The inquisitors courteously invited them to a parley. Of those who came, seventy were seized and put to the torture.

Sixty women also were tortured and thrown into prison, with none to bind up their wounds. Most of them died there.

The prisons were filled, and then the prisoners

led out one by one and put to death. "I can compare it," writes a Catholic eye-witness, "to nothing but the slaughter of so many sheep; and yet," he adds, "I do not hear that they behave ill. They are a simple, unlettered people, entirely occupied with spade and plough, and, I am told, show themselves sufficiently religious in the hour of death."

Much followed that is too horrible for us to hear; but yet it was not too horrible for our brethren to endure. They were sawn asunder, thrown from high cliffs, burnt, racked to death! "It was strange," says a Catholic historian, "to see their obstinacy. For whilst the son saw the father put to death, and father the son, they not only exhibited no symptoms of grief, *but said joyfully, that they would be angels of God.*

The whole of this little heroic band was slain, except a few who were sold for slaves.

The flourishing colony of four thousand perished, leaving not one trace behind. Their industrious labors, their conflicts, and their sufferings, are over now, but the long harvest of joy is only just begun.

* * * * *

And what had become, during these years, of the friends of Viterbo, the Reformers within the Church? They were scattered far and wide in place, and further still in thought.

Vittoria Colonna had passed, we trust, as she longed, to the rest beyond the storms, and the light beyond the clouds, with the Friend of the weary and heavy laden.

The gentle Christian heart of Cardinal Contarini had been sorely tried. In spite of all his patient efforts at effecting a reconciliation between the schismatics and the Church of Rome, the breach had widened. The Popes had never honestly furthered his endeavors; the conference for which he had toiled so perseveringly had resulted in a more marked separation; and, happily for him, he died before that General Council, which had been the goal of all his labors, contradicted all the truths he most prized, established and embodied all the errors he sought to reform, and defeated all his most cherished plans. We must hope that his gentle and affectionate soul passed into the inheritance purchased by Him on whose death and righteousness alone he relied, and received the blessing of the peacemakers.

With Pole and Carnesecchi it was otherwise. They lived till the day of decision. The narrow line that separated them proved the line of demarcation. The Council of Trent decided that tradition was of equal authority with Scripture; it condemned those who believed in justification by faith, exalted to higher honors than ever the "holy and venerable" images, and sealed all its decisions with the most terrific anathemas.

Pietro Carnesecchi preferred the voice of Christ to that of the Church—Pole placed the Church between him and the Saviour. The one was sent with every honor as legate to England—the other was thrown into a prison at Rome.

IX.

THE STRAIGHT PATH THE SAFE PATH.

The little glimpse of artifical light which Henry VIII. had made had faded away in England; but Mary, in putting it out, had gone so roughly to work, that she had torn down the old walls, and let the full stream of daylight in.

The city of London was echoing with the news of the death of Cranmer. The Papal Legate sat writing at a table in the palace of his cousin the Queen. Not long before, he had, by a solemn absolution, readmitted the nation within the pale of the Church. Every day brought tidings of some conversion to the royal and Papal cause—the capture of some noted Lutheran, or the death of some obstinate heretic. Yet Cardinal Pole had nothing of the air of a victor. His brow was furrowed, his eye was troubled, and his manner was irritable and uneasy.

A bishop entered the room. His bearing was authoritative and triumphant; he had no scruples and no fears. The name of Bonner has become a byword in every home in England—and with such men was the evangelical, and liberal, and gentle Pole now doomed to associate.

"I come," he said, "in the name of her Majesty and the estates of the realm, to offer your Eminence the mitre of the apostate Cranmer."

"I want no further dignities," replied Pole, irritably; "I have told you already, I only wish to be allowed to serve my God in quiet. I am an old man; I can not burden my few remaining years with further cares—why will you trouble me?"

"Does your Eminence scruple to wear the robes which have been polluted by a heretic?" retorted Bonner, fixing his little keen eyes on him; "they say the disease is infectious."

The Cardinal rose and paced restlessly about the room. He knew very well that his own reputation was not intact; he had narrowly escaped the Inquisition in Italy, and his very sense of the justice of the suspicion drove him to deed after deed of persecution to disarm it.

"But if I accept my royal cousin's gracious proffer," he said, "how can I serve the Church?—I am feeble and old: choose some younger and more vigorous man."

"A sound heart is better than a strong arm," said Bonner, pursuing his advantage; "your Eminence will not refuse your last hours to the cause so dear to your heart. Besides, our officers are faithful—the prisons are scarcely emptied for the stake, before the zeal of our servants fills them with fresh captives. Her Majesty and all the faithful will unite in the support and counsel of your Eminence."

Cardinal Pole sat down again, leaned on the table, and clasped his hands before his eyes.

"It will not answer—it will never answer!" he exclaimed; "I will remonstrate to the last. Men's convictions, right or wrong, are not to be burnt out of them; persecution only burns them in. Try gentle means—reason, tempt, persuade, unfold before them the glory of the Church of Ages—win their hearts back to the Mother of the saints."

"But if persuasion fails?" asked Bonner.

"By heaven! can you not leave the criminal to the Judge? Is not one hell enough?"

"But for the sake of the sound members, the the diseased must be amputated," Bonner rejoined; "when the Church can not reclaim the wanderers, she must teach the faithful by their punishment. In desperate cases the strongest remedies are the most merciful."

"What do you teach by burning?" demanded Pole. "One stake teaches more heresy than a thousand pulpits."

"The chastisement seems to have answered effectually in Italy," replied Bonner, dryly; "we hear no more of the Reformation there."

"I tell you for the hundredth time," rejoined the Cardinal, "that the cases are radically different. In England you have to contend, not with the relics of exhausted races, or the worn-out fragments of factious republics, but with a brave, obstinate, and united nation. They may bear the yoke long in quietness—it is their way; but depend on it, when the climax is reached, and the barrier once burst, the deluge will be terrific let my royal cousin look well to it that it does not sweep away her throne!"

"Well!" said Bonner, shrugging his shoulders, "I am no diplomatist. I am simply an humble son of the holy Roman Catholic and Apostolic Church. She has spoken—I have only to obey."

The Cardinal was silenced. "The Church," he said, "commands my feebleness as well as my strength; if she needs me for this weary dignity, I accept it."

He would not cast a stone at the martyrs, but he held the garments of those who slew them.

Pietro Carnesecchi stood at the window of his cell, looking out on the Tiber. His face was full of a grave and exalted joy. He turned from the window to a friend who had been permitted to visit him, and, raising his fettered hands, he said:

"I have learnt many things in this dungeon. Glimpses of heaven have come to me through those narrow windows, and sounds of everlasting truth and joy in the rushing of that river, such as I never saw or heard till now. I have learnt that there is no freedom like that of the heart which has given up all for Christ—no wisdom like that learnt at His feet—no poetry like the calm foreseeing of the glory that shall be."

The joyful assurance was with him to the last.

"He went to death," they say, "as to a triumph;" and the angels met him with the crown.

So far apart did two roads lead which seemed at first so nearly parallel. So much more joyful is it, even here, to endure all, than to compromise in aught.

X.

THE DISPERSION.

The years passed on. Olympia Morata was dead. She had lived some time at Schweinfurt, her husband's birthplace, as a quiet German matron. Her talents, her engaging character, and her misfortunes, had soon gathered a circle of friends around her. But at the siege of the place by those German princes who were enemies of the Protestant Albert of Bradenburg, she had suffered much from unwholesome food and lodging. The city was taken, and Olympia fled with her husband.

"If you had seen me," she wrote to Celio Secundo Curio, one of the most distinguished of the Protestant refugees, and then professor at Basle, "with my feet bare and bleeding—my hair dishevelled—my borrowed clothes all torn—you would have pronounced me to be the Queen of Beggars."

They escaped, however, to Heidelberg. Here it seemed Olympia would at length find a quiet resting-place, beneath the walls of the noble old castle, not then ruined by religious wars. She found rest there, though not in the way her friends had hoped. Her constitution was broken by hardship and trial, and the rugged northern climate. Her heart yearned over her Italy, but God called the exile to a better home. She sank into a rapid consumption, and died in her twenty-ninth year, full of quiet peace and hope.

The despotic and licentious Ercole of Ferrara had also passed to his account, with the highest recommendations from Pope Paul IV., as a "Defender of the Faith."

The good Duchess, after her husband's death, had retired to Montargis, a city sixty miles to the south of Paris.

True to her old principles, wherever she went, the exiled and persecuted Protestants found a home and a friend, and this at no small risk to herself. The persecutors of the age of St. Bartholomew's Massacre did not spare even princely heretics. The Guises did all they could to oppose her. The Duke even sent an army against Montargis in 1560, under Jean de Souches Malicornes.

The troops forced their way into the town, and succeeded in putting many Protestant refugees to death, and setting fire to their houses. The Duchess, and all who could escape, took refuge in the castle. De Souches threatened to batter it down, and pointed his cannon against the walls.

Rénée did not shrink; her gentle and generous

heart had stood many more trying assaults than this, and she sent this heroic answer to the general:—

"Consider well what you do; know that no one has the right to command me but the king himself; and that if you come hither, I will be the first to mount the breach, when I shall see if you have the audacity to kill the daughter of a king, who desires only to protect her subjects, and whose death heaven and earth will be bound to avenge upon you, and upon all your line, even upon your children in their cradles."

The general was perplexed, and the troops were withdrawn.

One evening, not long after this, the Duchess stood upon the ramparts of the castle, with a refugee recently arrived from Italy. It was Burlamacchi, one of the nobles of Lucca, and formerly pastor of the Reformed Church there. He, with some others, had attempted to effect a revolution at Lucca, and resist the establishment of the Inquisition. Both attempts had failed; the church was scattered, and the pastor had been compelled to flee.

"Do you remember," the Duchess said, in a low voice, "many years ago, as we stood on the terrace of the palace at Ferrara, with Calvin and Valdes, and Ochino, and Paschali, and Olympia Morata? Things are changed since then!"

Burlamacchi leaned against the wall, and hid his face. He could not reply.

"I remember," the Duchess continued, "that Paschali said then there was scarcely a city or a convent or a village in Italy which did not number some genuine disciples of the Saviour. He was right—for now there is scarcely a city or a village which has not sent its martyrs."

"It is true—it is true!" exclaimed Burlamacchi; "at Venice they have been sunk in the sea, calling on the Lord Jesus; at Rome, Bartoccio, and uncounted numbers besides, have perished in the flames, crying, 'Vittoria!' In Modena, Milan, Mantua, Cremona, Lucca, Pisa, Florence, Naples, nobles, peasants, priests, have gone to the stake and the scaffold, rather than renounce the Gospel of their Redeemer. They have succeeded," he added, bitterly, "the enemy has triumphed; for this time the light is trampled out of Italy."

"We have triumphed, signor," replied the Duchess, gently, "though not, indeed, by the way we would have chosen."

"The martyred Reformers do indeed live," he answered; "but the Reformation is dead, and Italy, our beautiful Italy, is lost!"

"Have any denied?" asked the Duchess.

"Some were too self-confident to fly," he said; "and when death looked them in the face, they shrank back, and did penance. Some fled to the Alps, and then, looking back on the paradise they had left, their hearts failed—they returned to apostatize or to die."

Neither spoke for some moments; at last Renée said, "The little band that met at Ferrara are broken and scattered now. Two are at rest; but Ochino! that is the saddest thought of all."

"What has befallen him?" asked Burlamacchi.

"He has embraced the cold and deadly falsehood of Socinus," she replied; "is it not strange that he could leave all for Christ, and then, when he had lost all besides, abandon his Master too?"

"Ah! how often," said Burlamacchi, mournfully, "it is easier to sacrifice than to submit! and yet he may be won back; prayer is stronger than logic, and we will pray for him and for ourselves. Has your highness any news of the other exiles?"

"There are churches at Geneva and Basle," was her reply; "Elizabeth of England has suffered them to worship openly in London; and from the rocks and glaciers of the Grisons the exiles write as full of joy and triumph as if from the very gates of Eden. The colony has become a mission to all the country round. You see," she continued, with one of her old bright smiles, "they have not trampled out the fire—they have only scattered it."

"It is true," he replied, more cheerfully, "we always grow better in the shade; nothing can ruin us but our own lukewarmness and divisions. But for Italy I fear the worst; the candlesticks once removed from the seven churches of old have never since been replaced. The sun rises again, indeed, but he rises on another shore."

"Let not our hearts be troubled," she said; "the martyrs live, the Saviour reigns, and the truth must triumph at the last."

"Yes," rejoined Burlamacchi, "this day has set in clouds; perhaps before another dawns, a night of storms and terror will have passed, such as the world has not yet seen."

"And we, my friend," replied the Duchess, "shall have passed beyond all storms before then, and shall, we trust, come down with the Saviour and the hosts of His redeemed, to bring to the earth the morning of the long day of joy."

She lived long enough to see that the Massacre of St. Bartholomew could not extinguish Protestantism in France; and three years afterwards, in 1575, she was called to be present with the martyrs she had succored, and the Lord she had served.

THE DIARY

OF

BROTHER BARTHOLOMEW.

"They be not all faithless that are either weak in assenting to the truth, or stiff in maintaining things any way opposite to the truth of Christian doctrine. But as many as hold the foundation which is precious, though they hold it but weakly, and as it were by a slender thread, although they may frame many base and unsuitable things upon it, things that can not abide the trial of the fire; yet shall they pass the fiery trial and be saved, which, indeed, have builded themselves upon the rock, which is the foundation of the Church. . . . . But how many millions of them are known so to have ended their mortal lives, that the drawing of their breath hath ceased with the uttering of this faith, 'Christ my Saviour, my Redeemer Jesus!' And shall we say that such did not hold the foundation of the Christian faith?"—*A learned Discourse by Mr. Richard Hooker.*

INTRODUCTORY NOTE.

The supposed date of this Diary must account for its quaintness.

The truths stated in it are, the Editor believes, not more evangelical than are to be met with in the letters of Bernard of Clairvaux; and these truths, and the errors which grow up beside them, not more inconsistent with each other than many of the beliefs which, in those confused times, contrived to find an honest livelihood in the same mind. The mixture of shrewdness and childishness in the good monk would be the natural consequence of an experience so limited as his, and of the union of the intelligence of manhood with that habitual relinquishment of all manly freedom of thought and action which his rule required.

Brother Bartholomew's practical piety must have had many parallels in days when the Bible was daily read in the Benedictine abbeys, and monasteries were the industrial schools and penitentiaries of the nations.

The earnestness of his religion may serve to show the strength of that principle of life which survived the malaria of the monastic system; whilst its deformed and stunted growth, in contrast with the quiet and steady progress of his friend, may illustrate the poisonous nature of the system which could paralyze and distort a life so real and so divine.

It is happy to think, that, amongst the millions who adhered to the ecclesiastical system of the Middle Ages, there were many who lived so near their Saviour, as to receive from His hands the antidote to all its poisons; but it is far happier to know, that there were thousands who lived so close to Him as to rise above its errors altogether, and to be content for His sake to be rejected of their generation.

THE DIARY

OF

BROTHER BARTHOLOMEW.

In the name of our Lord Christ, and all His saints, and especially of our Lady His mother, patroness of this our Abbey of Marienthal, I, Bartholomew, a poor brother in the same venerable Abbey, governed according to the genuine and original rule of the holy Benedict, have undertaken to write a history, from day to day, of the things which mine eyes shall see and mine ears hear.

The thought of this chronicle has visited me frequently of late, often intruding on my hours of holy meditation, for which reason I endeavored to scare it away as a presumptuous suggestion from the Enemy; but seeing that, in spite of all my conjurations, and crossings, and repetitions of the Pater Noster and the Sacred Hours, it hath continued to force itself upon me (being even spoken to me in visions by the holy Benedict himself), I have concluded it to be a good thought, well-pleasing to the saints, and have therefore resolved on executing it, and leaving these my humble memorials as a legacy to the Abbey, knowing that the common incidents of to-day are often as a strange and pleasant tale to those that come after : since which determination, my meditations have been no more disturbed—a further proof that the project is not from below.

In order to accomplish this design, parchment being somewhat costly, I have procured from the Prior the copy of an old manuscript, which none of us can read—not even our learned brother Lupacius, who has studied at Paris. The labor of effacing the former characters was great, they being carefully and thickly written, but I was cheered in my toil by the thought that I was destroying some of the works of the Evil One, the letters being of a very hideous and diabolical form, square and three-cornered, and very black, speckled moreover with a countless multitude of dots which skipped around them like wicked imps, making so ugly a confusion as no Christian could look at long without danger of distraction, much less have made. In every page, therefore, however I may fill it, it is a marvellous consolation to me to reflect that I am tilling so much ground reclaimed from the infidel.

I have lived all my life within the walls of the Abbey, and of the world beyond I know even as little as the Israelites did of the Promised Land when they believed the spies. Of my father and mother I know nothing, nor do any of the brethren. I was found one winter morning, a helpless infant, lying on the threshold of the convent, wrapped in a few rags, with a label importing that my mother and father were dead, and entreating the holy brethren, for the love of God, to bring up the orphan, and teach him to offer masses for the souls of his parents.

At first, I have heard, the monks were sorely puzzled how to handle or what to do with me. An especial convocation was convened, in which it was determined to feed and cherish me as they would any other young and tender thing, and, after being baptized, I was assigned to the guardians of the hospital, with a room for my special use. But, one after another, the patience of the holy men was quite wearied out with my ceaseless cries and complainings, until it was resolved to commit me to the keeping of a respectable peasant woman in our village, called Magdalis Schröder. With her I grew to a healthy and merry boy, but the good monks always insist that the suavity of my temper at present is nothing less than a miracle, considering that so unmanageable and ill-natured a babe was never seen.

In my youth I had occasionally strong desires to see something of the world beyond our valley, that before my profession I might know what I was renouncing; but the brotherhood always withheld me, saying, that such a wish was like Eve's desire to be made wise by eating of the

Tree of the Knowledge of Good and Evil—that in the world nothing was to be learned but evil, and in the convent the knowledge of good. Their will was everything to me, and I unresistingly acquiesced; but I have often since thought that the evil lies nearer home, and that if I had to choose, I would not fly for refuge to a monastery. But what am I saying? The holy Benedict pardon me! All I mean is, that if, as they say, the earth is the same everywhere, as the heart certainly is, perhaps the heavens are also the same, and as near. I say this to Mother Magdalis sometimes, when she groans under her burdens and cares; yet, for myself, I have no wish to change. Here I have lived, and here, if the Lord and the Abbot will it so, will I die.

Nevertheless, I was not always so content.

At one time, when I was young, my heart felt strong, and fluttered, for freedom, as the Prior's birds flutter in the spring, or as the young buds throw off their casings in the forest on an April morning, and tremble and open in the sun and the warm winds.

I used to go often and visit my foster-mother. She is a widow, but she has two children—the best, she says, a poor widow ever had. It is true, Karl is a little wrong-headed and fiery now and then, but Nannerl, certainly every one must agree there are not many like her. It was not because of her large, violet-blue eyes, and her fresh color, like a rose—if a rose could change hue as she does

NANNERL AND HER TWO CHILDREN.

Tales and Sketches.

(of such things I am no judge)—she was a strong and healthy maiden, and that is enough—but for truth and goodness, and singleness of heart, I never saw any like her. She was like a manuscript of a psalm of thanksgiving, illuminated all round with holy images in fair colors, so joyous and in harmony. I often thought, when I looked at her, of the blessed words, "If thine eye be single, thy whole body shall be full of light"— so full of light, pleasant, cheering, fireside light was she within and without. I never passed her mother's cottage any morning, how early soever —and I passed it often—but she was up before me, getting her brother's breakfast, or doing her mother's work, with her bright morning face, and her pleasant words.

Now it came to pass, when I went one evening to the cottage with a basket of broken meat from the Abbey, I thought they all seemed happier than usual; Nannerl's face was brighter than ever, but it seemed to be shining with some hidden joy. At length, when she left the room to put aside the contents of the basket, Mother Magdalis told me there was to be a wedding in the family—young Hans Reichardt, the Abbey carpenter, had asked Nannerl's hand. They had, she said, liked one another long; and before many weeks they would probably be coming to the Abbey church together.

I could not exactly comprehend why Magdalis should make such a festival of this; I could not tell why, but I had never much admired young Reichardt, yet I congratulated them all as honestly as I could.

"It is a good providence," said my foster-mother. "I am old, and the children have no father, and it is a blessed thing for them to have a home."

Nannerl's face glowed with quiet pleasure when I wished her joy of her new prospects. I did feel glad at their joy, but somehow I was less at home there that evening than I had ever been before—I felt left out of the circle. Hans Reichardt came to see his bride, and I took my departure early. Mother Magdalis's words rung in my ears, "It is a blessed thing to have a home." Home!—the word came to my heart with a new meaning that evening. *It means very much;* and for the first time I felt *this* the convent could never be; a shelter from wind and rain it might be—a refuge for the weary—a refectory for the hungry—a place to eat and sleep and live in— but home meant *something more.*

Who had shut me out from this? Who had a right to say that this word, this holy thing, might never be mine?

For many days these things rankled in my heart, and sad havoc they made there. Till then, I had not a want beyond the convent walls and the society of the brethren; now, my heart had looked beyond the old walls; and they girded me in like a prison. I was not then bound by any vows, and it was well.

I did not venture to tell any of the brethren what I felt; I did not believe it to be sin, but I knew they would all misunderstand me.

This lasted until one of our evening Scripture readings—for in our convent we still adhere to the rule of reading through a portion of the Scriptures in the winter evenings. I seated myself among the rest, prepared to be once more a weary listener to the oft-told tale. (Alas! how little I knew of its blessed meaning!) The reader stood at his desk, intoning the words in his lulling sing-song; the appointed monk went his rounds with the lantern, to see that none of us fell asleep. The monotonous voice of the reader —the uniform tread of the lantern-bearer—the monotonous recurrence of convent duties—all grated like so many instruments of torture on my impatient heart. In health, we do not notice habitual sights and sounds, but in a fever, the slow dropping of water from the eaves seems at each fall to eat into the brain. And this, I thought, is to be for life! My heart sickened and sank under the intolerable burden of countless tomorrows, all like to-day. And beside this weary circle of fruitless toil arose the haunting thought of *home*—fresh springs of love, ever fresh—life growing, widening, deepening, day by day around us, and all centering in that inner sanctuary of love, *the home.*

I was aroused from my dreams and murmurs by some words from the gospel, which fell on my ear suddenly, as if I heard them for the first time:—

"*For even the Son of man came not to be ministered unto, but to minister,* and to give his life a ransom for many."

For the first time, the idea of self-sacrifice came to me with all the exalted joy the thought can bring—the thought of laying down myself, my life, for others. I arose from that evening reading strengthened and refreshed, for I had a purpose—and life is never quite barren to us if we have one living purpose to sow in it, to grow and to bring forth fruit.

The thought of His life took possession of me. I longed, I prayed, I strove to be made like Him—the holy child Jesus—like Him who went about doing good.

I made a collection in the convent, to furnish Nannerl's house—I labored in the convent garden to rear vegetables for the sick—I traveled leagues through the pine forests, in the frost and snow, to visit them—but the more I read of the life of Jesus, the more unattainable the perfect model seemed. Are not the stars as far from the mountains as from the valleys? The more I heard of the law of God, the more I saw how far it carried its claims upon the heart; and the heart was precisely the thing which all my efforts could not reach.

I could labor for the sick, I could toil and plead for Nannerl and her husband, but I could not expel the repining thought from my heart when I came back from her bright fireside to these dull, cold, convent walls.

But yet again God came to me and completed the work He had begun. The second part of my text healed the wound the first had made. How strange it was that I did not see it all at once!—

"The Son of man came not to be ministered unto, but to minister, *and to give his life a ransom for many.*"

The ransom is needed—for whom? Surely, for the sentenced criminal—for those who, not being able to fulfill the perfect law, can read in it nothing but their condemnation—that is, *for me.* The ransom is paid—for whom? Surely for those who need it. *The ransom is paid;*—then the prisoner is free. *I am free!* "There is now no condemnation to those who are in Christ Jesus." It is faith in this which gives strength to walk, not in the flesh, but in the Spirit.

From that time, my whole life has been changed. *Jesus*, the Son of God, the Lamb of God, our Ransom, our Pattern, our Friend, He has redeemed me—I am His, and His cause is mine. The self-denial, which had been impossible as a sacrifice of expiation, became the joy of my life as a sacrifice of thanksgiving. With the eye of Him who died for us—and dying, saved us—watching our lives, what is not possible? I learned that before we can be servants of God, we must be made children of God.

Since then, I have lost those restless yearnings for an earthly home. I have a home in heaven, and my Father has sent me hither, for a little while, to call more of His children to Him, and to minister to all who need:—thus journeying, and singing as I go, I am hastening *homeward.* I am happy, and can rejoice heartily in the happiness of Nannerl and Reichardt. In the convent, as well as elsewhere, we can bear one another's burdens, and so fulfill the law of Christ.

And, perhaps, in this tumultuous world, it is well that there should be some set apart on high, so that the strife and eager chases of the present may sound to them faint as those of the past, with no seasons but the seasons of heaven;—like church-towers rising above the common homes of men, yet echoing with deep tones their joys and sorrows, and telling them, amidst their toils and pleasures, how the time is passing.

Yet, if any ask my advice as to leading a religious life, I usually say, "My child, in your home you are sure God has placed you. There He is sure to bless you. Be quite sure that He calls you away before you change. He knows what work to give His servants, and in good time He is sure to let them know."

April 9.—S. Gregory Nazianzen, Bishop and Doctor.

I am just returned from a preaching tour amongst the villages of the forest (anciently called of Odin), with two choristers and a deacon, to celebrate the mass, and preach the Easter sermons.

Much grieved at discovering in some of the peasants' houses a superstitious reverence and fear of the old heathen gods (or demons)—the people in many places using pagan charms and incantations against them, and even endeavoring to propitiate them with wheaten cakes and other offerings. I told them that either the old gods and goddesses were *nothing*, and therefore could do nothing either for or against them; or they were *fiends*, and God was stronger than they; and that, when affrighted at night, or in lonely places, they should have recourse to prayer and to the sign of the holy cross. Some places, where the apparitions and wicked demons seem to have been more than commonly malignant, I purified and exorcised, sprinkling them with holy water. Nevertheless, in my sermons, and at all times, I told the people, that it is only sin which gives the devil power over us, and that none but those whose hearts are turned to God, through hearty repentance and true faith, are safe anywhere. I mourn much that these things are not oftener proclaimed by our brethren; also, that they have given the peasants images of saints instead of their old gods—which they often confound, in their blindness, in a very profane manner.

As we went on our way, I and my companions made the woods resound, from time to time,

with psalms and holy hymns, thus lightening the
way; and thus also, towards nightfall, effect-
ually keeping the powers of darkness avaunt,
the deacon Theodore being of somewhat a fear-
some spirit. At other times, I meditated on
some holy text, the theme of my next day's dis-
course, refreshing myself with the living bread
wherewith I afterwards fed the people. At
night, we cut down branches from the trees, and
made palisades around our beasts of burden,
which carried the holy vessels and vestments;
lighting watchfires, also, to scare away wild
beasts and other evil things.

Once I awoke at dead of night, hearing a
strange rustling amongst the fir twigs which
covered the ground, and a cracking of boughs,
mingled with stifled, unearthly cries. Moreover,
by the moonlight, which came down in strange
and shifting patterns on the bare trunks, and on
the ground, I perceived some dark object flitting
rapidly away amongst the distant pine-stems.
Whereat I arose, and, stirring the watchfires,
commenced singing the fourth Psalm in a loud
voice. When I had concluded the last verse,
crossing myself on brow and breast, I laid me
down in peace and slept.

In the morning our best ass was gone. With-
out it we could scarcely proceed, the other beasts
being slow-paced and old; yet without it we
feared to return, the creature being a favorite
with our lord the Abbot. Wherefore, kneeling

down, we laid our trouble before God, pleading that it was His errand on which we were journeying, and telling Him of our sore need; our lord the Abbot being withal a man of a hasty spirit. How marvelously He heard the prayers of His servants, the sequel will show.

A few days thereafter, I preached in a certain village, on the commandments, dwelling, amongst the rest, on the sin of theft. Great power was present to smite the consciences of the hearers. Many wept, and before the close of my sermon, one came forth, and before them all cried out, "Lay on me what penance you will. It is I who stole the Abbot's ass."

The whole assembly were greatly moved, and would have fallen on the thief, but hastily descending from the pulpit, I went to him, and as he knelt before me, I said—

"Thou seest, my son, that the eyes of the Lord are in every place, seeing in the darkness of the pine forest at midnight, as in the assembly at midday. Thou canst not fly from Him, for He is everywhere; thou needest not fly from Him, for He is ready to forgive. It is because thou hast not known His grace, that thou hast despised His law. But if now thou repentest, and with thine heart believest, I, although a sinner as thou art, absolve thee from thy sin." He had been a very fierce robber, the terror of the neighborhood.

After the service he brought the ass to the

door. As I left the place, the people thronged around us to seek my blessing; and lifting up my hands I blessed them, many weeping and kissing my hands. But I turned and said, "Mourn not, my brethren, that ye see me no more; but look, I pray you, to Him whose arms were stretched out on the cross to save you—whose hands are lifted up always to bless you. Look to Him!"

The robber went forth with us, although the deacon Theodore much misliked his company. He spoke not a word for many miles, walking, with head bowed down, at my ass's head.

At last, as it grew dusk, and we were entering on a thick part of the Odenwald, said to be infested with plunderers, brother Theodore came to my side and whispered—

"Were it not better to send this man away? He may have too many friends here."

But I answered, in the words of the wise king, "The hearts of men are as the rivers of water; He turneth them whithersoever He will. Let us not hinder His work on this poor soul."

At length the shadows fell around us, and, coming to a glade of the forest, we alighted for our night's encampment. The robber continued with us, serving us much in hewing branches and lighting our fires, he being more skilled in such work than we.

After offering our vesper prayer and hymn, I lay down to sleep, none making me afraid.

The robber sat watching the fires, whilst brother Theodore lay, with half-closed eyes, watching him. But the peace of God kept my heart, and I slept soundly.

About midnight I awoke, startled by the crackling of the watchfires. The robber sat close to my head, stirring one of the fires with a huge pine-log. I arose and seated myself opposite to him.

"Father," he said, leaning on the log, his dark strong features glowing in the red light—"thou art a man of peace, but thou hast courage; knowest thou who I am?"

"I know, my son," I replied, "that thou hast been a great sinner; but I trust one stronger than thou is melting thy heart."

"I am he whom the peasants call Otho the Thunderbolt," he said. "My name has been a terror to thousands, yet thou fearest me not. I have many bold followers in this forest; if I were to give one of my gathering-cries, in half-an-hour you would see fifty men around these fires."

"The name of the Lord," I said "is more terrible than yours, my son; but to those who trust in it, it is a strong tower: the righteous runneth into it and is safe. The voice of the Lord is stronger than yours; and legions of His angels encamp around those that fear Him. I have not much courage, but I have faith, which is stronger."

"I know it, father," he replied; "I, too, know

that the voice of God is strong, for it has made my heart tremble like a reed. He is mighty, and He is against me, for I have sinned."

"Nay, He is for you," I said, "for He came to save the sinner."

Then he unfolded to me the terrible story of his life of violence, and I unfolded to him the good tidings.

It was a strange chapel—the wind roaring in the tops of the pine-trees, and driving the clouds overhead; and a strange audience—the wolves howling around the fires—the chief of a robber band; but are not all places holy for holy words?

And the heart which had never quailed before man, but had quivered in the grasp of the Almighty, melted as a child's at the story of the love and sacrifice of Jesus.

"Father," he said, "can you admit one like me within your holy walls? The meanest office would be welcome to me—the meaner the fitter for me, if only I might work for the poor I have robbed."

"Nay," I said, "go and tell thy companions what great things the Lord hath done for thee. Mayhap they too will repent and believe."

"I will return," he said, bitterly, "if you will not receive me; but it is scarcely possible for one like me to lead an honest life amongst those who have known me. They would say, The old wolf has clothed himself in sheepskin, but he shall not deceive us by that."

"Go, then," I said, "and seek to restore your comrades, and afterwards repair to Marienthal: there ye shall all find an asylum and a sanctuary."

Before the morning broke he was gone.

The sun arose, throwing slanting rays up across the pinestems, the birds awoke and sang, and the leaves trembled and glittered with the drops of dew—and we went on our way rejoicing: for, that night, had not the day-spring from on high arisen on one who sat in darkness and the shadow of death?

Otho the Thunderbolt, and three of his companions, are now inmates of our Abbey. We think it best to employ them as much as possible. They therefore fell our firewood, draw our water, keep our cattle, and help to clear more of the forest for tillage. The rest of their time they spend in learning and reciting psalms and litanies, and in listening to our solemn services. Otho, moreover, contrives to find leisure to weave mats and nets, the price of which he lays up for future restitution.

This event has greatly strengthened those amongst us who are truly seeking to lead a religious life, and has urged us afresh to prayer. But some, alas! continue idle and vain, caring for none of these things—for here, as elsewhere, our Lord and the devil have both their disciples.

June 7.—Vigil of the Nativity of St. John the Baptist.

We have entertained an angel since last I wrote. The holy Abbot Bernard, of Clairvaux, has stayed with us a day and a night—ever memorable at Marienthal. He came to preach the Crusade.

It is marvelous into what a ferment his coming has thrown the whole of Germany. People flocked from the towns and villages to meet him, bringing with them the sick on litters, that he might heal them with his touch—those esteeming themselves blessed who could kiss his hands. The churches were filled, and even the churchyards, when he preached, and men have taken the cross by hundreds. At Marienthal the peasants wept and sobbed at his sermon, although they could not understand a word he said—at which I marveled greatly.

Scarcely could they have received the Lord Christ himself with more devoted reverence: indeed, I wonder much that they should pay such homage to the words of His servant, and so little to His own. I fear for them, lest they be honoring the voice more than the words. Yet truly he is a man of a noble presence, and of a very lowly mind.

In the pulpit his eyes flash like flame, but in the confessional they are soft as any dove's. His stature is low, but his brow and bearing are so calm, and so full of gentle command, that the proudest bow naturally before him—not thinking of refusing what he never thinks of demanding.

He seems worn out by the fervor of his piety and the severity of his life; yet the ardor which is wasting his frame is mild as the first sunshine of May to all else. At the Abbot's table, more than once, I heard him laugh joyously as a child. Nevertheless, there is something in him I would shrink from encountering as a foe.

When one of us remarked on the austerities which had so emaciated him, he said—

"The cross of Christ is such a burden as wings are to a bird—bearing it aloft."*

To us he spoke as St. Paul might of the inward conflict, and the inward strength, the grace of God and the reconciliation wrought by Christ. "Blessed," he says, "are those to whom God has taught the meaning of the words, 'Ye are my friends; whatsoever I have heard of my Father, I have made known unto you.'"

In the Abbey he left behind him a holy calm. We felt that the place was holy ground, because He who dwelleth in His saints had been there.

He gave a lamentable account of the world and the Church—bishops and priests buying and selling holy things, Christian princes fighting one another; and, meantime, the Turk ruling in the Holy Land, and the heretics—Cathari, Paulicians, and Manichees—poisoning the wells of Christian life within the camp.

There are many of these heretics, he says, on the Rhine, and in Bohemia, and the south of

---
* See "St. Bernard's Letters."

France, who deny the Divine authority of the sacred priesthood, and mock at the holy sacraments, mimicking them in their secret assemblies —all the more dangerous, the holy Abbot says, because of the blameless moral lives of many of them, and their upholding their errors from the Holy Scriptures, which they know and pervert in a wonderful manner. Yet is he averse from killing them, having compassion on their lost souls, and dreading the effect of public executions in spreading their madness, and giving notoriety to their errors.

He is also very earnest against the recent slaughter of the Jews on the banks of the Rhine, which some have rashly styled a "crusade," saying, that the true weapons wherewith to conquer them are the Word of God and prayer. Many have already been converted by these means.

Note.—Why not the same for the Turks? They are, however, without question, very wicked and obstinate infidels, and have no right to the Holy Land.

Two of the companions of Otho the Thunderbolt were very urgent to be suffered to take the cross, and return with the venerable Abbot, who seemed nowise unwilling to receive them, "deeming," he said, "such an enterprise doubly beneficial, since their departure would be as welcome to their friends as their presence to those they went to assist."* But I ventured strenu-

* See "St. Bernard to the Templars."

ously to oppose their design, fearing that, to minds so recently enlightened, the distinction between spoiling the Turks for Christ's sake, and plundering the Germans for their own, might not be so clear as could be wished. The holy Bernard deigned to be guided by my remonstrances.

Note.—It is a pity that the holy Abbot should adhere to the novel rule of the Cistertians; but he is, notwithstanding, doubtless a man of God. Indeed, had it not been for our conviction of his especial sanctity, we certainly could not have received one of that rule at our Abbey.*

July 29.—SS. Peter and Paul.

I have done a deed this week, whether good or evil I shall know hereafter, but otherwise I could not do.

When I went to Magdalis's cottage this morning, I found her wringing her hands and weeping bitterly, the room unswept and in disorder, and Karl standing with folded arms before the fire, looking very sullen and determined.

"What is the matter?" I exclaimed; "what has happened?"

"Nothing!" replied Karl, gruffly, "but that

---

* The quarrels between rival monastic orders sometimes ran very high. The Cluniac monks refused the rites of hospitality to the Cistertians, and the compliment was returned, although the two heads of the orders seem to have been far more forbearing—the venerable Peter and St. Bernard having been, personally, cordial friends.

my mother does not want to spare me to be a soldier of the holy Cross."

"Nothing!" sobbed poor Magdalis; "will Father Bartholomew call that nothing!—for an only son to leave his widowed mother to the mercy of strangers, that he may go and be killed amongst the heathen Turks and Jews?"

I could not altogether approve of Mother Magdalis's view of the Holy Wars, but neither did I feel sure of the genuineness of my foster-brother's vocation to fight in them. He is at best but a willful lad, although sound at the core, and for some months he had been growing weary of the monotonous toil of his peasant life. Wherefore I represented to him that the call must be very strong which could make it a duty for him to desert his mother, and asked him, since the redemption of the Holy Land lay so very near his heart, when this loud call from heaven had been vouchsafed him.

He looked puzzled for an instant; then, drawing his hand impatiently through his long brown hair, he said—

"You know well I am no scholar: about calls and vocations I understand very little; but this I know—half the next village are going to Palestine, and the lord of Erbach-Erbach has promised to make me his armor-bearer if I will go. And how expect a young fellow like me to toil away his youth in earning a scanty pittance of daily bread, when he has the chance of seeing the world, and coming back rich enough to be head peasant of the district in a few years?"

"How many came back from the last crusade?" moaned Magdalis. "Ask the old men of the village that!—and who would not rather be a serf of the good monks of Marienthal, than a retainer of the proud lords of Erbach? And Nannerl, too, how she will grieve, and poor little Gretchen!"

"Gretchen will not care," said the young man, coloring. "Gretchen's grandfather was a merchant of one of the free imperial cities, and she says she will never wed a serf of the soil."

"What does it matter what that silly child says?" said Magdalis, half petulantly; "you will be killed, and then she will be as sorry as any of us, poor vain wench!"

Karl's lip curled, but he did not look altogether displeased.

"The War of the Cross is a holy war," he said; "and if I die, mother, you will know that I am safe, and Father Rudolph, who preached the crusade on the Rhine, says one wound from the Turk is worth fifty Pater Nosters."

Magdalis was too wretched to controvert either his theology or his purpose; but as I looked at his manly form, and his bold, bright eye, I felt still more doubtful as to his heavenly vocation to the Cross, and I said, "Well, I would not interfere with a pious vow, Karl, but I came to tell you that the old Abbey huntsman died last week, and I thought you might have filled his place, as you are a famous marksman."

Karl turned suddenly to me.

"Well, Father Bartholomew," he said, after a short pause, "I am no scholar, and, as I said, know little of calls and vocations—after all, it might be a mistake;—could you really get me appointed Abbey huntsman—and made free?"

"I might try, Karl," I said; "but far be it from me to tempt you to resist a call from heaven, or to neglect a sacred vow."

Karl rubbed his forehead and looked up and down, half puzzled and half convicted; at length he stammered—

"I am a poor unlettered man; I do not know that it was exactly a vow, Father Bartholomew; and even if it were, could you not perhaps manage that for me too?"

I could not help smiling as I shook his hand and took leave.

In a few weeks Gretchen is to be married to the Abbey huntsman. The saints intercede for me if I have done wrong! After all, Karl will be in the service of the Church.

And I sometimes wonder if the Saviour cares as much for His deserted sepulchre as so many now do.

Are not His living habitations far better?

"The poor ye have always with you."

"In that ye did it unto one of the least of these my brethren, ye did it unto me."

And St. Paul writes to each one of the faithful: "Know ye not that your bodies are the temples of the Holy Ghost?"

Why, then, travel so far to the site of an overthrown temple and an empty tomb?

"He is not there—He is risen."

He is not there *only*, for, where two or three are in His name, *there* is He.

St. Peter, St. Paul, St. Thomas, St. Bartholomew, and all the holy Apostles and Evangelists;

St. Stephen, St. Clement, St. Pothinus with thy companions;

St. Irenæus with thy companions;

St. Sebastian, St. Laurence, and all the holy Martyrs;

St. Augustine, St. Ambrose, St. Gregory, and all the holy Doctors;

All the holy Pontiffs,

All the holy Monks and Hermits,

All the holy Virgins and Widows,

Omnes sancti and sanctæ Dei,

Orate pro me,

if I have erred.

July 10.

On the eve of the Feast of the Transfiguration, a strange monk begged admittance into our Abbey. He bore letters of recommendation from the venerable Peter, Abbot of Clugni, and we received him gladly.

He is a noticeable man, tall, with a complexion

that tells of a southern sun; his eyes are very dark and piercing—they seem always still; and yet, whenever you look at him, they are fixed on you. His bearing is more that of a soldier than of a monk—and of a soldier more used to command than to obey; yet is he wonderfully lowly and submissive, and ready to perform the most servile offices if directed by his superiors. He calls himself Conrad. He says little, perhaps because he speaks German with a slight lisp, and with difficulty, nevertheless not as if his throat were sewn up like a Frenchman's, but with a manly force. He also talks Latin, so that I understand him easily, although brother Lupacius avers that his idiom is not that of the ancient Romans; no reproach, I trow, to a Christian man.

In no language, however, does he say much, his thoughts seeming for the most part turned inward, and not happy, although he has a singular way of seeing everything whilst apparently looking at nothing.

Most of us stand rather in awe of him, but the strange, taciturn man attaches me to him; also, he seemeth not to mislike my company.

August 13.

A company of Lombard merchants has been here to-day with silks from Greece and Asia, and other curious Eastern wares.

The Abbot bought some beautiful rare stones,

to ornament withal a copy of the missal which brother Theodore, a curious man in all arts and handicrafts, has lately illuminated.

Also some of the brotherhood purchased several ells of fine stuff for their hoods and scapularies. I marveled to see how curious they were in their choice,* running the cloth through their fingers —holding it up to the light—disposing it around them in cunning folds—and discussing its merits with the dealers and with one another, as eagerly as if it had been an article of the faith. Scarce could any lady at the court of my lord of Erbach have been more dainty. Methinks, if this had been our object, we might have found a more gallant costume.

Brother Conrad held himself apart the while, and once or twice I saw a smile pass across his face—but not of mere amusement.

The merchants spoke of a wonderfully magnificent Christian kingdom amongst the wilds of Asia. From their description, brother Lupacius, who studied at Paris, concludes it to be somewhere near the garden of Eden—but many of us think this a rash and profane speculation, deeming that the garden has been taken up into heaven.

The emperor of this country styles himself Prester, or Priest, John, although he has princes and kings amongst his servitors, himself prefer-

* See Neander's "Life of St. Bernard," p. 81, Miss Wrench's translation.

ring the title of Priest, as at once more lowly and more lofty—a singular mark of enlightenment in a barbarous man.

Note.—The merchants seem to understand rightly the controversy between us, the old Benedictines, and the Cistertians, speaking evil of these last, as sanctimoniously austere, and ill patrons of commerce and the arts.

August 24.—St. Bartholomew. Holy Patron, pray for me!

Our bees have prospered well this year, yielding a goodly store of honey and meat.

Monday.

Brother Conrad is foot-sore and ill from his journey. It was very long, and he seems unused to foot-traveling. Nevertheless, he will not consent in anywise to relax the severity of his abstinences.

This evening, I went to his cell with a healing decoction of herbs, which hath proved of marvelous virtue amongst the peasantry. As he did not answer my signal, I gently opened the door. He was kneeling on the floor, fervently grasping an iron crucifix to his breast. As I entered, he arose, and hastily threw his mantle around his shoulders, but I could see they were bleeding from the use of the discipline. He asked, rather haughtily, what I wanted. I prayed him to let me bathe his feet. He refused my assistance courteously, yet so that I could not press it. As I left the cell, he took my hand and pressed it to his lips, saying, "Brother, thou hast a good and innocent heart—pray for me."

I fear he has committed some great sin.

Thursday.

All the village is in uproar about the foreign monk. Yesterday, as brother Conrad was walking, he saw a stout peasant carle beating one of Manuel Reichardt's boys, for laming his mule by hard riding. Without saying a word, Conrad threw back his cowl, girded up his garments, and beat the man. At this the peasants are enraged, calling him a foreign meddler, but Nannerl takes his part, as also all the children, to whom he is ever gentle. Nannerl's boy was, however, a mischievous and idle rogue (very unlike his mother), and had no right to the mule. Moreover, such interference comporteth not with the dignity of the religious habit.

Our lord the Abbot, taking the matter into his consideration, has condemned our brother to penitence, and the seclusion of his cell. Abstinence beyond what he already practices is scarce possible.

Saturday.

Our lord the Abbot, after matins, enjoined on brother Conrad to ask forgiveness from the peasant carle.

His dark cheek flushed high: "I from a villain!" he murmured between his teeth.

"On the obedience of a monk, I command you!" said the Abbot, rather fiercely.

Conrad bowed in acquiescence, went to the village, sought out the peasant, and made the required apology in my presence.

The carle would have made him a present in acknowledgment of the condescension, but he would not accept it.

"The slave deserved the chastisement," he said to me, as we returned.

"The obedience of a monk includes submission in will as well as in act," I suggested.

"I know it," he replied; "I submit."

"The commandment of our Lord Jesus," I rejoined, "reaches the heart as well as the will; He said, 'Love your enemies.'"

He looked down, and spoke no more until we reached the convent; but in the evening, he came to my cell, and said—

"You are no hypocrite. Do you mean that it is possible, from the heart, to love those who have hated, wronged, and meanly slandered us—not only to forbear taking vengeance, but to love?"

"Jesus said of His murderers, 'Father, forgive them;' and thousands of them were forgiven, and are now amongst the blessed company of His redeemed."

"He was God," said Conrad; "I am a man and a sinner."

"Have you then, yourself, nothing that you need to be forgiven?"

He looked at me earnestly and sadly. "I understand you," he said, bitterly; "we must forgive, that we may be forgiven. It is hard to do it, but not to do it is hell."

"Nay," I replied, "we must forgive, because we are forgiven. We must love, because we have been so loved."

But he seemed to have fallen again into his self-enclosed state, and hastily taking his lamp, he left my cell.

Wednesday.

Brother Conrad seems to have been easier in mind lately, having been actively employed.

He had observed that we had to draw all our water for the household, the cattle, and the garden, from the stream at the bottom of the valley, which is nearly a quarter of a mile off. He asked why we did not dig a well. The Abbot assigned the labor, and the uncertainty of finding water, as the reason.

"If I am permitted," he replied, "I will engage to accomplish it in a week, with one laborer."

Most of us deemed this an idle boast, but Otho the Thunderbolt had confidence in the stranger, and freely offered to assist him.

They accordingly set about it at once. In a few days the water came gushing out of the excavation. Otho wondered at the sagacity with which he had fixed on the spot.

"I have been many years in the East, where water is scarce," he said in explanation. I suppose he was with the crusading army.

He has also shown us some new agricultural implements, used, he says, among the Provençals, and in Languedoc, a people marvelously skilled in all sorts of arts and handicrafts.

Friday.

To-day a horse was brought to the Abbey for sale. The creature was beautiful, but withal so wicked and ill-natured, that several of our best riders (and I grieve to say, there are more among us than befits a company of sober and peaceful world-renouncing men, who are skilled in the *manege* of chargers) were thrown violently to the ground.

The horse was about to be sent back, when Conrad, who had been watching us apart, offered to mount him.

First whispering in the animal's ear, he sprang on his back, and rode him round the court and whithersoever he would, guiding him like a lady's palfrey.

When he dismounted, we all crowded round him, marveling at his skill. But he said carelessly, "I learned it from the Arabs. There are many among them who ride far better;" then disengaging himself from us, he retired to his cell.

Brother Conrad puzzles us all sorely. Some of the brethren fear he may have been a follower of Mahound, for he spoke in some heathenish jargon to one of the Italian merchants, of which none of us could understand a syllable. And, as brother Lupacius saith, what could he mean by " learning from the Arabs?" how can one learn anything Christian from an Arab?

Yet I feel a strange liking for him; to me he is always gentle and friendly. Only sometimes I fear he may have mistaken his vocation. Natures energetic as his, and accustomed to action, will scarce find scope or employment in the dead calm of our life.

December

The whole Abbey has been in a tumult for some weeks. The sub-prior is dead, and we have been engaged in electing a successor.

He lay sick for many weeks, being well stricken in years. During his illness, there was much plotting and conferring in the convent; four of the elder monks gathering groups of two or three at a time around them in corners, at our hours of recreation, and talking earnestly in a low voice.

These monks were very courteous to one another; yet, if one of them saw another thus engaged in converse, he would join the group, which was sure soon afterwards to disperse.

These same monks were very tender in watching the symptoms of the sub-prior's malady.

Also, the office-bearers have been marvelously diligent in their business of late—increasing notably the while in courtesy to all.

At length the sub-prior died and was buried.

For some days, the whole brotherhood stepped more softly, and spoke with subdued voices. I mourned the old man from my heart, for to me he had been as a father, and he had many strange tales of the olden times. Yet were his last years so quiet and noiseless—his voice has so gradually become hushed among us—that it scarcely makes a silence, now that it has ceased. May he rest in peace! many masses will I offer for his soul.

We met in the chapter-house, and after solemnly chanting the *Veni Creator Spiritus*, the lots were cast.

To the surprise of us all, the lot fell on brother Conrad, but he was not to be found.

Whilst some of the younger brethren went in search of him, the rest began to whisper together. At first, the four elder monks, whom I have mentioned, seemed relieved to find that neither of the four besides themselves was chosen; but, as brother Conrad's absence was prolonged, they drew together, and conferred in angry whispers. "An intruder!"—"a foreigner!"—"a foundling of the gallows!"—"an Arabian magician!" and many other rash words, dropped from them.

The good men suffered the heat of argument to

carry them away; and, ere long, the whispered murmurs rose into loud debate, and the debate into a tempest of wrathful words; and so eager and passionate was the discussion, that brother Conrad stood five minutes amongst them before they perceived him.

At length, our lord the Abbot arose, and after gesticulating some little time in vain, he succeeded in imposing silence.

Still, however, there continued a low grumble of discontent, as the echo of thunder among the hills when a storm is gone, and we wonder whether it will return.

"Brethren," said the Abbot, "behold him whom you have chosen to succeed our venerable sub-prior. May the choice be blest!"

But many of the brethren glared angrily on brother Conrad, and the storm was beginning to rise again.

Brother Conrad stood with his arms folded on his breast, calmly awaiting a pause, with that peculiar smile on his lips which I have observed before, until the Abbot was obliged again to interpose.

"Brethren," he said, "are we not a sacred council of priests, guided by the Spirit of the Highest? Behold the man of your choice."

Then there ensued a sullen calm, and Conrad's voice was heard.

"I came not hither," he said, "holy father, to

rule monks, but to save my soul; let the holy brotherhood choose some fitter man."

We were accustomed to this formula of humility in the newly-elected; but, to our surprise, brother Conrad persisted in his refusal, and was not by any means to be moved from it.

We accordingly proceeded again to the election, and this time the choice fell on one of the four elder monks.

With this the assembly was obliged to be content. The new sub-prior has been solemnly installed, and brother Conrad is honored in the convent as a model of humility.

On the next morning, as brother Conrad and I were journeying together to administer the sacrament to a sick man, I said, "I rejoice to see that your heart is not set on seeking great things for yourself."

He laughed, and replied, "I do not understand the monks, nor they me. If I had desired the greatness of this world, I would not have sought it in an obscure monastery of the north. I have commanded thousands of soldiers, and to me it is no point of ambition to rule a few monks. I came hither to fly the world, not to seek it. I came hither to live in quiet, and to save my soul."

Brother Conrad is right, and I love him for his honest words; nevertheless, I marvel that he should speak so slightingly of our venerable Abbey—chartered as it is by the Emperor, containing the sacred relics of a supreme Pontiff—

our blessed Lady herself having marked out the site in a vision, our founder being in the calendar, and our Abbot ranking next the mitred Abbots and the episcopal throne. He can scarcely be informed of this, or he would never have used words so singularly inappropriate as an "*obscure monastery,*" or "*a few monks.*" Not that I am proud of these privileges: no! holy Benedict knows that we are nothing but a company of poor and humble priests—the servants of the servants of God.

January 26.—*St. Polycarp, Bishop and Martyr.*

A post arrived to-day, with messages and letters for our lord the Abbot, and a letter, sealed with a noble escutcheon, for brother Conrad. The messenger brings sad tidings of the apostasy of some of Bishop Otho of Bamberg's new converts in Pomerania, and the sufferings of others. Hearing and reading of such things, how it shames my languid and lukewarm heart! Thou art the same to us as to them; oh make us the same to Thee!

I took the letter to brother Conrad in his cell. On receiving it his hands trembled, and his face turned livid in its paleness. When he had read it, he tore it passionately in twain, murmuring, "The curse of God!"——then suddenly checking himself, he said to me, "Leave me, brother Bartholomew, you can do me no good now." I had no choice but to leave the cell, for so stern was his countenance, that I deemed it folly to resist his will.

January 30.

For these many days none of us have seen brother Conrad. He refuseth meat, and denieth entry to all.

February 1.—*St. Ignatius, Bishop and Martyr.*

To-day, I knocked at the door of brother Conrad's cell; receiving no answer, I at length ventured to enter unbidden.

He sat on his bed, with his eyes bent on the ground. His crucifix lay on his knees; his face was pale and drawn, as that of a man who had passed through some great agony of bodily pain; but it was perfectly calm, and so was his voice when he addressed me, saying—

"Wherefore do you come here? you can do me no good."

But I seated myself beside him, and said, "Brother, I came to read you some of the words of peace, fearing that you have suffered."

He did not reply, nor did his features relax; but he bowed his head, and receiving no further encouragement, I opened the Psalter at the 32d Psalm.

"Blessed is he whose transgression is forgiven, whose sin is covered. Blessed is the man unto whom the Lord imputeth not iniquity, and in whose spirit there is no guile."

"Do you come hither to torment me before the time?" he exclaimed, looking sternly and abruptly at me: "in my spirit there *is* guile. My transgression can never be forgiven, nor my sin covered. The words of peace are very swords to me, for I can not repent. Those who forgive not shall never be forgiven, and I can not forgive!"

I was silent, and after a few moments he proceeded:—

"Listen, if you will, to my wrong. I have told it to none beside. I had broad lands in Arragon, and castles. I loved, and believed myself beloved, and was betrothed. In an evil day, I took the Cross; she decked me with her colors when I went, and I bore them triumphantly through the thick of many battles. I returned. Came with my retainers to my father's castle. There was feasting there: she, my bride, was there, and my younger brother, a scribe, a lawyer, a man of smooth words and a comely face, whom I had cherished as my own son, for we were orphans—she was there, *his wife!* My lands and castles were my own, and the king was my friend; but what were they or he to me? they could not restore her to me, or to the truth and beauty of soul with which I had clothed her. I left my country in disguise, and came hither a monk, resigning my titles and estates to them. They took advantage of my absence to slander me to my king; he trusted me, and revealed their treachery. There is the letter they have sent me, thanking me for my generosity, and begging me formally to transfer all my hereditary rights —*and she has signed it.* That is all my story. I have done what I can—I have sent them what they asked for. I will not curse either of them —but God, you say, exacts more. I have tried, but I can not forgive. You can do me no good —I am lost."

He said these words with the calm of fixed conviction, as one to whom the terrible thought was no strange or doubtful thing, but ascertained and familiar. But I could not withhold my tears.

When I could speak again composedly, I took the crucifix from his knees, and said, " Brother, whose image is this?"

"I know what you would say," he answered; "but it is in vain. He is God. His heart was tender and compassionate; mine is hard—it has been frozen hard in its own tears. He forgave, but I hate. I sin even as I speak, and can not repent. I do not murmur against God. He is just. I am lost—and I deserve it!"

There was such intense and fixed anguish in the slow calmness with which he uttered these words, that I felt any words of mine were powerless; and kneeling down, I called, at first in silence, and then aloud, on Him who delighteth in mercy.

What I said, I do not exactly remember; I remember only that I poured out my whole heart before God, calling on Him who is so near to the broken-hearted to have pity on my brother—to heal the heart men had broken, and to bind up its wounds. I knew and felt that the Lord was near us—as near as when the sick and fearful touched the hem of His garment, and were healed, and the guilty outcast wept at His feet, and was forgiven—and as gracious. I was sure that He heard, and sure that He would keep His promise, and give what we asked. Before I rose, Conrad had sunk on his knees beside me, and when I rose, he still remained kneeling.

I waited some time: then placing the crucifix in his hands, I said, "It was for no light sin that the Son of God left His glory, and became obedient to a death such as this: nor did He suffer such things in vain. My brother, you *are* lost; but the Lord Jesus came to seek the lost. You have mistaken the object of His coming altogether. He came not to judge, but to save. Look on Him your sins have pierced, and live."

There was no tear in his eyes—no sign of emotion on his face; but as I left the cell, he grasped my hand, and said, in a scarcely audible voice—

"There is hope."

February 4.

This evening, brother Conrad rejoined us at the reading of the Scriptures. We are reading through the Book of the prophet Isaiah. The chapters read to-day were from lii. to lvi.

"Surely he hath borne our griefs, and carried our sorrows: yet we did esteem him stricken, smitten of God, and afflicted.

"But he was wounded for our transgressions, he was bruised for our iniquities: the chastisement of our peace was upon him; and with his stripes we are healed.

"All we, like sheep, have gone astray; we have turned every one to his own way; and the Lord hath laid on him the iniquity of us all."

And again—

"Ho, every one that thirsteth, come ye to the waters, and he that hath no money: come ye, buy and eat; yea, come, buy wine and milk without money, and without price."

Methought the living words never brought to my heart such a warm feeling of the unmerited and unutterable love of God before; and as the lantern-bearer went his rounds, casting the light on one after another, I saw that brother Conrad's face was wet with tears, and he did not try to hide them—a strange thing for so proud a man.

February 12.—St. Eulalia, Virgin and Martyr.

I never saw a man so changed as brother Conrad. His heart seems opened; it is as if a hand which knew the secret had touched some hidden spring, and the closed vessel had sprung open in an instant. Instead of his soul being a dark thing folded up in its own gloom, it seems an open house full of peace and light, and warming all who come near him. The old smile of contemptuous pity has given way to one of kindly interest. In place of the dead mechanical submission with which he used to obey the commands of the superiors, it seems now his joy and his "meat" to minister to all as the servant of Him who came to minister.

This evening, as we returned from a visitation in the forest, we passed Nannerl's cottage; the children (she has three now) were standing at the door waiting to catch the first glimpse of their father as he returned from his day's work at the Abbey. When he came in sight, they all ran out to meet him. The two eldest clung to his coat, the youngest tottered after them until he caught her in his arms and covered her with kisses.

"What is it," said Conrad, when we had passed, "to be able to call God Father!"

"Yes," I replied, "and heaven *home.*"

God gives strength by giving peace.

To Conrad as to St. Paul the Son of God has been revealed; and the Spirit of God fills every corner of his ruined and desolate heart with the music of "Abba, Father."

February 14.

The poor people are beginning everywhere to suffer from the scarcity of the late harvest, added to the inclemency of the season. They throng our gates, imploring charity for the love of Christ.

Our lord the Abbot has emptied the Abbey granaries of all the superfluous corn; and this week we have sent brother Theodore to Bamberg, with a trusty escort, to sell some of our most richly illuminated manuscripts, with the gems wherewith they were studded. Brother Theodore almost wept to see his beloved manuscripts thus stripped; and scarce could all I said about the living epistles being even more precious than the written ones, assuage his grief. "The collections and labors of a century," he says, "scattered in a week, and betrayed perchance into the hands of the ignorant and profane, or of some rival order!"

Also we have sold some of the church plate and decorations, and sundry of the more costly vestments, to buy corn withal. Some murmur at this as a desecration of holy things, but brother Conrad saith, "It is but laying them up in a safe place, until we want them, with a sure Keeper."

He himself hath been very busy of late copying manuscripts of the Holy Scriptures, a new occupation for him until within the last few months, he being more used to handle the sword than the pen. At the first, his letters were very uncouth and unchristian-like, but he laughed at his mistakes until he conquered them, and now scarcely can brother Theodore write more rapidly or in more beautiful and legible characters. He laboreth at it day and night, designing to sell these copies for the famishing peasants. Also the copying of the holy words nourisheth his own soul: so that, in watering, "he is watered also himself."

It is piteous to see the poor starving people thronging the Abbey courts: mothers holding up their crying children, themselves complaining not—old men tottering from feebleness, and stout youths from famine. We are expecting supplies from Bamberg.

March.

Brother Conrad seems daily to grow in grace and in the knowledge of the Scriptures. To-day he said to me, after matins—

"Once, looking on the height from which I had descended, I thought myself a man of marvelous humility, until looking up I saw how low my Saviour had to stoop to reach me. Now I can never wonder enough at my pride and His grace. Some," he added, "paint humility with downcast eyes, looking as if she thought every one was saying, 'See how humble she is!' but true humility looks freely up to heaven, knowing *what* she is, and *where;* and then forgetting herself in thinking what God is."

He is like one moving softly in the calm of a royal presence. Yet I sometimes tremble at his questions about our Holy Mother Church and her doctrines. His mind is direct and simple as a child's; and having caught the thread of a truth, he follows it on through the Scripture, without ever heeding what nets he may tread through, or what sacred enclosures he may trample down in his path. I fear whither this may lead him.

This evening we had been sitting in the dusk, discoursing of the legends of the saints, and their appearing amongst us—of the warrior St. James—of him who was pierced through with many arrows, yet not slain—of the virgin Margaret, daisy and pearl of Paradise—of the lamb-like Agnes, her woes and her triumphs—and of many others, knights and ladies of the court of heaven.

Afterwards, when we were alone, he asked me—

"Why pray to the saints when we may speak directly to God?"

I was somewhat startled at the abruptness of the question, but I said—

"In our monastery we may all apply directly to our lord the Abbot, yet many choose rather to prefer any suit through me, knowing that the Abbot has a favor unto me."

"That may be," he replied; "but the Abbot is not our father, nor has he expressly commanded us to make known all our requests unto him."

The saints, or He who sanctifieth them, preserve us from all rash speculations! nevertheless, the growth and fervor of brother Conrad often shame my cold and slothful heart. I seem not to grow, and sometimes, in looking back to the early days of my Christian life, I am ready to cry, " Where is the blessedness I spake of then?" It seems to have faded away like a gleam at sunrise on a gray and rainy day. Can it then be with us as with the Church? Are the early days necessarily those of freshest love and purest zeal?

This would seem as if eternal life were doomed, like corruptible things, to decreptitude and decay. But no, it *is not so*. St. Paul speaks of *growth*—Conrad grows; the fault is in me—my heart is so dead, my hope at times so feeble, and my prayers so mechanical: can I have mistaken my *vocation?*

> "Rex tremendæ Majestatis,
> Qui salvandos salvas gratis,
> Salva me Fons pietatis.
>
> "Recordare Jesu pie
> Quod sum causa tuæ viæ,
> Ne me perdas illa die.
>
> "Quærens me sedisti lassus,
> Redemisti, crucem passus;
> Tantus labor non sit cassus."

April 13.—*St. Justin the Martyr.*

Our supplies of corn are arrived, and the villagers come daily to the Abbey gates for their portion. It is blessed thus to be stewards of God's storehouses, to give His people meat in due season, though it be only meat for the body.

April 23.—St. George the Martyr.

Yesterday a young Frenchman visited us from the University of Paris. We gave him a night's lodging, and he repaid us by proving various theological and other theses.

I marveled at the readiness and skill with which he tossed the ball of argument, and caught it again more deftly than the expertest *jongleur;* but brother Conrad sat silent and displeased—he affecteth not such juggler's play with truths.

Many curious questions were, however, started by the learned student—as, "Whether angels could strictly be said to fly, seeing spirits have no place, whereas flying is motion, and motion change of place."

"Why the nose was placed above, instead of below the mouth."

"What God would have done if Adam had not listened to the seductions of our mother Eve, and eaten of the forbidden fruit." *

Whilst he was subtilely debating this last point, brother Conrad suddenly rose, and confronting the stranger, said—

"When a man is shipwrecked, it is no time to be discussing the conduct of the helmsman, or how the rope was manufactured which is thrown out to save him."

The student was silenced for a moment, then he said—

---

* See Neander's "St. Bernard."

"That, reverend sir, may admit of argument; permit me to state the matter syllogistically."

"I am no scholar," rejoined Conrad, "but this I know: when our Lord shall come again, there is one question which will place us among the saved or the lost—'Do you know me as the Redeemer of your soul?' And if we can say Yes, all the wisdom of angels will be opened to us afterwards in His presence."

The Frenchman was proceeding to debate the point, when our brother laid his hand gently on his arm, and said—

"Young man, I think you are a disciple of Peter Abelard; he is a great man, but our Lord Jesus Christ is infinitely greater. Read His Word; follow Him; He can save you—Abelard can not."

The student colored.

"Master Peter has been foully slandered," he exclaimed; "but all admit his wisdom now. Who disputes his orthodoxy here?"

None of the brotherhood offered to enter the lists with so fierce and skilled a combatant, but Conrad said quietly—

"I slander none. I knew Abelard at Clugni; he was a man of mighty intellectual power, and has, I trow, passed through hard conflicts. To his own Master he standeth or falleth: but I believe his scholars trifle with truth as he would never have dared. There is nothing so far from the childlike heart to which God reveals His secrets, as the childish vanity of those who play with things before which the angels veil their faces. Beware, as you value your salvation, that whilst you are making confects and dainty dishes with the Bread of Life, your own soul do not starve."

"A worthy man," whispered the student to brother Lupacius, when Conrad had left, "but lamentably behind the age."

"You were hard on the stranger," I said to brother Conrad in the evening.

"Was I?" he said. "It makes me shudder to hear sentenced malefactors, such as we are, playing with the message of pardon and deliverance the Sovereign sends them at the cost of such anguish to the Deliverer. That man can never utter truth who has never himself felt it unutterable."

June.

It is long since I have handled the pen, having been laid on my bed by severe sickness. Even now my hand trembleth, yet must I record my thanks to Him who has raised me from the gates of the grave.

"The living, the living, he shall praise thee, and declare thy truth." The famine was followed by a grievous plague. Want and hunger, and irregular feeding, have made fearful ravages amongst the peasantry. I, myself, with brother Conrad, closed the eyes of many who had been abandoned of their kindred ; not without hope for some, that their eyes would open one day to welcome the morning of the resurrection.

Nannerl's youngest child died. How she watched and tended it, never heeding herself!

Brother Conrad sat with me day and night during my illness; and when I began to recover, he would read to me for hours together in the Sacred Scriptures. We seemed never to weary of the blessed words. To me they were as refreshing draughts.

When I left my room for the first time, at the door I met Otho the robber. He seized my hands and pressed them to his lips. They say he had watched there morning, noon, and night, waiting to do any little service, and was not to be tempted from his post by entreaties or remonstrances.

How could I have dreamed that Thou, O Lord, wouldst have called forth such streams for me from the rock!

They led me into the convent garden. I sat for an hour or two there in the sunshine. How the birds sang that day!

July 1.

Brother Conrad has taken my place in the hospital—I his, by the bedside. He is wondrous grateful and patient.

At times, with the fierceness of the fever, his mind wanders, and then he seems to dream himself engaged in mortal combat, either with the infidels or other fiercer foes, even the spirits which believe and hate; yet he seems scarcely ever to lose sight of Him who overcame by dying; at some moments appearing to cling to Him as a drowning man to a plank.

July 4.

To-day, as I stood in the sick-room, just as the stars were going out in the gray of the morning, he spoke to me very feebly; I went to his bedside.

"I have been lying awake long," he said; "I have had a fearful conflict. I sank through an abyss—an abyss of darkness. My sins weighed me down and down through the bottomless depths. Beneath me was *nothing:* everything I clung to melted away and sank down with me—the earth, the stars, all men, and all they have made. Below the abyss of darkness was an abyss of fire; slow noiseless flames burned on and languished not; the smoke of their torment went up for ever and ever. I could not speak; there was no sound in the dead air, and still everything I grasped slipped from my touch, and I and they fell on together, noiselessly. I despaired utterly, yet, from the depths of my sinking heart, I grasped Jesus."

"Then my hands clasped something which did not give way. It was the root of the tree on which He bore our sins. It went below the depths of the fire, and was not consumed; in the universal dissolution it stood firm, for it had foundations. It rested on God, and I rested on it, and as I clung to it, one drop of the precious blood fell on me—the blood of the Son of God! The fever was cooled—the fire was quenched—in the place of hell stood the open sepulchre, and on it sat angels in white; in the place of the abyss of darkness, above me was an abyss of impenetrable light. The angels floated away into the heavens, singing, 'He is not here; he is risen.' I looked after them, and when they were lost in the light, other voices joined them; and in the distance they sounded low and sweet as a voice from the depths of my own soul; and they sang—

"'There is joy in heaven;' and, 'He seeth of the travail of his soul, and is satified.'

"So, with their songs in my ears, and my head on the foot of the cross—below me the empty tomb—I fell asleep. Now, I have been lying awake long, wrapped in a sweet calm. It was a dream, brother Bartholomew; but hell, and the cross, and the resurrection, are no dreams; I am awake, but the night is around me no more; all is day— eternal, unutterably blessed day!"

I knelt beside my brother's bed, and gave thanks in silence. Then I gave him some fresh fruit; and, exhausted by the effort he had made, he slept again, and has scarce spoken since for this day.

July 8.

This morning, as I watched beside him, he said, as if to himself—

"Yes; it is true! He has gone down to the depths for us, and is set on the heights for us. He that believeth *hath everlasting* Life! I believe; therefore I live—live for ever a life of unspeakable, undefiled, unfading joy. 'They shall never perish.' 'He that believeth not is condemned already.' There is, then, no middle state between imperishable life and condemnation. *Here* we may pass from death unto life—there, there is a great gulf fixed which can *not* be crossed over. The fire of God's just wrath twice seen—*in the cross*, forsaking His own Son —and *in hell*. His blood must be upon us either to cleanse or to condemn. Brother," he said, turning to me, "was the work of expiation *finished* on the cross?"

"Unquestionably," I replied; "having by Himself purged our sins, He is seated as one resting after a completed work, at the right hand of God."

"Then," he said, deliberately fixing his penetrating eyes on me, "there can be no purgatory. *The cross is the only purgatory!* For those who believe in it, no second purgatory is needed: for those who reject it, no second is possible—there remaineth no further sacrifice for sins."

I feared to engage him in debate just then, dreading recurrence of fever, but I conjured him to leave such dangerous speculations until his soundness of mind and body is restored.

He smiled, but said no more, desiring me to read to him from the 10th chapter of St. John. When I had closed the book, he said—

"He is the Door as well as the Shepherd of the fold: the channel, as well as the source of life. Then, it is the Lord who unites us to the Church, not the Church to the Lord. Where He is, the Church is; where He is not, there is nothing but death."

I said, "The Church is the steward of the manifold grace of God."

"Yes!" he replied; "and it is required of stewards that they be found faithful. If, therefore, the Church, priests, sacraments, saints, seek to come between us and our God, they at once hide the light and cease to shine. In eclipsing they are darkened."

July 9.

To-morrow he is to leave the hospital for the first time.

July 11.

Brother Canrad's first attendance at the offering of the adorable sacrifice since his illness.

It was a high festival, being the day of the commemoration of the holy Benedict.

The silver and golden vessels of the altar were all uncovered; the church glittered and glowed with rich decorations and stained light. The choristers sang with voices like nightingales or angels.

But in the afternoon, Conrad said—

"How much of what we call church-music must be mere noise to heavenly beings!—the melody in the heart failing."

Again he thinks that the sacrifice of the cross being complete, it is mockery to profess to repeat it; and being divine, none but God can offer it.

Also, he deduces from the writings of St. Peter and St. Paul, that there are only two priesthoods in the Christian Church—the unchangeable priesthood of Him who hath entered into the holy place by His own blood, there to make intercession for us; and the priesthood of the whole living Church by virtue of her union with Him, set apart to offer spiritual sacrifices.

July 20.

Brother Conrad seems to become confirmed in his new convictions. He hath a perilous way of tracing things out to their consequences, which I fear may lead him to consequences I shudder to think of.

I never have felt tempted to this.

I also believe in the perfect pardon obtained by the perfect atonement; but, nevertheless, I thankfully receive the absolution of the ambassadors of heaven.

I also believe in the sufficiency of the one Mediator; but, nevertheless, I am glad to avail myself of the intercession of the saints.

I also believe in the high priesthood of the Son of God; yet I dare not question the existence of a Levitical order in the Church.

I conjure him not to speak openly of these things. He promises to do nothing rashly, but, saith he, "I dare not teach the smallest lie, since the truth is my life."

Also he saith, "Every truth taught me is a talent intrusted me, therewith to trade for the glory of my Lord. In hiding, I waste them."

He says he believes some may cling so close to Christ, that all their errors lie dead and nugatory outside; but, nevertheless, he asserts that all which is not truth is falsehood, and all falsehood is pernicious—tending to lull the slumbering, and to harass the earnest; that all which is not armor is a weight burdening us and hindering our course; that if Jesus himself neutralizes the poison *for us*, it is still poison when we present it to others.

August 10.—*St. Laurence.*

Otho the robber is dead, having caught the fever from us.

"Thou receivest sinners."

August 20.

Woe is me! to what is my brother fallen!

A few weeks since he went to visit a sick man. The man had led a very abandoned life;

his heart seemed closed to all brother Conrad's appeals; but as he was leaving, the dying man called out to him, "Father, you are a holy man; when you come to see me again, bring me the last sacraments of the Church, and I will give you all the money I have left, to offer up masses for my soul."

Conrad was shocked at the request, and going back to the bed, he said—

"The pardons of God are free. They are to be had by those who want them for asking, but not for gold."

And he refused to receive any money to pray his soul out of purgatory, even telling him that God offered us no choice besides heaven and hell, conjuring him with tears to accept the pardon so dearly bought and so freely given.

But the man persisted, asking, with oaths, what priests were for, if not to save the souls of their flocks.

And so, unshriven and unanointed, he died.

At his death, the relations came to the Abbey and complained to our lord the Abbot of Conrad's conduct.

At first the Abbot, being a man of an easy temper (although fiery withal), would not believe the report; but on our brother being called and questioned, he deliberately and unhesitatingly confirmed the conversation in every point.

They threatened, exhorted, and disputed with him—but in vain.

The discussion seemed only to confirm brother Conrad, whilst it made our Lord the Abbot very angry, so that at last he swore, if Conrad did not abjure his errors within three days, he would excommunicate him, and hand him over to the secular arm.

He made no reply, and was sentenced to be imprisoned in his cell.

The three days elapsed swiftly.

At length, on the eve of the appointed day, I obtained leave to repair to his cell, and make one more effort to save him. But verily, when I entered therein and saw with what marvelous sweetness and composure he sat awaiting the morrow, all the skillful exhortations I had framed wellnigh died away on my lips. Yet I believe I spoke to him faithfully of the Holy Mother Church, reminding him that she who had born and nourished countless hosts of saints and martyrs was worthy of all reverence, and conjuring him not to suffer himself to be cut off from her communion; but he said with a smile—

"My brother, it is God, and not the Church, who hath begotten and nourished the saints and martyrs; 'begotten by the resurrection of Jesus Christ from the dead,' and 'nourished and cherished by the Lord Himself.' This outward framework of ordinances and institutions is not the Church. It has cost me much to learn it; but truth is worth everything."

Then I entreated him to remember the holy

words with which she had sustained him, and her divine offices, gently leading him from infancy to manhood. Where martyrs died he might surely be saved; in leaving her, what security could he have? "This," he replied: "'my sheep know my voice, and they follow me, and none shall pluck them from my hand.' His voice is in the Bible; anything which seeks to silence that, can not be from Him. The Church can neither give life nor take it."

I forebore to argue further, seeing that it was vain, but we knelt once more together and prayed.

Can the devil give such heavenly composure? Can any but God inspire such prayers? Can he be right?

Holy Benedict, and Bartholomew, and Mary, mother of God, forgive me, and pray for us both!

I can not hate the heretic, but a heretic myself I will never be.

* * * * * * *

It was midnight; the altar lamps were lighted, the solemn service commenced; the incense, the lights, the awful music—they float before me like a dream—only, in the midst, one form stands out real, as if I could touch it now—one brought there to be degraded and cursed, and yet with a countenance as calm and radiant as that of the martyr Stephen, when, looking up, he saw the glory of God, and Jesus at the right hand of God.

The service ceased; the lights were extinguished one by one, and in the silence of the awe-stricken assembly, and through the arches of the lofty roof, echoed only from time to time the terrific words, "Anathema! anathema! anathema!"

And the excommunicated heretic was led back to his cell.

My brother—my brother Conrad—thou who wast my companion, mine equal, and mine own familiar friend; we took sweet counsel together, and walked in the house of God as friends!

What if, whilst they were pealing anathemas, the Lord Jesus was whispering, "Come, thou blessed of my Father!" What if——

[Here occur an erasure and a blank in the manuscript.]

August 15.

Brother Conrad's cell was this morning found empty.

We have searched for him everywhere, but in vain; we can discover no traces of him.

In my heart I can not help half rejoicing; and our lord the Abbot is, I trow, not sorry; yet to have lost thee, my brother, my son!

Fragments of Letters found amongst the Secret Papers of the Abbey of Marienthal, at its destruction, during the Thirty Years' War. [Supposed never to have reached their destination.]

FRAGMENT OF LETTER THE FIRST.

In the name of Him who has called us from idols to serve Him, the living and true God—and to wait for His Son from heaven—grace and peace!

I, Conrad, write these words unto thee, Bartholomew, my friend, and my brother, knowing that thou wilt often have wondered at my sudden disappearing—to tell thee of my safety, and of the love and gratitude with which I constantly remember thee; giving thanks for thee in all my prayers.

I send this packet to the house of our friend Magdalis, there to be left for thee by a trusty hand. If thou desirest to hold further communication with me, outcast as I am, the same hand will be ready to receive thy missive; if not, these lines can not endanger thee.

I made my escape by wrenching out the bars of my prison windows. I believe I do not dread death, having met it often, and having now learned to see through it—yet life is precious when we can lay it out for our Saviour; and I was glad to deliver the Abbot from blood-guiltiness, and thy tender heart from much sorrow.

I reached the top of the hill which bounds our valley, at the morning twilight. The village lay dim in the mist, the Abbey tower rose up through it, and the voice of the river came to me like the farewell of a friend; of thee I could take none! My heart misgave me: I was about to cut the last cable which bound me to the shore of happy days—the birthplace of a new life; but I turned away. The boat was launched—the little creek, apart from the tides and currents of the main, was left behind, and with it my regrets.

There are but two calms, the calm of the grave and of heaven—the rest of death and of perfected life. To rest before the voyage is over is to miss the haven.

I passed through valley after valley, keeping on the skirts of the forest: and at evening, when the long shadows crept down over the meadows, and the herds of goats crept on before them in the sunshine, I stole out to beg a morsel of bread of the goatherd, and to drink of the stream. With one of these poor herdsmen I changed clothes, and in this disguise entered Heidelberg.

It was a solemn joy to lie awake at night, with nothing between me and the infinite starry heavens—nothing between my soul and God.

It was a feast to awake in the morning, in the free forest, with the open sky above me—to feel that I might go whithersoever I would; and yet to know that all my goings had a purpose—the purpose of Him who guideth us with His eye.

I felt I had issued from the dull and smoky lamplight into the daylight; from a narrow monk's world into the unbounded God's world: and the world was a household, and I His child!

I prayed earnestly, that if there were yet any in the world who lived simply by the eternal life He had manifested, and the rule He had given, I might find them—that we might not be traveling the same road in the same service, and yet walk as strangers to one another.

For many weeks it seemed as if I were not heard.

The life of the cities was as a strange discord to my ears; they seemed like cities of Cain— music was there, and workers with all manner of tools, in all manner of metals; but God was not there. All the noise was but to drown the voice of the River of Life, which, meanwhile, flowed on beside them, bearing them swiftly to eternity.

Priests were there, and cathedrals, and they sang truths which might have saved the souls of all who heard them; but they sang them in a language the people could not understand. Was not this also mere din to drown eternal voices?

They made the church windows opaque at noon, with beautiful colors, that men might see the altar tapers.

And there were processions, and preachers, preaching pilgrimages to Jerusalem, and recounting the merits of sacred images, and dead bones; but of the journey each man is going, whether he will or no—of the living God, His love, and His light—of His defaced image in man, and its restoration through the Second Man, the Lord from heaven—of the mystery, now a mystery no more, which changes us from homeless and aimless *vagabonds* into *pilgrims* journeying home, with hands and hearts full of blessings—I heard in the high places not a word.

Oh, if men did but know what Voice they are rejecting—what are its words, and its tones!

Some, indeed, were toiling earnestly to reach the heavens, making themselves wretched to please God, as if He had never given His Son to make them happy—toiling, as if the Light of the heaven of heavens had never come down to men, saying, "Come (not to heaven—*that* you can not) but to *Me:* I am the Resurrection and the Life; in Me you shall live and rise."

It was all the old heathendom—with a Christian name.

And again I prayed earnestly, that, if any still adhered to the simplicity of the faith once delivered to the saints, I might discover them. So I journeyed on, speaking from time to time, to those I met, of the blessed message, if by any means its music might strike on a string that could echo it. Some were careless, and some mocked, and some received the good tidings eagerly, yet as a new thing. None seemed to recognize in them a familiar voice.

At length, one day, when I was about three

leagues from one of the free cities, I fell in with a pedlar, walking beside his mule. He did not look like a son of the north; there was something in the grave cheerfulness of his countenance and bearing which interested me, and I accosted him.

He displayed to me his wares; some few of them were costly silks and stones, for the castle, but the greater part were woollen and cheap ornaments, for the peasantry.

Then he asked me my calling, for by this time I had changed my herdsman's dress for that of a burgher, earning the price by copying manuscripts.

"I, too, am a merchant," I replied; "but all my property is invested in one jewel. Your goods perish in the using, mine multiply."

He looked at me with peculiar earnestness. "Incorruptible things are not bought and sold," he said, significantly.

"No!" I rejoined: "Freely ye have received, freely give."

He paused, and fixing his eyes on me with a gaze of eager inquiry, he said in Provençal French—

"Blessed are ye when men shall revile you, and shall separate you from their company, and shall reproach you, and cast out your name as evil, for the Son of man's sake."

My father's castle was near the Pyrenees, and I knew the Provençal dialect well, and replied by continuing the quotation—

"Rejoice ye in that day, and leap for joy; for behold your reward is great in heaven; for in the like manner did their fathers unto the prophets."

He held out his hand, and we embraced each other as brethren. When He shall come with clouds, there will be many rapturous recognitions; but few will surpass the pure joy of that day to me.

"I thought," he observed, "when first you spoke to me, that you were one of us—and yet I scarcely knew why."

"Are there, then, many of you?" I asked, eagerly.

For a moment he glanced at me half suspiciously.

"You must know as well as I do," he replied, laconically: "the birds of the air have their nests!"

Then I related to him my history, at least as much as was needful, and when I had finished, he grasped my hand again, more cordially than before, saying—

"Blessed are those who have never been within the walls of Babylon!—more blessed they who have burst her bonds and come out of her!"*

And he briefly sketched to me the story of his own life.

His name was Peter Waldo; his native place

---

* It is not to be wondered at, if the Vaudois, and other Christian sects of the Middle Ages, like the early Reformers, concluded the form of Antichristian power predominant in their days to have been the final one. They are constantly spoken of as having done so.

Lyons. The sudden death of a friend, at a feast, had first turned his heart to God and His Word. In reading, like myself, he became convinced that the Church of the Pope was not a divine institution—not the true Church; but the dead image of a church, moved not by the breath of life, but by machinery. Because he believed, he spoke, and then he found that many had believed and spoken the same things before. It had not been left for him to disinter the pearl—thousands possessed it already. The truth, in making him free, had not isolated him, but had, for the first time, brought him into a brotherhood of Christian people. Henceforth, having received the promise of an eternal inheritance, he joyfully confessed himself a stranger on the earth, living not to himself but to Him who died for us. He caused two translations of the Bible to be made into the vulgar dialects of France and Piedmont, spending his whole wealth in multiplying copies of these, and in assisting the poor of the flock. The priests and magistrates cast him out of Lyons, and now they persecute him from city to city; but everywhere he scatters precious seed, selling perishable goods, that he may be enabled freely to give the imperishable; preaching the gospel of the kingdom, and gathering together the children of God that are scattered abroad.*

The multitudes which follow this way in all

---

* For this account of Waldo and the Christian sects of the Middle Ages, see Mosheim, Milner, Bost's *History de l'Eglise des Freres*, &c.

places, but more especially in Bohemia, the south of France, and amongst the Alps of northern Italy, are incredible—but I withhold details, from reasons which thou mayest well surmise.

There are also some wild and fanatical people, led away by their own fleshly minds, or by false teachers, who suffer themselves to be misled by an unchastened zeal, to resist the authorities and pull down the churches; and these the persecutors take pains to confound with the simple Christians, massing them all together as Manichean heretics: but they are no more allied than art thou, my brother, to those that burn them.

Before I close, I will give thee a brief account of their manner of assembling and worshiping, and my admission amongst them, refraining from indicating the place otherwise than as a city in Swabia.

It was at the house of a poor weaver. Peter Waldo led me to the door at the dusk of the evening. We were admitted in silence, and the door barred after us. Then passing singly through a dark, narrow passage, the master of the house pressed the floor at the end of it with his foot, and immediately a trap-door sprang open, revealing a stone staircase. We descended into a low damp cellar, where twenty or thirty people, men and women, were already gathered around one whom they seemed to recognize as their teacher and president. He approached us, and embracing my companion, welcomed me amongst them. When it was stated that I wished to join them, he said—

"Then you have learned the meaning of the peace of God?—for in the world we have nothing to offer you but tribulation."

"I have," I replied; "to me all things are dross compared with the knowledge of Christ Jesus my Lord."

"It is well, my brother," he said; "for if we be dead, we believe that we also live with Him —if we *suffer*, we shall also *reign* with Him. The kingdom of God shall yet be set on high amongst men, and the high places of the proud shall be cast down. For the day of the Lord shall be to us a day of redemption."

Then the whole assembly joined in a circle round me,* whilst I knelt before the president, and he laid the book of the Gospels on my head, repeating, in a low, impressive voice, the Lord's Prayer, and the first verses of the Gospel of St. John.

"Blessed," he said, in addition, to me, "art thou! for flesh and blood hath not revealed it unto thee, but our Father which is in heaven."

And as I rose, the brethren greeted me with the holy kiss of brotherhood.

I thought, brother Bartholomew, of another midnight service—of the extinguished lights, the degradation and the curses—and I felt that even here I had been repaid an hundredfold.

* This account of the form of admission is historical.

"For I am persuaded," as thou knowest, "that none of these things can separate us from the love of God which is in Christ Jesus our Lord."

The president then read some chapters from the Bible; and after a short explanation and a prayer—in which they prayed also for the persecutors, and for all in authority—and the singing of a hymn, we separated, drawn close to one another, and to our Lord, by the Spirit of adoption, and the presence of Him whom no splendid offerings nor gorgeous ceremonial can charm amongst us, but who is ever with the two or three gathered in His name.

Every one who attended that meeting was there on pain of death if discovered, so that no mere "smooth words" would have been sufficient to sustain us. The Word was preached with manifestation of the Spirit and power—for, brother Bartholomew, it is a certain truth that the Spirit of God is sent forth from on high, and abideth perpetually in the living temple of the living God, as with every quickened soul.

The Church is *not* orphaned.

There is a Vicar of Christ on earth, and an Infallible Teacher, *the other Comforter*.

But it is not the Pope.

FRAGMENT OF LETTER THE SECOND.

Not receiving any answer from thee, I yet venture to write thee again, believing that thy letter may have miscarried, and that mine can bring thee into no trouble.

I have traveled through many places since last I wrote thee, and everywhere found fragments of this blessed brotherhood, bound together by no secret vows or concerted signals, distinguished by no peculiar garb, yet fitting together as exactly as the fragments of a torn letter; recognizing one another as the children of one family by the mysterious tie of *kindred*—loving one another with the natural affection of new-created hearts.

I have found them among the industrious craftsmen of the trading cities; in Languedoc, amongst the noble and learned of the land, but chiefly amongst the recesses of the mountains—God's citadels of old for His oppressed people. Especially amongst the Alps of northern Italy, on the old Roman highroad from Italy to Gaul, they are gathered in great numbers. Elsewhere, they meet and part in secret, or are scattered in families, or one by one; but there they are gathered together in villages, and meet, in the summer, in the open air, pealing their thanksgivings, as loud as they will, to heaven.

There are no churches so grand as theirs, brother Bartholomew—cathedrals of God's own building: gigantic rocks, mountains clothed like saints in white, girding them around: for their organ and instruments of music, the voices of many waters; for their sacrifices, the offering of **redeemed and thankful hearts**.

An "old, bad race of men," their enemies call them; and some of themselves say, that the Apostle Paul himself first planted their Church, and that it has been watered by the constant influx of Christian exiles, persecuted first by Imperial, and since by Ecclesiastical Rome, men who counted the reproach of Christ greater riches than the treasures of Egypt. There *is* an apostolic succession, my brother, but it is not continued by the laying on of men's hands.

They speak much and reverently of one Claude, Bishop of Turin, who died about three hundred years ago, as a pillar of their Church. They are a brave and industrious people, hardened by toil and danger—for though some of their valleys are fertile, it tasks their strength to the utmost to eke out a subsistence from their mountain fields and pastures; and though, as yet, no persecution has wasted their valleys, they live in constant perils, and, as it were, with their lives in their hands— or rather, in God's hands.

In winter, many of the men will travel fifteen or twenty miles on the Sunday, swimming through rivers, and scaling mountains, to hear the Word of God, and meet their brethren and pastors; and this, not because they deem such meetings necessary to save their souls, but because of the joy it gives, and the burning of the heart, when a few disciples meet together in the name of Jesus—and He in the midst. Many noblemen and women of rank join them; some relinquishing wealth, and country, and kindred, to serve their God in peace; and others residing in the castles which crown the heights of their valleys. There *is* a religious order—God's clergy, the lot of His inheritance—set apart from the world, not by distinctive vows or habit, but simply by holding forth the truth which the world hates, and living the life of holiness which the world despises—separated from the wanderers by going straight forward—marked out from the darkness by shining—cast out by men, and set on high by God.

There *is* a holy war, but its weapons are not carnal; and a taking of the cross, but it is not a sign of glory amongst men.

I am living now with Henri, a poor weaver of Lyons, the native city of my friend, Peter Waldo. Indeed, so many of the simple Christians here follow this craft, that they are commonly called the *tisserands*, or poor men of Lyons. But long, I believe, I shall not be able to remain here, the Abbot Bernard, of Clairvaux, having excited the city, of late, against us. I remember thy speaking of him as a Christian man—alas! how many, even of such, know not what they do!

Our life is very quiet and simple. I maintain myself, and assist the family of my host, by copying and translating manuscripts of the Scriptures: thus also sowing, whilst I reap. At leisure hours, I take rounds amongst the neighboring villages and towns, sometimes with a pedlar's wares, sometimes without. The common people for the most part hear us gladly, and not a few believe. Of these, some remain attached outwardly to the old ecclesiastical system, and some openly forsake it; this we leave to every man's conscience, our chief aim being to unite souls to Christ, and then to leave them with Him.

We have had trouble in our family lately, Henri having been laid on his pallet by fever and prostration of strength for many weeks.

His lying there, so uncomplaining, often even triumphing amidst his pain, seems to hallow the cottage into a temple for all of us. As I sit at my desk in the other corner of the room, I hear him repeating whole psalms and books of the Bible to himself—for thus it is our wont to make up for the scarcity of the copies of the Sacred Scriptures.

At times, he calls us all to praise the Lord with him; and then, the children joining us, we sing a hymn around his bed.

Before meals, it is customary with us either to kneel in silence for the space of twenty or thirty Pater Nosters, giving thanks in the depths of our hearts, or our brother Henri will offer up some simple grace, such as—"Thou who didst feed the five thousand, feed us"—"Thou who givest us this bodily nourishment, deign also to feed our souls."

Henri's poor wife is generally almost as patient as he is, although it is so much sadder to see those we love languish and suffer, than to suffer ourselves. But enduring as she usually is, the other day her faith seemed to fail;—her husband's recovery so long hoped for and so long deferred, and my manuscripts having failed to sell; one little sickly child crying fretfully on her knee—the others clinging, hungry and half-clad, around her: she hid her face, and sobbed aloud.

"O Henri!" she murmured, "what have we done, that our prayers can not reach the Lord?"

He took her hands in his, and said, "Alette, they have reached Him. He is only keeping back the help until the best moment comes."

"Our need can scarcely be sorer, Henri!" she said. "Can He love us, and know it all, and not help?"

"He is helping us, Alette; He is teaching us now one of His best lessons—the lesson all have had to learn in turn. He is teaching us to trust and *wait*. He is watching us, to see how we are learning it. Let us look up to Him, Alette, that we may hear His voice in the storm. Let us ask Him to bless us in the trial, and I am sure He will bless us after it."

And we knelt together, and prayed, and were heard.

Ah! brother Bartholomew, there is no discipline like God's. *We* seek to discipline the heart by hardening it—*He* by melting it. And there is no comfort like God's. Our medicines weaken the constitution in relieving the disease; His strengthen the heart, while they heal the wound.

It is a grievous mistake to abstract ourselves from all the bracing air of everyday life, and the softening training of home, to the mechanical routine, and the dull, close atmosphere of a convent—to substitute our dead machinery of rules and abstinences for the living school of God.

It is a blessed thing to be *immediately* under the guidance of His hand, cost what it may.

I have taken my revenge on my younger brother, and on her. I have left them a New Testament, copied by my own hand, with the promise that they will read it.

LETTER THE THIRD—THE PRISON AT COLOGNE.

The Abbot Bernard has succeeded in scattering our flock at Lyons, aided by the excesses which some, in their untempered zeal, committed. Some of us have fled to the Alps, some to Hungary, Bohemia, Austria, and Swabia. I myself went northward once more; but they have captured me at last, with many others. This must be my last farewell to thee, my brother, for tomorrow we die!

This evening, we made of the portion of bread and water which they gave us a holy supper, trusting that He whose word made the water wine would not regard the imperfectness of the symbol. His presence made the prison fare a heavenly feast.

It was the last meal we shall eat on earth; it

seemed more like the first in heaven. To-day we have once more shown forth His death; to-morrow, we shall be with Him for ever, and then the long to-morrow of the day of the resurrection! For to-morrow we are to die at the stake!

This has the Abbot Bernard effected (not that I believe he himself wished to compass our death). If we meet one another, by and by, redeemed and cleansed by the same precious blood, how he will wonder at his own work!

But, for us, how is it possible to resent, when so soon we shall stand before Him with whom we have none of us anything to plead but *Himself!*

"Thou hast redeemed us by thine own blood."

We have a sure anchor, reaching to that within the veil, even Christ *in us*, and "*in heaven*"—"the hope of glory."

The last storm is coming on me—the vessel tosses—the flesh trembles; but, my brother, *the Anchor is firm!*

[For many years a blank occurs in brother Bartholomew's chronicle; then it recommences in a feeble and tremulous hand, and after noting one day, closes abruptly.]

Marienthal, November 1.—*All Saints.*

It is long since I have written anything.

Things have changed since brother Conrad left. The whole convent seems to look suspiciously on me, as his friend, and perhaps the accomplice of his flight. In clearing myself from this latter imputation, I have sometimes been led to say more than I meant against him, and afterwards my heart has reproached me bitterly. He was ever with me, as a son with his father; and sometimes I tremble, thinking that I misled him, and that I myself have been rash and presumptuous in my belief, taking too much, and too boldly, from the Bible, and looking with too little reverence to the fathers and rulers of the Church.

And then the seducing thought comes— "What, after all, if he be right and thou wrong?" And in the tumult and confusion of the many voices in my old brain, I can not always tell which are the devils and which the angels.

Mother Magdalis died a few weeks after brother Conrad disappeared, and a stranger, whom I mislike and mistrust, occupies her cottage. It is singular I should never have heard from brother Conrad; sometimes I think he may have written, and his letters miscarried, or *been withheld*, for why else do they watch me so suspiciously, and never suffer me to visit and preach to the poor peasants around, as I used to do?

Once, Nannerl told me (she always loved him since he rescued her boy), that amongst other heretics, Cathari, Pauliciens, Vaudois, and Picards, whom they burnt at Cologne, a few years since, was one of a lofty and commanding presence, said to be a Spanish nobleman—that he touched the people so by his calm and heavenly words, that many wept; and then he prayed them not to weep for him, for he was only going home by a rough way, but for themselves, that Jesus might have pity on them, and forgive them their sins. It might have been him. It may be only Nannerl's fancy. It was certainly like him. However it be, God rest his soul! and yet, why do I pray thus? Surely, if he died so, he must have been at rest these many years. Yet the decrees of the Holy Catholic and Apostolic Church, and the Vicar of Christ on earth! God help me! I am a poor old man, and my brain is sorely confused at times. Many of the monks point pityingly at me, as at one half-crazed; but I am not that—only tried, and very tired.

Also, the new Abbot is a jovial man, who loveth hunting, and wine, and pleasure, so that the convent echoeth oftener with the voice of mirth than with that of prayer; and for such things my old ears are out of tune.

My flesh faileth—my heart faileth; I am very lonely and desolate; I seem to be as a wrecked vessel, rotting, useless, on the shore. And yet, at times, I have gleams of a better hope. Have I not clung to the cross of my

Lord? and is He not living—and His promise very sure?

O blessed Lord Jesus, I am a weary old man, sorely tired with this burden of life; wilt Thou not soon say, " Come to Me ?" for Thou knowest I need rest.

SKETCHES

OF THE

UNITED BRETHREN OF BOHEMIA AND MORAVIA.

SKETCHES OF THE

UNITED BRETHREN OF BOHEMIA AND MORAVIA.

PART I.

THE FIFTEENTH CENTURY.

I.

John Huss had been dead for eight years; and during the greater part of that time Bohemia had been blazing with the fire kindled at his stake. The words he had spoken under the roof had indeed, as he foretold, been pealed forth from the house-top, though not in the sense or with the effect he could have wished.

The eternal truths he taught had doubtless been working their way, like most heavenly agencies, in silence, purifying the hearts which received them, to see further than their teacher; but of these, historians have, in general, spoken only parenthetically, like indiscriminating almsgivers, bestowing the largest share of their attention on the most clamorous. Of the true successors of Huss, preacher of the gospel in Bethlehem Chapel, we know very little; whilst of Ziska and his Taborites—their intrepidity and ferocity, their victories and slaughters, their violent dissolution of five hundred convents, and their torturing a poor priest to death for denying transubstantiation—we hear far more than we could wish.

In the spring of the year 1423, the Hussite army was encamped before Prague, to chastise an attempt of the citizens to elect a king.

"Twice," said Ziska, "have I saved Prague from the Emperor—now I come to destroy it!"

At first the soldiers murmured. The old royal city, enthroned on its twin hills, the crown of Bohemian nationality, the shrine of Calixtine faith, had a sacredness in their eyes. Was it not the holy city of Huss? Had not they themselves defended it with their life-blood?

But loyalty to the blind old chief who had led them through so many perils to so many victories, whose blindness had on them the double claim of suffering, and the transcendent energy which vanquished it—the habit of obedience, and the enthusiasm of personal devotion to their general, overcame the spell of association; they invested Prague, and prepared for the assault.

For a brief space, the then contending parties

—Calixtines, Taborites, and Roman Catholics—whose strife had been deluging the city with blood, were frightened into agreement by the presence of one stronger than they.

The gates were thrown open, and a peaceful procession issued slowly from them.

At its head was John Rockyzan, the cathedral preacher, and virtual leader of the Calixtine or "Moderate" party.

He came to intercede for Prague. He pleaded the services Ziska himself had rendered her, and the love he had borne her. His eloquent voice on Ziska's heart prevailed. The city was spared; and, as in the days of the old Hebrew combatants, whose wars the Hussites imagined themselves commissioned to imitate, a pile of stones was reared on the camp, as a memorial of the covenant; whoever first broke the covenant being doomed to be crushed beneath the memorial. But the election of a king was prudently waived, and Ziska, with his troops, made a triumphant entry into Prague.

II.

Another thirty years had clasped. Ziska, his successor Prosopius, the scourge of Saxony, and their army of Taborites, had passed out of hearing. That mighty creation of human will and force had been crushed and utterly dissolved; but the truth, and the hearts it had regenerated, remained, stronger than all storms. All that was combustible had blazed and been consumed; what was not combustible "burned, and was consumed not"—the starlight outliving the fireworks, to glorify God by its quiet shining.

From the ruins of the armies of Tabor had arisen the Church of the United Brethren.

One winter's day, in the year 1456, two foot-travelers were ascending one of the lower hills of the northern mountain-range of Bohemia. They walked fast, for the air was buoyant and frosty, and they were conversing eagerly; their steps keeping pace with their words. Both were clad in the clerical garb; one in the monastic habit, the other in that of a secular priest. They were uncle and nephew; and there was in them that mixture of resemblance and contrast which so often causes us to make involuntary comparisons between members of the same family. Neither was young, and there was little apparent difference in their ages. Both were genuine Sclavonians; both were tall and dark, with muscular limbs, and the firm tread of mountaineers; both had straight features and broad, massive foreheads. But in the expression, in all which thought and life stamp upon the features, there was a stricking contrast. On the brow of the monk time had ploughed long furrows, but from beneath, the large eyes looked forth serene and trustful as those of a thoughtful child; but from amidst the countless petty and anxious lines which wrinkled the face of the priest, gleamed a pair of eyes restless and distrustful as those of some small animal perpetually on the watch against attacks it had no strength to resist. The soul of the one was as a harvestfield on which time had drawn broad furrows, the depositories of precious seed; whilst that of the other was as a highway cut up and kept barren by the daily trampling of a thousand cares.

The uncle was John Rockyzan, he whose eloquent intercession had saved Prague thirty years before, now acknowledged chief of the Calixtines, and Archbishop of Prague, by the choice of the States, though unconfirmed by the Pope. The nephew was Gregory, of the Abbey of Raserherz, leader and provisional Elder of the United Brethren of Bohemia: although, had you addressed him by that title, he would probably not have recognized himself; for if he led the infant Church, it was by no official staff, but simply because he pointed out to her the straight path, and she desired to walk in it.

"The Brethren are unreasonable with me," said Rockyzan, impatiently, in answer to a remark of Gregory's. "I am, after all, their best friend; but because I work by a slow and safe process to effect their object, like impatient children, they are always fretting and teasing me. Has any man denounced more boldly than I have the corruptions of the Roman Church? Have I not declared her to be the Western Babylon, and the Pope the enemy who sowed the tares among the wheat? Have I not said publicly, in the hearing of priests and courtiers, that we Calixtines do not go far enough, cleansing only the outside of the cup? And even in that for which you most bitterly reproach me, the compact which I negotiated between the Calixtines and Rome, have I not most effectually served your cause?—for has not the civil war which ensued, disastrous as it was, been the means of sifting from amongst you the turbulent men who would have renewed the barbarities of Ziska, of the chalice, and the Taborites, and thus left you, in the midst of defeat, really strengthened, because purified?"

"It is true," replied Gregory, gently; "the hand of the great Husbandman has turned the sword into a pruninghook."

"And who," pursued Rockyzan, "has toiled more than I for the triumph of the gospel? When I found that the Pope was only trifling with us in his pretended compact, refusing to confirm me in she arch-episcopate, did I not labor, and scheme, and negotiate for years, to re-knit the old ties which once bound our Bohemian Church to that of the Greek empire? And I should have succeeded, if the Turks had not taken Constantinople whilst the negotiations were pending;— was that the fault of my double-mindedness, as they call it?"

"It was proof that our strength lies elsewhere than in political machinations," remarked Gregory. "You have indeed schemed and toiled enough: all that I desire for you now is, that you should cast from you all those subtle webs of policy, and go forth in the strength of dependent loyalty."

"It is well," resumed Rockyzan, "for men like you to speak thus; your path is straight, and you may thank God for it. You have none but yourselves to consider; I have all Bohemia in my heart. The peasant may go to his work singing under his load, but he who is gifted with the power, or set in the place of the ruler, must not shrink from burdens though he sink beneath them."

"My kinsmen," interposed Gregory, "you mistake your calling. Christ rules His Church, not you; you are the minister, not the master; as servants, we have no course but to do His bidding, leaving the responsibility and the result with Him. We do not uphold the truth; it upholds us."

Rockyzan was silent for a few moments before he rejoined:—

"Had I done as you say, declared myself openly one of you, what voice would have filled the cathedral of Prague with gospels and denunciations? Who would have fed the deserted flock? Who would have pleaded for you with our noble sovereign, George Podiebrad, and obtained the district of Litiz as a Goshen for you, as I have done?"

"Is not the living God on our side?" said Gregory. "If He is *not*, let our cause perish; if He *is*, who can hinder it?"

"You are so one-sided with your solitary monastic habits," replied Rockyzan; "St. Paul was not above that tact and management, that politic accommodation, which you abhor; was he not all things to all men, if by any means he might gain some? I would gain all Bohemia for the gospel."

"That was precisely what St. Paul gained by his distinct and decided position," Gregory quietly remarked; "those who do not compromise can afford to conciliate."

"But what would you have me do?" demanded Rockyzan, impatiently, after a few moments' hesitation.

"What your conscience dictates," said Gregory, looking steadily in his face; then laying his hand on Rockyzan's arm, he continued, with appealing earnestness—"John Rockyzan, we know one another well; you have power, but you have not peace; I want you to sacrifice much, that you may gain all. You see before you honor, power, the favor of your king—a position from which you might rule your country; but they lie one step out of your path. You intend to turn aside to gather them, and then to return and use them for your Master. You are mistaken. Talents gained in disobedience to Him can hardly be used in obedience; there is a tendency in motion in any direction to perpetuate itself; you will either toil on with your burden of earth until, weary and dispirited, you are compelled to cast it from you, and return, after the loss of precious years, to the point from which you started; or you will not return; you will never return; you will labor with your restless heart and your burden of cares, and the end of all your travail will be to be *lost*. O my kinsman, bear with me, and listen to my words: you are come to a cross-road in your life; you know the way; walk in it. 'If any man serve me, let him follow me.' There is no serving Christ but in following Him with a single heart."

Again Rockyzan asked, "What would you have me do?"

"Ask your God that question," replied Gregory, with increasing earnestness. "He will show you—not, indeed, the whole scheme of your life—but *the next step;* if any man *will* do His will, he shall know of the doctrine. I can only tell you what I will do. We believe that the system of the Church of Rome keeps men afar off from God, instead of bringing them nigh to Him; tossing the hearts of the faithful with doubts, and lulling the consciences of the careless with dreams. We believe that she has hidden the cross on which our sins were blotted out, and closed the sepulchre which our risen Lord opened for us, by the dead doctrines and hollow ceremonies which she has built over them; her refusal of the sacramental cup to the laity being but a type of the cup of salvation which she withholds from them. With her false doctrines and ceremonies we have nothing to do; but the cross, the riven tomb, and the free cup of life, are our all. She conceals and withholds them, but God has revealed and freely given them to us; therefore we must offer them freely to one another. This is the sole object of our little community at Litiz. For some time, as you know, we have accepted teachers from the Calixtines; but, in spite of our earnest remonstrances, they send us men who only pull down what we seek to build up. We have, therefore, no resource but to recognize those amongst us whom God has endowed with gifts of governing and teaching, and to trust Him for the result. Our high priest, our master, our bishop, our chief pastor, is none else than the living Son of God; our canons, His Word; our guide and counselor, the Eternal Spirit, whom He has sent forth to abide in His Church, and build it up. Our prayer for our Church is, that if she ceases to minister to the world as a living body, she may never pollute it as a corpse; that if she ceases to *live*, she may cease to *be*. We are now about to enter on the serious work of seeking and appointing our pastors; if you like to join us, you can."

All this while they had been toiling up steep after steep, until at length they reached the height of the Donnersberg, the highest of the group of volcanic mountains, which they say once arose as islands out of the lake of Bohemia, and through which the Elbe has cut itself a stormy passage.

Around them lay mountains, upheaved, wave on wave, by the tossings of a fiery sea, girding in their fatherland on all sides, and guarding it, the fruit of such convulsions now reposing in calm strength beneath the heavens. Snow covered the heights, glowing in the warm light of the low sun. Over the sunny upland pastures the white frost was steaming up in soft transparent clouds; from the dim white fog below arose hills of dark pine woods, and red masses of leafless oaks.

Beyond spread the broad plain, teeming with life; valleys nestling in the heart of the lower hills; spires glittering through the thin mist; rivers linking together the cities with silver chains: and over all floated the still, clear sunlight. They paused and looked, and listened to the silence. At length Rockyzan exclaimed—

"See how our country lies before us, guarded by her mountain walls from all the world without, linked together within by life-giving waters! My hand shall never be the one to break her sacred unity! Let us have a Bohemian Church, or none!"

But Gregory replied, sadly—

"My kinsman, there is another mountain, from whose holy calm God looks down on the whole earth, and throughout it the Father's eye watches our scattered family, unknown to men, yet the only thing amongst men on which the heart of God can rest. Before Him that scattered family is *one;* the living stream which unites them is the truth. There is no unity in God's sight, no unity which will stand the test of fire, but unity in the truth. All other unions are mere congealings, freezings together, of heterogeneous elements, which the day will dissolve. In forming any spiritual confederation on any but God's principle, you are marring God's unity, uniting what He has sundered, and sundering what He has joined together. The only schism in His sight is, I believe, to make anything but Jesus the centre and the bond of union—to reject those whom He receives, and to receive those whom He rejects. From this may He preserve us!"

But Rockyzan's eyes were riveted on the fair scene before him. He "lifted up his eyes, and beheld all the plain, that it was well watered everywhere, as the garden of the Lord, as the land of Egypt; and he chose him all the plain." He also, like One we know, was taken up to the top of a high mountain, and shown a kingdom and its glory. But, unlike Him, he did not repel the tempter with lowly dependence on Divine words. The thousand dewdrops in his eyes outshone the one sun, and he said—

"I can not join you yet: Bohemia needs me. I must be Archbishop of Prague, and from my throne on the mountains in the centre of my country, I will send forth messengers of the gospel to every corner of the land; and then, when all Bohemia is penetrated with the truth, as one man we will arise, and throw off the yoke of Rome! The eye of the politician sees further than that of common men. He who guides men must move slowly." And taking a hurried leave of Gregory, Rockyzan went back to Prague. Gregory visited his brethren among the mountains, and then returned to Litiz. Their paths parted, only crossing once afterwards. The eye of the politician saw far, but the eye of the Christian saw further, for it saw through the clouds to the heavens. Few men consciously choose the service of Mammon; none unconsciously serve God.

III.

Things followed the course foretold of the disciples in the last conversation our Lord held with them before His death. In the world the little faithful flock of Bohemian Brethren had tribulation; but in Him they had peace.

The little church at Litiz grew in stature and in numbers, and many similar bodies sprang up in different parts of Bohemia—quiet, peaceable communities, whose sole bond was union with their Saviour, whose sole object was to minister to all men for His sake. Why, then, did all men speak evil of them, and all parties unite in persecuting them? We only know that they did so, and men had done the same before to Him in whom no fault could be found.

Rockyzan retained his power and place, and his influence with the King of Bohemia increased. For some time he used this influence cautiously, but constantly, in favor of the truth and its calumniated confessors. But at length the United Brethren were summoned before the Consistory at Prague.

The moment came when Rockyzan could no

longer unite the two services. The choice which had been so long unconsciously made had now to be decisively acted on. It was no longer prudent or safe for him to assist the Brethren; he therefore abandoned them. To excuse his own vacillation, he accused them of precipitation and turbulence; to prove his sincerity, he persecuted them. The king, it is said, wavered. The earlier teaching of Rockyzan himself, the convictions of his own conscience, the blameless lives of those he was called upon to attack, weighed heavily upon him. But Rockyzan was at his sovereign's elbow, to remind him of his coronation oath to extirpate heresy; to urge him to save himself, the more "moderate," and the "truth," by sacrificing the "extreme party." None can tempt like the fallen, and George Podiebrad yielded.

Thus Rockyzan began with waiving his convictions, in order to gain influence to promote them. He ended in turning the influence thus gained against the cause for which he had persuaded himself he sought it. The process in his mind was perfectly natural. The first act of unbelief, by which he virtually said, "I will uphold God's truth by disobeying Him," led logically to all the rest. The same question is being daily proposed, in divers manners, to some amongst us now. How are we answering it? Love is our surest logic. Whom are we loving best?

The Church of Bohemia was called to pass through one of those periods which will fill eternity with deathless memories, echoing in "songs of deliverance," and in wailings of unpurifying remorse.

In the depth of winter the sick were dragged from their homes, and cast out into the fields to die. Some were seized, and sent back to their friends without hands or feet, maimed and wounded, as living tokens of the fate which awaited those who persevered. Some were tortured, and sent to heaven with strange tidings of the welcome which those whom the Son of God is not ashamed to call "brethren" met with on earth, dragged to death, burnt alive, even little children burnt at the stake. And the Brethren of Bohemia endured the fiery trial, and multiplied. They met together as usual to read the Word of their God; (how living and significant was every page read by the firelight of persecution!) to pray, as those pray who have no defender but God; and to show forth their Lord's death, as those do who have no hope but His coming again.

One evening, a body of them had assembled in a private house in Prague, to pray, and to celebrate the communion of the body of Christ. Amongst them was a venerable man, whom they revered as a patriarch. His hair had grown gray, his manly form had acquired a slight stoop, and the voice which pronounced the fatherly benediction was the tremulous voice of an old man; but his eyes were still bright with an expression of childlike trust and love. It was Gregory of Raserherz.

They were preparing for the distribution of the sacred elements, when an interruption was caused by the sudden appearance of a messenger, who whispered something to Gregory, and then as suddenly disappeared.

When he had left, Gregory calmly addressed the congregation. The messenger, he said, was sent from one of the judges, who was a secret friend of theirs, to entreat them to disperse instantly, or he himself would be compelled to come within a short space of time to arrest them. Gregory expressed his own conviction that they should best fulfill the wish of Him who had said, "Let these go their way," by accepting the friendly warning, and quietly dispersing.

But there were amongst the assembly many enthusiastic young men, students of the University of Prague, who had embraced the oppressed cause with all the chivalrous ardor of youth— men who, like St. Peter, had not counted the cost, and therefore deemed their resources of endurance and fidelity inexhaustible—and many of these murmured openly against Gregory's counsel, declaring that they were ready to die for the truth, but would never consent to such a denial of it as this cowardly flight.

To their untempered zeal, stakes, racks, and scaffolds were as "trifles." Gregory knew they were *not* trifles; but the assembly was partly borne away, and partly silenced, by their enthusiasm, and he resolved to cast in his lot with them.

Whilst they were proceeding to the celebration of the communion, the door opened, and the judge appeared, followed by a band of armed men.

The assembly was mute, until the voice of the judge broke the silence with the remarkable words—"It is written that they who will live godly in Christ Jesus shall suffer persecution." Then, with a strange inconsistency,* suffering himself to become the instrument of a cruelty which he abhorred, against men whom he revered and had sought to rescue, he added—

"Follow me to prison."

And giving the word to his followers, the leaders of the assembly were forthwith bound and led away.

It is said, that of those who had so confidently invited persecution, not one had the courage to endure it.

* * * * *

An assembly of priests and magistrates, ministers of Christianity and of justice, were gathered in a room in the city of Prague, to try whether

---

* This is not the only example of such conscious inconsistency during this struggle. Lupacius, a friend of Rockyzan's, after deserting the United Brethren, wrote them a letter full of earnest exhortations to persevere in their course, and wise advice as to the best method of doing so.

by laying an old man on the rack they could induce him to renounce the convictions of his whole life, and betray his fellow-believers.

Gregory of Raserherz and John Rockyzan met once more; the nephew on the rack, the uncle watching to see whether torture would do for Gregory what prosperity had done for him.

But the high and holy One who inhabiteth eternity dwelt with that gentle and lowly spirit; and the sorer his enemies pressed upon him, only so much the closer did they drive him into the sanctuary of that Blessed Presence.

They could not succeed in wringing from Gregory one murmur or one word of recantation; but they did succeed in subduing his enfeebled frame with the extremity of pain.

He fainted, and lay for some time unconcious.

But He who spoke of old to His people in visions came near to Gregory in the cloud.

As he lay there, insensible to all around, he saw, as in a trance, a tree spreading its roots over the earth, and its branches to the heavens. It was covered with delicious fruit, and the birds found shelter under its branches, and ate of its fruit—filling the air with their sweet and happy songs. Three men guarded this tree.

The dream was significant, and time interpreted it.

The torturers believed their work was done—they thought him dead; and for a moment

Rockyzan's conscience awoke, and in an agony he exclaimed—

"O my poor Gregory!—would to God I were where thou art!"

But the old man recovered, and after procuring his release, Rockyzan, in spite of a solemn remonstrance from the Brethren, relapsed into his old course of action.

They concluded their last letter to him with the words, "Thou art of the world, and thou wilt perish with the world;" and he revenged himself by deliberately exciting a fresh persecution against them.

I only know of two subsequent events in the lives of Gregory and Rockyzan; both were consistent.

The United Brethren wished to give a more systematic organization to their community; and true to their faith that the Lord Jesus had not grown weary of guarding His Church, they met together in His presence, to seek His direction in the choice of their pastors.

Seventy of them met in a house in the town of Lotha; men of the higher and lower aristocracy, burghers and ministers of the gospel.

This was in 1467, fifty-two years after the burning of John Huss at Constance, and fifty-two years before Luther's burning of the Papal bull at Wittenberg.

After fasting, and reverently addressing God

in prayer, and listening to Him through His Word, they chose twenty men, and out of these nine as candidates for the sacred office. Gregory of Raserherz, hitherto the Provisional Elder, had been the most earnest in counseling a measure which was to deprive him of all his official authority; and he now offered up a solemn petition that God would choose their pastors for them.

Then, like the primitive disciples in the choice of a successor to the fallen apostle, (unmindful, perhaps, that this proceeding took place before the day of Pentecost,) they left the matter to the decision of the lot. The billets were drawn from an urn by a little child; and the three on which the decisive word *est* was written, fell to the lot of the three men whom, six years before, Gregory had seen in his vision on the rack guarding the fruitful tree.*

They were accepted with joy and gratitude, and installed into their office with a hymn of thanksgiving. They subsequently sought and obtained ordination from the bishop of an ancient Vaudois colony in Austria.

This was the first definite organization of the Church of the United Brethren of Bohemia and Moravia. Was not this act of joyful renunciation a beautiful close to our glimpses of such a life as Gregory's?

It is remarkable that these Austrian Vaudois,

* V. Bost's "Histoire de l'Eglise des Frères."

probably descended from the French Christians dispersed by the persecution in the days of St. Bernard, had scarcely thus linked themselves with the young Church of Bohemia, when they themselves were crushed and scattered by an exterminating persecution. They laid their hands on the heads of their successors, and blessed them, and then were taken to their rest.

The last voice that brings us tidings of John Rockyzan is from his deathbed.

He died, it is said, without hope.

PART II.

THE SEVENTEENTH CENTURY.

I.

MAGDALEN.

History will tell you what kings were reigning, and what armies were fighting, in 1619—what subtle webs of policy were being spun in French and Austrian cabinets; how all Germany was quivering with excitement at the clever chess-playing of the Union and the League, and the preparatory agitations of the Thirty Years' War, the hero around whom all were to group, the mighty and lowly Gustavus Adolphus, not having yet appeared; she can also tell you of the solemn and joyous confederation which had taken place not long before between Lutherans, Reformed, and Calixtines, in Bohemia, in which even the United Brethren were included—thereby gaining quite a respectable position amongst the Bohemian national institutions;—but of that history of "holy and humble men of heart," of spiritual conflicts and eternal victories, which is written in heaven, she can tell you very little.

She will lead you through the steep, narrow streets of Prague, the most picturesque, she says, and romantic of European cities, whose walls and towers are dented with the sign-manuals of so many wars—and she will show you the mountain throne where the royalty of Bohemia sat for centuries, looking over her broad domain, the Moldau lying as a faithful guardian at her feet, ready to convey her behests whither she would; she will point out to you church after church, sacred with the relics of Bohemian martyrs—and palace after palace, gorgeous with the pomp of Bohemian nobles; she may even guide you to the portal of the house of the noble family Von Loss, whose young chief has been one of the Directors of the kingdom, and advocates of the United Brethren under the Emperor Rudolph; but she can not admit you within. Nevertheless, if you please, we will enter.

It was a grand old room, high and long, more of a gallery than a hall; in the deepening twilight, with its lofty Gothic windows, its strongly-shadowed pictures looming from tapestried walls—rich paintings of Titian's, quaint, hard, symbolic, family portraits of the Middle Ages—it had something of the mystic light of a church; yet it was apparently the ordinary sitting-room of the family, for it was full of rich, massive furniture. A fire blazed on the hearth at one end, to keep off the chill of an evening in early autumn; and near it sat the young daughter of the house, and an old man in the sober dress of a Protestant minister.

The maiden was dressed gracefully, but plainly; you would scarcely have remarked her costume, had she been introduced into your drawing-room now, but for the rich Vandyked collar which has become characteristic of the century of the great portrait-painter. Nor am I sure that you would have remarked her face; it was not striking— its beauty lay deeper: had she been the only specimen of Bohemian beauty Titian had seen, he might probably not have said that he had seen the ideal of a female head at Prague; yet its poise on the long throat was so firm and graceful; the brow, as it lay bared by the throwing back of the long curls, was so innocent and calm; the eyelids, and dark lashes, threw such a soft shade on the cheek, and the mouth had such a happy smile on it as she sat at her easel, that Magdalen Von Loss was certainly one of those works of God on which we may still look, and say thankfully, "It is very good."

She laid down her brush among the brilliant colors and tinctures which she had been using, and bringing her work to the old man, she knelt before him, and placing the painting on his knee, playfully covered the book he had been reading.

"Now, father," she said, (he was not her father, he was a Moravian pastor, called David Jablonsky, but she and her brother had acquired the habit of calling him so in their infancy, having been left to his guardianship, and had continued it since from reverence to his pastoral office, and his venerable and endearing character,) "now put down that great learned book—it is too large to read anywhere but in a pulpit—and let dear old John Huss enjoy his own thoughts a little, and look at me. I think two hundred and four years is long enough for him to have been talking to our incomparable Czeskan nation: now it is our turn."

He placed a mark in the book, and let her lay it on a table beside him; then taking her drawing to the window, he looked at it for some minutes in silence.

It was from a hymn-book of the Brethren which she had been illuminating; the subject was from the *Te Deum*—

"The noble army of martyrs: praise thee."

At the bottom of the page she had sketched in solid and sombre colors the martyrdom of Huss. Around the stake were gathered soldiers and priests, some with countenances breathing out slaughter, others turning away their heads in compassion; in the distance were shadowed forth the forms of many Bohemian martyrs; mothers weeping over the innocent faces of their dead children, widows over their slain husbands, young girls chafing the hands of old men perishing of cold in the snow-fields. The face of Huss was turned heavenwards, illumined as if by some glorious vision. The smoke from the burning fagots arose in blue wreaths around the text, parting at each side to give glimpses of two medallions, and at the top melting away amidst sunset clouds. In the medallions, in shadowy purples and grays, she had sketched Huss's well-known dream—on once side priests and magistrates laboriously effacing the pictures of Jesus on the walls of his chapel of Bethlehem—on the other, angels restoring them in fairer colors. Above, in aërial transparent tints, such as bathe the clouds at sunset, was a meek, exulting band, bearing palms, and casting chaplets of victory at the feet of one whose form was half shrouded in light, one hand only coming distinctly out from the glory, to crown the martyr—and that hand was pierced.

"I like this, Magda," the old man said, at length; "it is the best you have done."

Then passing to her drawing-table, he turned over sheet after sheet of brilliant illuminations—historical sketches, portraits, borders of arabesque, rich branches of brown and golden autumn leaves, ferns and mosses, and delicate garlands of spring flowers.

"My child!" he exclaimed, taking her hands in his, "God has given you many gifts—spend them all for Him."

She smiled: "This is my myrrh and frankincense," she said, "which I would lay at the feet of Jesus."

She knew Him, as yet, more as the Divine child, heralded by angels, than as the crucified Saviour, rejected of men, and dying for them.

Jablonsky reseated himself in the arm-chair by the fire. Magdalen piled the logs so as to make a cheerful blaze, and then seated herself on a footstool at his feet.

"Now, father," she said, clasping her hands on his knees, "tell me of our forefathers."

A sunbeam crept in through the deep windows, danced amongst the liquid colors, and lit up her happy, eager face, as she looked up and listened eagerly while David Jablonsky went over the oft-told but unwearying tale of the martyrs of Constance, and their prophecies of better times; of the dove-like messengers sent out over the earth by the isolated Church, east, and west, and south, to see if anywhere they could meet with their kindred—who returned, finding no rest for the soles of their feet; of the fierce wars of the blind Ziska and his Taborites, their valor and their defeat, God not consecrating such weapons; of the noble band of Christian heroes which arose from the ruins of the old cause; of Rockyzan the double-minded, driven with many winds and tossed; of the single-hearted Raserherz, resting on the rock, and his dream; of the old Austrian Vaudois, casting their mantle on the young ministers of Bohemia, and then being borne aloft in chariots of flame; of the Jamnici, or cavern-dwellers, who followed Jesus into the desert, hiding in dens and caves of the earth, reading His Word by firelight, stealing out at night over the snow in search of food, treading in each other's footsteps, the last brushing out the traces of the rest; of one who was offered a year's respite, but preferred to die whilst his heart was warm, with five of his condemned brethren; of these and countless others, beloved of God, whom the world rejected, and now the heavens receive until the time of the restitution of all things.

The history of the Church of Bohemia was rich in such treasures; some of the sufferers had been amongst Magdalen's own ancestors; she had been fed with such stories from her infancy, yet her eye by turns moistened and kindled, and her cheek glowed as she listened. The history was ever fresh to her, for it was *true*, and its heroes were those ever-living ones whom she hoped to meet, and whose memories she delighted to garland with her fairest offerings.

"And now," she observed, when he ceased, "that rough season of ploughing and sowing is over, and we are reaping the harvest. If John Huss could see us now, how his heart would glow! The old chapel of Bethlehem restored to us, and wise men and princes filling it with their offerings and thanksgivings; our glorious old brethren's Church, no longer despised, but honored of all men—admitted into the Consistory with Calixtines and Lutherans; all Europe, they say, resounding with praises of our discipline, all Bohemia filled with our churches and Bibles: has not our God done great things for us?"

"We have certainly sought great things for ourselves," he replied, thoughtfully; "I have little doubt John Huss would have rejoiced could he have foreseen these things; but I much doubt if he would rejoice to see them now. They have such different measurements of things in heaven from ours on earth."

"But surely," she said, "we must thank God when He gives us rest and honor, and fills our cup with blessings?"

"We must eat and drink and give thanks, Magda, and go on our way; food is given us to strengthen us for action, not that we may take our ease, eat, drink, and be merry."

"But," she said, "surely, as our Father loves us, He delights to see us happy? It would not please Him, when He has spread a feast and furnished a palace for us, that we should take lodgings in a hut beside it, and refuse to eat anything but black bread, because the palace and its fare are too good for us. Would not this be the mistake which you so often told me the monks made?"

"We must not throw away God's gifts, my

child," said Jablonsky; "we must reverently gather up the fragments, and *use* them. But we are stewards, not proprietors; *think what that means;* for a steward to build himself a palace and buy himself jewels with his lord's money, would be, not only waste, but robbery—robbing both the master and the servants. The monk mortifies himself that he may live to God, and he fails; but God quickens us that we may die to self. The ascetic renounces the earth that he may approach God; he is mistaken—God is nearer us than anything we can offer Him, but His presence necessarily extinguishes our brightest glories, as well as glorifies our meanest services. It estranges us from the world far more effectually to be sent into it (as Christ was, and all His are,) from the heavenly places, than to be toiling away from earth to heaven. The sun puts out our torches as well as the storm, but it extinguishes them in light."

"But are we not *free*, father?" she asked—"free both as ransomed captives, and as adopted children?"

"Faith in our redemption sets us free, Magdalen," he replied; "love to the Redeemer makes us servants again."

"I do not understand you," she said impatiently; "do you mean that the Emperor Rudolph did not do us a service when he granted us the Majestäts-Briefe?* that my brother and the nobles

---

* Letter of grace.

are not right in spending all their energies to secure the establishment of our brethren? that we may not rejoice that our Church is honored instead of being despised? and that we may worship in our old temples instead of in caves and wildernesses?"

"Dear child," said the old man, gently taking her hand, "we shall see. The glory of the Church in this age is not to be clothed in purple and fine linen, but to be bearing the cross after her Lord, the servant of all men for His' sake. She is necessarily a paradox amongst men; her laws are totally distinct from those of the world, as her nature is. When she is weak she is strong, when she is poor she is rich, when she is despised she is glorified, and this not because weakness and poverty and reproach are in themselves good things, but because, being always really weak, she is then only truly strong, when the consciousness of weakness leads her to abide close to her Lord."

"But," pursued Magdalen, rising and stirring the firelogs, then going to her easel and laying her hand on her beloved drawings, "would you have me renounce these happy, beautiful dreams, my painting and books, and all I delight in, and strip my soul bare to tread the Dolorous Way?"

"I would have you renounce nothing, my child," replied Jablonsky; "what will be the end of our heaven-born life in the resurrection, is its **tendency now.** The new life must overwhelm and rule the old; we must be clothed upon, not unclothed; mortality must be swallowed up of life. I believe, as at the first opening of our Christian life, so ever after, God would have us receive before we renounce. I do not mean that you may not have to renounce much that is dear to you, that you must not have perpetually to resist the evil nature which abides within us till death: you may be called upon to pluck off the right hand and to pluck out the right eye—but it is by listening to His voice, and learning to know it well, and follow it, that you will find strength for this. Love is the element of Christian life, and self-sacrifice is on earth the element of love. Simply ask Him to fill your heart with His love, and your life with His presence, and then all that is displeasing to Him will be expelled from both, simply because there is no room for them. You need not pluck off the dead leaves, the young buds will gently push them off when the spring comes."

"I need not, then, seek trial?" she said.

"No," he replied, with a smile, "you need only seek faithfulness."

There was a great spring against the door, as of the forefeet of some large animal. Magdalen ran to open it, and was nearly thrown down by the rough embraces of old Rudolph, her brother's favorite stag-hound. "Down, Rudolph, down!" his master exclaimed; and kissing his sister, he advanced with his arm round her into the room.

He was many years older than Magdalen, though still young. "Magda! Herr Pastor!" he exclaimed, shaking Jablonsky's hand, "give me joy; I have the best news for you: we have succeeded at length, the states are unanimous, we have cast off our allegiance to the traitor Ferdinand, and offered the crown of Bohemia to Frederic Count Palatine of the Rhine; he has accepted it, and will be here in a few weeks. Our armies are united with those of Bethlen Gabor from Transylvania and Hungary before Vienna; Ferdinand and his priests are trembling in his palace, the emperor has not a firm place to set his foot on in all his dominions. Our cause is the cause of heaven; in a few months our Bohemian Church shall be the Queen of Protestant Germany."

"And our Queen, the lady Elizabeth of England!" exclaimed Magdalen, clapping her hands; "they say she is the noblest and most beautiful lady in Europe!"

"We shall see that," rejoined her brother, laughing, "when our little Magdalen stands by her side bearing her coronation robes."

Magdalen colored, and Henry Otho took up her sketch of Huss's martyrdom from the table.

"This is good, Magda," he said, "as far as it goes, but we will have another class of confessors of Christ now: men with strong arms and brave hearts, ready to do and dare all for the right. Why have you left old Ziska out of your army of martyrs?" he continued, pausing before a portrait of the one-eyed warrior, and gazing on the wild, energetic countenance, the deep furrow down the brow—the stamp, they say, of military genius—the stern features lit up to a fiercer glow by the flickering of the fire-light.

Jablonsky laid his hand on the youngs man's shoulder as he stood thus, and said earnestly—

"I know you will deem my warning the mere querulous timidity of an old man; but once more, before you plunge Bohemia in civil war, I entreat you to remember to what Ziska's victories led. God bears with the world, but He judges His Church. He will not suffer her to prosper in disobedience to Him; and can it be obedience to resist your sovereign, and to return evil for evil?"

"Father," said the Count, respectfully but impatiently, "the die is cast, we must now await the issue; to advance may have been rash, to retreat is impossible."

"It is never impossible," the old man replied, opening the door, "to refuse to do wrong;" and with these words he left the room.

"Endurance is always beautiful in women," exclaimed Henry Otho, pushing the fire-logs together with his foot, "but only the last resource for men. Besides, we are not fighting for our religion, we are simply preventing the emperor from committing a thousand crimes. It may not be lawful to avenge ourselves; but what law can withhold us from binding the arms of a madman?"

The brother and sister sat up until late, dwelling on the glorious future which lay before Bohemia and the truth.

Jablonsky also watched until a late hour that night, alone, with his Saviour, entreating with tears and agony of heart that, if possible, the cup of retribution might this time pass from his people, that the disciples who took the sword might this once not perish with the sword.

"They are blind," he pleaded, " but they mean to serve Thee. Oh, forgive the error, and reward the intention! or, if we must suffer, may our sorrows teach us and glorify Thee! and carry Thou Thy lambs in Thy bosom!"

II.

THE CORONATION.

All Prague was full of music and splendor.

Pastor Jablonsky sat in his study, thinking of his Sunday's sermon which he was to preach in Huss's old chapel of Bethlehem, when Henry Otho entered the room, leading his sister in her court dress.

A robe of blue velvet with ermine borders fitted tightly around her form and fell in dark massive folds from a girdle clasped with pearls. Her only ornament was her coronet, from which her brown hair fell in rich clusters.

"Magda is frightened at the idea of encountering all the strange eyes, Herr Pastor," said her brother, "you must reassure her."

"It is a solemn thing, is it not, father," said Magdalen, "the crowning and anointing of our king and queen before God?" And, kneeling before him, she added, "Give me your blessing."

He laid his hands on her head, and blessed her, and she went out with a glad heart.

The old man's thoughts went back to the time

when her mother had come into his study, dressed just as she was, and had begged him to take charge of her little Magda while she was at the Emperor Rudolph's court; and he left the house to follow the orphan maiden.

He saw her step into the family state coach, formed like an open van, but gorgeously painted and embossed with gold—not forgetting, in her pomp and excitement, to thank the attendants for every little service—her brother on horseback beside the carriage, proudly guarding her.

Every one was in the streets that day in Prague; the winter sun shone brilliantly in honor of the "winter king;"* and flags of many colors, with triumphant inscriptions, flaunted from house to house. The Moldau was crowded with boats full of peasants in holiday attire; the Sclavonian youths and maidens thronged into every gate, singing old Czeskan national songs; regiments of Bohemian infantry marched up the streets, with spoils from the suburbs of Vienna, followed by the enthusiastic cheers of the people; troops of Hungarian and Transylvanian cavalry pranced on with their wild eastern music. The city was full of happy stir and bustle and life, the tramp of infantry and the prancing of horsemen, shouts of joyous voices, thrilling bursts of military music, grand pealings of old church hymns, resounding through the narrow streets, caught up

---

* The name commonly given to the Palatine, Frederic, in Bohemia.

from hill to hill, from the Visselirad to the Hradshin, and floating down the Moldau to the plain.

As the old pastor moved through the throng, his pulse beat quick with the common enthusiasm; and he thought, "If men's hearts bound so high to greet an earthly sovereign, what will it be when the Ancient Nation and the whole earth shall go forth with songs and everlasting joy on their heads, to meet the King of kings, no stranger to His redeemed, singing, 'Blessed is he who cometh in the name of the Lord?'"

In the evening, the brother and sister came to him apart, to tell him of the day's events.

Henry Otho related how Magdalen had outshone the queen herself in beauty and grace; how many eyes had rested on her, how many lips had murmured praises of her simple grace, and how the queen herself hat addressed gracious words to her, saying that her court must not be without such an ornament; and then he spoke of the enthusiastic reception of the new sovereign.

"And now," he added, "we are a nation again at last; we have a Bohemian king, a Bohemian court, a Bohemian Diet, a Bohemian people, and a Bohemian Church."

And Magdalen came afterwards, and told how in all the assembly there had been none so noble and manly as her own brother, and the queen had mentioned him to her, "the dear, beautiful, good queen."

"Oh, father!" she said, "she is so gracious and gentle—I could love her as a mother—and yet so noble and queenly, my whole heart bowed before her; and when the people cried 'God bless her!' I could not help weeping, and praying that no harm may ever touch that royal heart."

"See, Magda," he replied, "all these sacred and blessed relationships has God given us to bind us in happy subjection to one another. Great is the peace of those with whom all these relationships are as links to Him—all centred in Him; great shall be the peace of the earth when this shall be the manifest law of all."

She looked earnestly in his face for an instant, then, kissing his forehead, she glided from the room.

Then returning and holding the door in her hand, she said—

"Why was it that the rich, magnificent choruses which filled the old cathedral when they crowned our king and queen seemed to bear me with inexpressible longings to the very gates of heaven, yet left me still longing *outside*, whilst, when we sing our quiet hymns together in church, all the heavens seem opened, and I lie as nothing beneath and amidst their glory, yet happy as a happy child?"

"Is it not ever so?" the old man answered: "the pomp of man's religion only expands the soul in vague emotions, as if *it* were the Infinite, and *leaves it empty*. God's religion brings down the Infinite into the soul, and *fills* it. Let your heart be but as a flower meekly opened to the sky with all its stars, and the heavens shall drop dew into it, and the dead earth shall distil living sap into it. Only keep your soul lifted up, and God will take care that it shall grow."

III.

THE INCORRUPTIBLE INHERITANCE.

It was a crisp, bright spring morning in 1620.

David Jablonsky and Magdalen von Loss were prolonging their walk on their return from one of those invigorating early morning services of which the Moravian Brethren were so fond, Henry Otho being absent with the staff of Frederic's army.

They had mounted to the top of the Visschrad. Down its precipitous side they looked on the river, the low golden sunbeams crisping the sides of a hundred masts, sparkling in a thousand ripples, glittering capriciously, through the morning mist, on roof and spire and tree along the valley of the Moldau, and in the distance clothing with delicate saffron and violet tints the woods and the tops of the hills; whilst the clouds were as bird-of-paradise plumes, fresh rose-leaves, pearly shells, scattered at random from God's treasure-chambers, and all—the colors of the clouds, and sky, and hills, the laughter of children from the city, the songs of birds—all fresh, and delicate, and pure, and light, as the soft fragrance of the budding earth which wrapt their senses imperceptibly as in a delicious dream.

On the other side lay Prague, the city of their fathers; church, and palace roofs, and gilded pinnacles, and white walls shining with sharp edges of light; the old Bohemian cathedral on the Hradshin crowning all the city.

"And all, all," said Magdalen, softly, "working together *for good;* all the ministers of life and love! Oh, happy earth, with God shining on it, and happy, happy creatures we, to live on it, beloved of Him!"

"*You hath* He reconciled," murmured the old man; "all power is given to Him in heaven and in earth, and in the fulness of times *all* things shall be gathered together in Him."

Then, after some minutes of happy silence, she said, as they descended the hill—

"What hinders the world from being Eden still to hearts redeemed and set free, and at peace with God?"

"His presence does indeed make a temple and an Eden about the faithful heart here," he replied, "as it will make heaven hereafter; but, dear child, this earth is not all Eden, not Eden *for all*, for there are on it dead souls turned away from the light of God—thousands who sin without repentance and suffer without being chastened. For millions on it, Magda, this world is an hospital, and a charnel-house, a place of sin and pain; there are men to whom the morning for which we watch shall come as a sudden destruction, and a terrific close of life and hope for ever."

"But that can be no cause," she said, shuddering, "why those who love God, knowing His great love, should not let some songs of joy ascend to greet Him from His fallen creation?"

"It can be no cause why we should not be thankful; but it is abundant reason why we should not sit still and dream, painting fairy visions on the darkness," he rejoined. "In Him we are indeed commanded to rejoice always. His love to us, and the union of the believing heart to Him, can not be more perfect than at the first moment when, in faith, we touch but the hem of His garment; our life is eternal, and 'hidden' above all storms, and therefore our peace is in its nature absolute and unchangeable as the peace of heaven. To dwell in the sense of this is our strength; such holy, reasonable joy is, in itself, service. The very presence of a heart so manifestly at peace with God and all He sends, is a gospel."

"Then why speak of this beautiful earth so often as a mere wilderness to be passed through?" she exclaimed: "I feel so at home here; and would not God have us feel so, while we remain?"

"Magda," he replied, gently, "it is most important that our peace should rest on objective realities, not on inward emotions. Truth is always the happiest thing to believe in the end: for the storm comes to all, and truth is the only thing that stands it. Now, when God said,

'This is not our rest.' He meant what He said; yet surely He did not mean this for ill news, but for the gladdest tidings men can hear. We have a '*better* country,'—a city that *hath* foundations; and we are hastening home, not empty-handed, but with hands and heart full of His gifts, to minister to all, as we journey, and with lips overflowing with His blessed invitations. And ever as we go, the Great Comforter is fashioning in our hearts, through fire and flood, the graces which are of great price in the sight of our Lord."

"You will forgive me," she resumed; "I am afraid I must be very cold-hearted; but earth is so warm and familiar to me, with my brother and you, and so many to love, that I can not help weeping sometimes, when I think of leaving it. I am not weary of life, you know, and I do not need sleep or rest; and the grave is so lonely, and the heavens, with the spirits and their unwearying harps and songs—we know so little about them."

"Dear Magda," he said, "God will teach you all His lessons in His own time; but have you forgotten the *Resurrection?* Look beyond the parting to the gathering, look on beyond the dim, unclothed, spirit-state in which the human heart finds no resting-place but the '*for ever with the Lord*'—to that bright morning when He who once appeared to cheer a weeping woman who loved Him, calling her 'Mary,' shall come again to breathe on us an eternal peace, and to gather the whole redeemed family into the Father's house. Then shall the pedestal of His cross become the footstool of His throne—then shall the earth, unfettered and impregnated in the new life, 'give forth her increase,' an Eden in the keeping of an Adam who has endured temptation, and vanquished the tempter—the second Adam, and His heavenly Eve, created, whilst He slept, from out His pierced side, bone of His bone, flesh of His flesh. This, Magdalen, is the glorious hope for which we wait; no mere unclothing of a wearied spirit, that it may lie down and rest, but the outpouring of the fulness of life; no mere selfish deliverance from conflict and pain, but the redemption of the whole Church from all fetters, the emancipation of the whole creation, the day of the triumph of our Lord, *the marriage supper of the Lamb.** This is the overwhelming joy which lies before us—for this the whole family in earth and heaven wait—for this result of the travail of His soul, the Conqueror also waits, sitting at the right hand of God."

Much more he said, which I may not now repeat; but as he spoke, tears gathered in Magdalen's eyes, and she said—

"Father! I am but a child; I have much to

---

* I do not at all mean to attribute these definite thoughts as to the future to the whole body of the Moravians. I believe there have always been individuals amongst them who have in some measure rested on them.

learn; these things overwhelm me. I seem stepping into a new and infinite world, and my heart trembles."

"Fear not, my child," he answered—"God teaches very patiently. He will take thee by the hand, and lead thee gently on. The Almighty One is also the meek and lowly in heart; He gives wisdom liberally to all that lack and ask for it, and upbraideth not."

Magdalen read her Bible much that evening, with a new reverence—read of the new creation, commenced in the soul of the feeblest believer, destined to find its completion when we shall awake in perfect likeness to the risen Lord, and its final home in the new birth from dissolution of the new heavens and the new earth; and she lay down to sleep with the joyful consciousness that she was a learner in a school of inexhaustible truth, having for her teacher Him who knows all things because He has made them, knows the heights of God, and the depths of man, by being both.

And the morning found Him still about her path as He had been about her bed—and the day's work shone to her with the light of her eternal home

IV.

THE BATTLE.

Magdalen had need of something to strengthen her. She had plenty of petty trials to prove whether the new hopes which had arisen on her heart were mere pictures of light—glowing, but opaque—or transparencies letting in real light on the dark corners of life.

The affairs of Bohemian Protestantism looked more and more gloomy every day.

Frederic threw away half his advantages by mismanagement, and let the rest slip away by his indolence and indecision. His generals were jealous of each other; his Bohemian subjects were jealous of the Germans; and there was no strong will, no plastic mind, to mould the discordant elements into harmonious combination. Men who should have supported one another only jostled one another, because there was no one to fix them in their places; and whilst the Protestants were hesitating and quarreling about their rank in the procession, the Emperor Ferdinand and his Catholics came and stole away the ark.

Henry Otho von Loss, and other wise and disinterested men amongst his party, doubtless saw this, but they saw it as the guardian angel is said to see the errors of his charge—with fruitless foresight.

They labored, and entreated, and contended, but their voices seemed only to serve to increase the clamor, until at last they had no resource but each to do his own duty, and leave things to arrange themselves as they would.

All this fretted Henry Otho's temper intolerably; like a strong wave struggling against an ebbing tide, to spend all his strength, only to find himself at each successive effort further from the goal, it was very bitter; and, in addition to this natural disappointment, he felt all that a Christian feels who has entangled himself in a thousand cares and schemes, and yet fears to look straight up to God, lest one clear glance from Him should pierce through all the laborious fabric, and smite it to pieces in an instant. Not that he was precisely conscious of this, but he felt less at home with himself, and therefore hurried the more impetuously on in the path he had chosen.

Magdalen had entered heart and soul into all her brother's schemes for liberating Bohemia and the truth, but she was less involved in the details of their practical execution; doubts of their consistency with the calling of the Church to lowly patience, and rendering good for evil, occasionally crossed her mind, and of late she had not sought to banish them, but had simply asked for more light.

At first, in the ardor of her new interest in Divine truth, she had sought to communicate it to her brother; but he grew first weary and then impatient, so that she ceased to speak to him on the subject, and endeavored to enter as much as she could into his cares.

But even this did not always please him: "What could women understand of such things?" And then, if she took refuge in her painting, he would say, " These were no times for such child's play."

At first Magdalen was surprised and indignant at this—she for whom his watchful love had always been providing some new pleasure; and often she was sorely perplexed and tried; but her tact and gentleness seldom failed: not that it was any great merit in her; she loved her brother literally as herself, and often some burst of repentant tenderness would make up to her for a thousand words, harsher than any he had ever spoken; for the kindness, she knew, was meant, the harshness not.

She was always ready to welcome him with some playful or loving word, or some proof of thought for his comfort; thus working out the prayers which, with so many tears, she daily offered for him.

So she was daily gaining wisdom in the lore of life, the blessed art of watching and ministering to the sick at heart.

God was training her for further lessons.

He was leading her consciously "with His eye," teaching her with His own voice the way in which she should go; and, though with the rougher lessons of external providence, He was as surely training and directing the yet unsubmissive heart of her brother.

And the old pastor looked on, and helped, and counseled—and where he could do neither, prayed for both his children, thus laboring together with God.

*　　*　　*　　*　　*

It was the eve of the 8th of November, 1620, the eve of one of those decisive days on which centuries of a nation's destiny are suffered to depend. All Prague, the Imperial and Bohemian armies encamped in its neighborhood, all Bohemia and Protestant and Catholic Germany, lay awaiting the issue of the battle to be fought on the White Mountains.

Once more Magdalen von Loss and her brother sat in the old room, with its family portraits and tapestry, its oaken cabinets, and high, deep windows—chatting by the blazing hearth.

Insensibly, as the twilight deepened, their conversation wandered off from national prospects and dangers, to the old days before care had set in on them—to plots and ambuscades concocted behind the tapestry, to tears shed over difficult lessons, through which could be seen no glimpse of hope—bitter griefs, forgotten the next day; to Henry Otho's gracious condescensions, and Magdalen's unlimited reverence; quarrels cemented into indestructible alliances; blame borne for one another, and pleasures hoarded up; all the world of love and trust they had been to one another—the orphan brother and sister.

They chatted merrily of it all, not daring to look forward, or to touch any deeper chords.

Then all the household met in the great hall to commit themselves and one another to the care of God; and His peace came down on them as they prayed, so that the young Count took a hopeful leave of them all.

"Magda," he whispered, "forget all my cross words: things have gone wrong sometimes, but one way or another God's cause must triumph: after to-morrow we will be His happy and trustful children again. Good-bye."

Magdalen bore up bravely, only after he was gone weeping and praying for him, till she fell asleep from weariness.

But they were soft, childlike tears, falling through the light of happy hopes.

Henry Otho von Loss lay by one of the watchfires in the Protestant encampment, on the White Mountains. The country was glowing with the feverish flicker and glare of many watchfires, gleaming here and there on the forms and arms of men, scattered over the ground in every attitude of hasty slumber.

With the exception of the patroles and those who had to plan to-morrow's movements, the two armies were asleep.

The night was still, yet beneath the stillness there was an undercurrent of stir and preparation; some groups talking in hushed voices, others stealthily changing their position, the crackling of fires, and the occasional challenge of sentinels.

Above, the calm was absolute, the moon passing noiselessly in and out amongst white clouds, and all the heavens full of her peaceful light.

As he lay there, musing, he saw a dark figure approaching the height, which on nearer approach he recognized to be that of Jablonsky. He beckoned the old man to him, and they sat down together by the fire.

"What brings you hither at this hour?"

"I came to see what was the character of an army sworn to defend the holy cause."

"And you found little satisfaction? The camp is a barren field for missionary labor—at least, until after the battle."

"And yet where is there more need of a life hidden beyond the grave?"

"Did they listen to your message?" said Von Loss.

"Some listened and some mocked, and some turned away, and some began to tell me of Christian homes and early childish lessons, until they wept and made promises for to-morrow. The hearts of men are the same everywhere."

"But did you find the men generally sanguine about the issue of to-morrow?"

"To be candid with you, I did not; your army, they say, is so mixed; the Bohemians seem indignant at having to fight under Germans, and beside foreigners from Hungary and Transylvania, whom they look on as little better than Turks and barbarians."

"Father!" said the soldier, rising and standing before him, "must not the cause of the Almighty triumph?"

"It must, it shall," said the old man, firmly, "though not perhaps by the arms of the mighty. Our banner of victory is the cross. The cross, and not the sword; for we also conquer by sacrificing, not by avenging ourselves. The cross, and not the crucifix; for He who was once nailed to it now rests in triumph, having obtained for Himself, and for us, an eternal victory."

"I understand," said Henry Otho, in a low voice; "but if, perchance, we have chosen wrong ways to His end, must not His end nevertheless be reached, and His cause prevail?"

"His triumph is as certain as His Godhead," replied Jablonsky, solemnly; "living or dying, vanquished or victorious, we only further His supreme and blessed purposes. He has undertaken, not only to save His people, but to guide them, and He will do it."

"It is well," replied Von Loss: "whether my earthly life serve, by being trampled into soil, to nourish other lives, or, by spreading into a forest, to shelter them, I can trust Him implicitly with it; for me, and for His Church, *it is well*. My blood may flow in vain, but my Saviour's can not. Kneel once more, father, and pray for me, for does not His blood cleanse from all sin?"

The old man prayed in few and simple words, for his heart was full; and then embracing Henry Otho, he hastened back to Prague.

On the next day, the cause of Bohemian Protestantism received its death-blow. The Bohemians gave way the last, but to die at their posts was all their valor could achieve.

As the consequence of that day, the pastors were driven first from Prague, and then from Bohemia; the churches were closed; those who could emigrate, did; those who could not, kept the faith in secret, or betrayed it, or were put to death.

The Reformation was crushed in Bohemia until this day.

V.

THE VICTORY.

Eight months had passed, bringing round to Magdalen and her brother the eve of another battle.

But the issue of this conflict was certain, the armor proof.

It was the 20th of June, 1621.

On the morrow, Henry Otho von Loss, with twenty-six defenders of the Protestant religion, was to die on the scaffold.

They allowed Magdalen to enter the cell, in the castle of Prague, in which her brother was imprisoned, and to spend an hour with him there. They had been praying together, and now they sat quietly hand in hand, fearing to make those last moments pass more quickly by any movement or burst of emotion. The thousand fragments and reminiscences and farewells, which that hour could never have contained, were all condensed into the one prayer—

"Father, we commit one another to Thee."

"Tell Pastor Jablonsky," he said, "that his

words are with me to the last. I am sure he has been praying for me, and has been answered."

They had not suffered any of the pastors of the Bohemian Brethren to visit the prisons. The Jesuits distinguished them with this especial hatred.

"After all my mistakes, Magda," he murmured, "that He should suffer me to die for Him!"

She did not attempt to speak.

"Magda," he resumed, "my sister, you will suffer, but trust His love; it is not charity or kindness, Magda, it is love—love deeper than mine. And, sister, do not struggle with sorrow, it is of no use; *sink down on Him*. He can heal, He will sustain you. And—oh, do not grieve an instant for me! You are the martyr, not I."

She sank on his shoulder, and they wept together; but the step of the jailer echoed through the narrow passage, and the long embrace had to be unclasped.

Once more they stood hand in hand, and Henry said, calmly, "By and by, my sister, after the little while, we shall have time to say all we would."

"At His feet," murmured Magdalen—for his sake, with a strong effort, repressing her tears.

They parted in silence.

Magdalen went home alone. She entered the house without speaking, and, quietly passing through the hall and up the staircase, she opened the door of the family sitting-room, and softly closing it again, she sat down before her drawing-table, and leaned her head upon her hands.

She was still leaning thus to avoid the pain of seeing, when she heard a soft step in the room, and looking up, she saw pastor Jablonsky standing close before her.

She was not weeping, but tears ran fast over his cheeks as he looked at her, and she stretched out her hand to him, and said gently—

"Life is not so very long, father, after all."

He could not answer, but he sat down beside her; and folding her hands on her knees, she said no more.

She sat long without moving, when a rough head was thrust under her hand, and in another moment old Rudolph's paws were on her lap.

Then her tears fell fast on his shaggy head; he looked wistfully in her face and moaned, and licked her hands as if to comfort her, until, hiding her face on the old man's arm, she wept bitterly.

And Jablonsky whispered—

"*Now Jesus loved Mary and her sister and Lazarus.*"

On that evening the confessors were removed to the Town Hall. The scaffold was already erected before it; and as they passed, many of their brethren and fellow-prisoners greeted them from the windows with hymns, and the people thronged around them and wept. *

---

* The following scene is strictly historical.

On the morrow, they all dressed as if for a wedding; and one by one, as they were led out to execution, they cheered one another on to the combat. The farewell would not be long.

When it came to the turn of Henry Otho von Loss, a Lutheran minister accompanied the guards. Von Loss had been amongst those who, perhaps, from too fond an attachment to the Church of their fathers, had refused to receive the Lord's Supper from the hands of a Lutheran: but when he saw the minister, he arose from his seat as if in a kind of ecstasy, and said to him—

"How I rejoice to see you, man of God, that I may tell you what has happened to me! I was sitting in this chair, grieving bitterly that I could not receive the Supper, having desired, as you know, a minister of our own Church. I fell asleep in my grief: and lo, in a dream, the Lord appeared to me, and said, 'My grace is sufficient for thee: I cleanse thee in My blood.' At the same instant, I felt, as it were, His blood flow over my heart; and since I awoke, I have felt singularly strengthened and refreshed."

Thereupon he broke into these words of triumph—

"Yes; *believe*, and thou hast eaten the flesh of the Son of man. I have no more fear of death. My Jesus comes to meet me with His angels, to lead me to His marriage supper, where I shall for ever drink with Him the cup of joy and gladness."

He ascended the scaffold full of joy, first prostrating himself in prayer, then having risen, and laid aside his garments, he again knelt, saying, "Lord Jesus, receive me into Thy glory!" and whilst he was uttering this last word, he received the death-blow.

Thus did the cause of external Protestantism in Bohemia fail, and thus did the Church of God triumph.

It was night—a summer's night; and under the calm stars a funeral procession bore the body of Henry Otho von Loss to his tomb amongst the recesses of the hills.

The mourners were a band of outlawed Protestants, yet they sang hymns as they went—hymns of hope and victory—and the soft music was peaceful as the songs of angels, transpiercing the calm.

One woman followed the bier, leaning on the arm of an old man. When they reached the new-made grave, he left her to perform the last rites over the dead, and she stood a little way off alone, her hand resting on the head of an old stag-hound.

The corpse was lowered into the grave, and the earth fell on the coffin.

Then arose the beautiful Moravian Funeral Litany,* floating through the silence with its responsive music.

At first all joined—at least, all who could for

---

* I do not know whether the Litany, from which the following extracts are taken, existed so early as this. It is now used in the Easter Morning Service, in the Moravian cemeteries.

THE SCAFFOLD.

Tales and Sketches.

weeping, for amongst the mourners were many faithful old servants of the family—in the hymn,

"I know that my Redeemer lives—

the eternal song of triumph of the resurrection.

Then Pastor Jablonsky said—

"Glory to Him who is the Resurrection and the Life! He hath been dead, but now He liveth for evermore; and he who believeth in Him, though he were dead, yet shall he live. To Him be glory in the Church which awaits His appearing, and in that around His throne."

And the assembly responded—

"For ever and ever. Amen."

Then the minister's voice arose again, at first feeble and broken, but gradually gathering strength from the power of the words he uttered:—

"Our Lord Jesus Christ,
By Thy human birth,
By Thy meritorious tears,
By all the miseries of Thy life,
By Thy languor and Thy pains,
By the distress and anguish of Thy soul,
By Thine agony and bloody sweat,
By Thine insults, stripes, and wounds,
By Thy painful death,
By Thy return to us, or
By our resting in Thy bosom"—

And with one voice the people cried—

"Comfort us, O Lord our God!"

Then, turning to the mourners, and especially to her who stood apart, he lifted up his hands, and said—

"The Lord bless thee and keep thee.

"The Lord make His face to shine upon thee, and be gracious unto thee.

"The Lord lift up His countenance upon thee, and give thee *peace.*"

And all the little band responded—

"In the name of Jesus. Amen."

Then leaving the grave, Jablonsky went again to Magdalen—for it was she—and led her home.

"My child," he said, trying in vain to check his own tears—"My child, God is indeed teaching thee the lessons of the wilderness."

"But He is with me," she replied; "and He teaches me also that it is the way to our rest."

And the next morning, like another Magdalen to another sepulchre, whose opening has made all burial-places for us only sleeping-places, she came early, when it was yet dark, unto the tomb.

And kneeling on the fresh earth, she said with her whole heart, amidst her sobs—

"Master!"

And Jesus said by His Spirit to her heart—

"Peace be unto thee! Go unto my brethren, and say unto them, I ascend unto my Father and your Father, unto my God and your God."

She and her brother were *His.* His Father was their Father. It was enough. She also had learned the meaning of the words Death and Resurrection.

The Great Hope of the Church had become the great hope of her heart.

She also went forth in His strength, to witness by her life that the Lord was risen indeed.

VI.

THE PEACE.

Magdalen never married. Without father or mother, or brother or sister, an exile from her country, cut off from all ties of kindred, she passed the prime and close of her life, which was a long one. Can you conceive anything more desolate?

In a little cottage in the suburbs of Dresden, an old paralytic woman lay on a low bed. Everything about her was scrupulously clean, and a young girl, having just completed her arrangements about the room, was seated by the fire, knitting.

"Why does not she come?" said the old woman, querulously. "It is long past her time; but the strong and healthy never think how slowly time passes on the sick-bed."

"O grandmother," said the girl, "I am sure she always thinks! The snow is lying thick on the ground, and every now and then it beats in heavy drifts against the window. Perhaps the Fräulein may not be able to come to-night." But the latch was softly raised before she could finish her sentence, and the Fräulein entered, and, after a few preliminary inquiries, took her usual place beside the old woman's bedside, and began to read to her from the New Testament.

It had been rather a hopeless task, and if Magdalen's eyes had not been directed rather to Divine promises than to visible results, she would have grown weary of it years before; for, although the old woman always listened attentively, and was very much aggrieved if the daily visit were omitted, she seldom vouchsafed any more cheering declaration than—

"Well, all these things are very good; but the comforts of this life are very needful, and the poor body must be cared for."

But to-night, when she had laid aside the book, and had arisen from her prayer, and had presented the sickly creature with a warm shawl of her own knitting, the old woman's heart seemed touched at last, and grasping Magdalen's hand tight for some moments in her own, she said—

"Well the comforts of this life are very needful; but the Great Gift of God, and His grace in the heart are above all."

It was reward enough for labors a thousand times more irksome. Tears gathered in Magdalen's eyes, and she went home with a glad heart, too happy to heed the cold, but not too full to notice how the pure moonlight lay in silvery streaks on the pure, smooth snow, roofing common houses with alabaster, fretting the bare trees with fairy tracery, and to thank God from her heart for all the changing beauty of this fair earth. Magdalen's religion was no mere inward emotion: it was a reception into her inmost soul of the truth, which is the "incorruptible seed" of the new life; it was the living relationship of a redeemed sinner to the living God. Being received into the family, and taught the freedom of the child, she had also been taught the "perfect freedom" of those who, having no object in life but His service who guides every step of their lives, labor under no cares, and can meet with no hindrances.

Two little faces were peeping out of the door of a house in Dresden.

"Why would she go out this bitter weather?" said one.

"We will go to meet her if she does not come soon," said another.

But in a few minutes they caught a glimpse of her coming quickly up the street.

Joyous welcomes were on every lip, laughing reproaches, and tender, loving words, and in a few moments the children had "Sister Magdalen" in by a blazing Christmas fire; one chafing her hands, another taking off her snowshoes, a third removing her wet cloak, a fourth bringing a warm shawl, and a fifth busy little fairy preparing a basin of hot pottage.

These were all orphans of Bohemian martyrs, to whose maintenance and education Magdalen von Loss had devoted the remains of her brother's confiscated fortune and her life.

Then, when she had rested, there were narratives of the day's doings and learnings to be given, and counsel to be sought; and in reward for lessons well learnt, and tasks well done, came the general plea for a story of old Bohemia.

The firelight shone cheerfully on the eager child-like faces, and on the gray hair and quiet happy eyes of the story-teller. Then were the old heroic tales she had listened to by the fireside at Prague poured forth afresh into the young fresh hearts;—for when will the harvest end, to be reaped from the seed of one holy life, laid down for the brethren, and laid up in the book of Church History written in heaven?

"Oh!" said one of the children, "we will be more useful than ever, and more like our fathers, when this bitter frost is passed, and we can go out again. I wish there were no such thing as frost."

"Do not murmur at the frost and snow, dear child," said Magdalen, smoothing back the eager little girl's hair; "the fire never burns so brightly as in the frosty weather: and the snow, you know, is God's mantle, under which the flowers are kept warm against the spring."

"That is one of Sister Magdalen's parables," the children whispered thoughtfully to one another.

The spring came. One of Magdalen's orphans

was betrothed to the pastor of Lohmen; she had given the children a holiday amongst the wild beautiful gorges of the Saxon Switzerland; and now she and the young betrothed stood alone on the rough bridge which connected the heights of the Bastei with those on which are the ruins of the castle of the robber knight of Thuba.

On one side of the narrow bridge they could look down into the deep hollow of the Grünbachthal, tall firs seeming like rock-plants in the crevices of the gigantic perpendicular walls of rock, and the deep green fields resting peacefully below.

But they were turning in the other direction, where, on the left, the Elbe wound beneath the heights of Königstein and Lilienstein, flattened as if for the pedestals of fortresses; and on the right, through wooded hills, to the broad plains of Dresden; whilst beyond, the setting sun glowed on the mountains which girded in Bohemia. The soft air was full of light and of the fragrance of the flowers it had opened; snowdrops and blades of grass trembled and shone in the interstices of the natural masonry.

"How glorious and wonderful all this is!" said Magdalen; "think, my child, what it will be when every city shall be a holy city, every cottage a temple of God; when the grace of God shall rest on all hearts as it now does on all nature; when the Church, from her heavenly dwelling-place, with its ever-open gates, shall minister to men as even angels never can;—helping as those help who have been tried; comforting as those comfort who have suffered!"

"Did you always love nature," asked the maiden, "as you do now?"

"I always loved her," Magdalen replied, "but I think never so much as now; the love of years of familiar kindness is stronger, my child, than the glow of early feeling. In my youth my thoughts danced like fairies in the sunbeams, often with the glancing of their bright wings hiding the deeper beauty of God's works. Now I can look and listen, and never tire of being still, and letting the beautiful pictures lie upon my heart."

"But, Sister Magdalen, you did not glide all at once into this calm?"

"No. Thirty years ago all my life was laid waste and rent asunder. It was by the grave of my only brother that I learnt the calling of the stranger traveling to the heavenly home; and the lesson has been worth the cost"

"But is there no way of learning these lessons but through suffering such as that?" asked the bethrothed bride, shuddering.

"God has a thousand ways of teaching us, my child," she answered. "He can teach by giving as well as by withholding. It is her blessedness that best keeps the bride apart—the unchangeable love of her Lord, and her waiting for Him. There is another way of reaching the power of His resurrection than through the grave of our hopes. The Lord Jesus is Himself the resurrection and the life; as in union with Him all things are ours to *possess*, so in communion with Him all things are ours to *use*. By sitting at His feet we may learn a thousand lessons, else to be taught by rougher voices. May He keep us there!"

"But Bohemia?" said the girl, as she looked towards the southern hills; "do you believe our country is lost to the gospel for ever."

"We do not know, my child, what seeds are ripening under the soil. Perhaps our old Church may yet arise with a purified heart to teach Christendom the great lesson, that with us it is not to be as amongst the Gentiles, 'for he that is great amongst you, let him be your *minister:*' it is my constant prayer."

Thus sitting at His feet, and ministering to Him in His brethren, her peaceful being shedding balm around her, her whole womanly nature developed and satisfied by the interchange of childlike dependence and motherly care, she passed on to her rest. Can any life be desolate with such companionship and such service?

Need any Christian life be without them?

"Fear not, little flock."

"The Father himself loveth you."

"For the Lord redeemeth the souls of his servants, and none of them that trust in him shall be desolate."

PART III.

THE EIGHTEENTH CENTURY.

I.

THE OLD MAN'S PROPHECY.

The Reformation, as to external establishment, was crushed in Bohemia, but the living streams were still oozing through the land, and secretly nourishing the roots of many plants of our heavenly Father's planting.

Throughout the seventeenth century we catch accidental glimpses of secret meetings, for receiving the Lord's Supper, of Christian families; of one dying without desire of extreme unction, being, he said, already anointed and sealed of the Holy Spirit, and as sure of his salvation as of the existence of the sun, yet in whose life the priest could find no fault, and in his death only occasion for the prayer that he also might die the death of the righteous. Indeed, so many of these "hidden ones" were there, that when, in 1716, Charles XII. of Sweden wrung from the emperor toleration for a stated number of Protestant churches, 70,000 were found ready to attach themselves to one of them.

One evening, in the year 1707, five young men were gathered around the deathbed of an aged Christian, a descendant in spirit, as well as by the ties of natural kindred, of the ancient Brethren of Bohemia.

These were the five Neissers, nephews of George Jœshke. The calm of death in the peace of God pervaded the room. No one spoke. A little boy stood by the bedside, his hands clasped in those of the dying man. It was the son of his old age. Jœschke was about to rest from a life of many labors—faithful preaching of gratuitous salvation—faithful living in the peace of the reconciliation of Jesus—labors which might have seemed to be worse than fruitless, for the band of the old Christians was constantly diminished by death, whilst the numbers of the compromising constantly increased. But the old man did not despair; he rested on the promises, which rise eternally above the storms. Like the Alpine hunter, through the clefts of the clouds he looked down on the world.* He conjured the young men to be faithful to the truth which had made them free.

"It is true," he said, "that our liberty is destroyed; that the greater part of our children are more and more entangled in the love of the world,

* *Vide* "Schiller's Wilhelm Tell."

and fall off to the Papacy; that, from all appearances, one might say the cause of the Brethren was lost. But, my children, a great deliverance will come for those who remain. You will see it. Whether it will take place in Moravia, or you will have to leave this Babel, I know not. I think, however, you will have to quit this ountry, in order to find a place where you may serve God according to His Word. When the hour comes, be ready. Beware of being amongst the last, or of being left entirely behind. And now, I commend to you this little one, my only child. I commend him especially to thee, Augustine Neisser. He also must belong to Jesus. Lose not sight of him, and if you leave the country take him with you."

Then, with tears, he blessed the child and his nephews, and not long after, he rested in peace.

I know not whether we should call this confidence, prophecy, or simply faith. At any rate, it was abundantly fulfilled.

II.

REBUILDING FROM THE RUINS.

It was the 15th May 1725. A company of about thirty persons were gathered in a marshy spot, on a declivity by the highroad from Loban to Zittau in Saxony.

All around them arose an uncleared forest—tall pines looking old and sombre amidst the fresh green of the budding forest trees. On a leveled space amongst the bushes they were laying the foundation of a house.

It was a strangely assorted company. A Saxon nobleman and his bride, a young Swiss baron, with their friends; and on the other side, nine or ten mechanics and peasants, with their families. But the bond which united them was far more real then the distinctions which separated them. The noblemen were the Count von Zinzendorf and the Baron de Watteville, to whom all their property and influence were as nothing, except as a trust for their Master; and the mechanics were men who had suffered imprisonment and loss of all things, and had left country and kindred for the sake of Christ and His gospel.

Amongst them were the brothers Neisser and old George Jœschke's son. The Count spoke earnestly and affectionately to those present on the object of the building they were about to erect, of the faith which had once made them exiles and provided them an asylum.

"Rather," he said, "than that this building should not tend to promote the glory of Him in whose name it was founded, might fire from heaven consume it!"

Before he began to speak, five travelers came along the highroad, way-worn, and poorly clad. They stood apart, and listened in reverent silence.

Then the Baron de Watteville drew off a ring, the last jewel he had retained, and laying it on the foundation-stone, knelt there, and prayed aloud.

The power of the Holy Ghost overwhelmed every heart as he prayed. When he ceased, the whole of the little band were in tears. And the five strangers came forward, and said—

"Surely this is the house of God: here shall our feet rest."

That house was the first in the settlement at Herrnhut. The travelers were also exiles from Moravia for the sake of the faith. They had escaped from prisons, and across mountains, by deliverances which would have seemed miraculous, were not answers to prayer the "daily bread" of the disciples. Amongst them was that David Nitschmann, who was afterwards the first missionary to the West Indian slaves, and the first bishop of the restored Church of the Brethren of Bohemia and Moravia.

III.

SEEDS BORNE BY THE WINDS.

In a room in the island of St. Thomas, in the West Indies, some years after the foundation of Herrnhut, Count Zinzendorf was awaiting the arrival of some prisoners whose release he had procured with difficulty from the tyrannical planters. When they arrived, harassed and emaciated by three months of imprisonment, he saluted them —as they used to salute the early martyrs—by reverently kissing their hands in the presence of their oppressors.

These were some of the exiles of Herrnhut, men of the old martyr-race of Bohemia.

A few days after, you might have seen the Count conducting a service amongst some hundreds of slaves, "the Lord's freedmen"—men in whom love to their Saviour, and faith in His love, were strong enough to overbalance the infliction of bodily sufferings such as we shudder to hear of.

After a prayer from one of the slaves, he was commencing his address with the words of one of his favorite hymns, when suddenly the whole assembly broke out, in their own language, into the triumphant hymn—

"My Lord, my Lord, Thou hast redeemed me?"

Accustomed as he was to uncontrollable manifestations of feeling in the Moravian assemblies, the scene entirely overpowered him.

These were some of the converts of the imprisoned missionaries.

* * * * *

On one of the Christmas holidays, about thirty years ago, amidst the snowy rocks and glittering icebergs of the north, a company of Greenlanders were gathered around the Mission-house at Lichtenfels, singing Christian hymns, and accompanying themselves with instruments.

They were too happy in the presence of their Saviour to heed the cold. "It was to them," as they afterwards said, "as if they already stood before the throne of the Lamb, singing the new song of the redeemed." And those who listened could not refrain from tears.

And within the houses grouped around them, you might have witnessed the sober and peaceful lives of Christian families, or deathbeds illumined by the "sure and certain hope" of those who depart in Christ—and all knit together in the imperishable love of Christian brotherhood. Yet not many years before, these very men had been savages, wandering from place to place, without thought of God or duty, with no social bond but the necessities of selfishness—no hope beyond the deathbed.

Patiently had the missionaries labored for this end, enduring hunger and cold, and worse trials from cold and hardened hearts; through fifteen years trusting to the promise that they should reap, when not a sign of the harvest appeared. But at length, after the long polar winter, spring and summer had burst on them as it were in a night.

These were more of the fruits of the seed which had so long been buried and trampled under the soil in Bohemia.

If there was need of "long patience," was there not reward for it?

But it would take far too long even to name the blessings which were showered on the colony of Herrnhut, and flowed from it, in those days of fresh love and life, when "the multitude of those that believed were of one heart and one soul, neither said any of them that aught of the things which they possessed was his own, but they had all things in common." We, in our "majestic sobriety," may reprehend such excesses of zeal and love; but they, in their "gladness and singleness of heart," would have been far too happy to care about our reproaches: for "with great power" did many amongst them bear witness unto the resurrection of the Lord, "and great grace was upon them all."

But one thing which happened amongst them is, unhappily, so singular in the history of religious controversies, that I can not refrain from mentioning it:—

The infant community at Herrnhut had been much disturbed by a certain controversy (I believe it was about the human nature of our Lord): there seemed danger of a violent rupture —but *they prayed together*, and read the First Epistle of St. John; and such a sense of their blessed and eternal oneness in the Lord Jesus, and such a glow of brotherly love, were diffused amongst them, that the schism was healed so perfectly as not even to leave a scar behind. All causes of division literally melted away, like a cloud or a snow-drift, in the light of Him whose manifest presence shall by and by dissolve all ice-bonds and ice-barriers amongst us for ever.

The Moravian Brethren have done little towards expanding before us new worlds of science or art—towards cutting new vistas into the depths of astronomic space, or geologic time—but who can count the souls to which they have opened that eternal kingdom where all shall know even as they are known?

They have done little for symbolic architecture and the glory of beautiful temples—but of the habitations of God which they have built through the Spirit, He only knows the glory and the number.

Their sole theology was JESUS—the eternal

Son of God, the crucified and risen Son of man, the Sacrifice, the High Priest, the Universal Bishop of His Church; the Way, the Truth, and the Life.

The foundation of their community, and their bond of fellowship, was no system of doctrines or Church government: it was "Christ Jesus the Lord"—"the same yesterday, and to-day, and for ever." For any mistakes they may have made in carrying out a church principle so catholic and so divine, our weak nature is responsible.

It is possible that, fixing their eyes too exclusively on the dying, rather than on the risen, Son of man—on the intense but finished agony, rather than on the eternal and actual joy it has purchased, dwelling on His bodily sufferings with a prolonged excitement of feeling which seems hardly scriptural; their piety may occasionally have lost itself in religious sentimentalism; but the love they bore Him was no mere barren emotion; and the crosses they bore after Him were neither self-imposed burdens nor mere devotional ornaments—and we may surely pardon —as He who is touched with the feeling of our infirmities doubtless has—the extravagances of a love which braved polar winters, and equinoctial summers, and long years of seemingly fruitless toil, for His sake.

With their failures we have nothing to do, except to warn us how unwise we all are when we abandon ourselves to any teaching but that of the Word of God—or to blend with our confessions when, as members of the one family, we say—"All we like sheep have gone astray;" but the example of their single-hearted devotion and brotherly love is ours to rejoice in, with thanksgiving for ever; and the best part of it is, that these things are existing amongst us still.

Now, whilst I write, two Moravian brethren are laboring within the infected walls of a lazar-house in Southern Africa, having deliberately suffered themselves to be immured there for life, in order to reveal to the wretched inmates "the unsearchable riches of Christ." What they are now suffering, we know not—but we do know that when they die there are others ready to fill their places.

With such a golden cloud of witnesses, linking the very air we breathe with the depths of the inmost heavens where the first Martyr rests in the light which shone on his dying eyes, who shall say that the ages of faith and love are past, and that the heart of the Church is palsied and grown chill?

Are not fresh springs of life ever gushing forth in our midst? Is not the very existence of the Church of God on earth a perpetual miracle? Is not a new creation commenced in every soul to which God says, "Let there be light?" Does not the morning glow around every awakened heart?

Is not *their* Father *our* Father? Is not the

Lord Jesus Christ the same to-day as when yesterday He said to them, "Follow thou Me," and, "My grace is sufficient for thee?" Is not the Holy Spirit still with patient love and undiminished might gathering and chiselling the living stones for the living temple? May we also go forth every morning refreshed and strengthened by draughts from the Well of Life? May not we also walk all day "in the light"—thus having fellowship one with another? May not we also lie down every evening with hearts and consciences "white and clean" as the robes of the Blessed before the throne—washed in the same "precious blood?"

And, oh, if our hearts thrill at the recital of holy deeds done ages since, must they not throb with redoubled life at the thought of such lives flowing parallel with our own day by day?

The love wherewith we are loved is as great, the arm on which we are invited to lean is as strong, the time in which we have to labor is as short, the eternity to which we are hastening—and which is hastening to us—is as long, the position in which we are placed is the very best in all the battle-field our God would choose for us. There is not a difficulty in our path which shall not be compelled to work for us, if we meet it in communion with our Lord. Are we also *overcoming?*

NEW BOOKS.

Melbourne House. By the Author of "The Wide, Wide World," etc. 2 vols. 12mo, ...

A most touching and beautiful Story, in which, through the history of a little girl, most important truths are taught in a very interesting way. With most readers, Little Daisy of Melbourne House will be as great a favorite as Ellen Montgomery of the "Wide, Wide World." This Story has all the freshness of her first work.

Ellen Montgomery's Book Shelf. By the Authors of the "Wide, Wide World," and "Dollars and Cents." 5 vols. 16mo, illustrated, in a neat box, ... 6 00

The Volumes are also sold separately, as follows:

Mr. Rutherford's Children, ... 1 20
Sybil and Chryssa, ... 1 20
Hard Maple, ... 1 20
Carl Krinken's Christmas Stocking, ... 1 20
Casper and His Friends, ... 1 20

This interesting Series of Books has long been out of print, and frequently called for. This new and handsome edition will be hailed with delight by youthful readers of various ages.

Egypt's Princes. By the Rev. G. Lansing, American Missionary at Cairo, 12mo 1 50

A most interesting book—giving life pictures of Egypt as she now is. Equally well adapted for the Sabbath School Library, or the Christian Fireside.

NEW BOOKS FOR THE YOUNG.

Sea Drifts. By Mrs. Georgie A. Hulse McLeod. 16mo, illustrated,.. 1 25

A beautiful religious Story of Boarding-school life, the scene of which is laid near Newport, R. I. It is well adapted for girls verging into womanhood, and will prove alike entertaining and instructive.

The Martyrs of Spain, and the Liberators of Holland. By the Author of "The Schönberg-Cotta Family. 16mo,.. 1 25

It has been well said, that the charm of this lady's writings consists in their truthful adherence to the spirit and customs of the olden time. We have here those qualities applied to Spain and Holland. Few religious writers are more favorably known to the reading public, than this attractive writer.

Good for Evil, and other Stories. By A. L. O. E., 0 90

A series of Short Stories by this eminently popular author, which possess all the interest of her longer stories. It has six fine illustrations.

Cortley Hall. By A. L. O. E...................... 0 90

Containing "The Straight Road the Safest and Surest," and the "Stories of Jewish History,"—the first highly entertaining, and the second very instructive.

Human Sadness. By Countess de Gasparin. 16mo, 0 90

The Countess de Gasparin's famous work, "The Near and the Heavenly Horizons," has rendered her name familiar to the lovers of good books. The present work will be found well adapted to those who are in affliction.

NEW BOOKS FOR THE YOUNG

The Book of Animals. With numerous Illustrations. Square, ... 0 90

    A very pretty book for children, plentifully illustrated, and abounding in interesting Stories.

The Child's Bunyan, or the Story of the Pilgrim's Progress told for Little Children. 18mo, ... 0 60

The Cripple of Antioch. By the author of the "Schönberg-Cotta Family." $1 25

    A fascinating narrative of Christian life near the beginning of the Christian era. A book which, when once taken in hand, is not easily laid aside till the end is reached.

The Cedar Christian, and other practical Papers. By the Rev. T. L. Cuyler. 16mo 90

    "Genial, open-hearted and fascinating in his style, both spoken and written, Mr. Cuyler has made for himself a land-wide reputation, and written his name everywhere as a household word."—*Evangelist.*

Ned's Motto ; or, Little by Little. By the author of "Win and Wear," &c. 1 25

    This may be truly reckoned among first-class books for the young. Ned is the son of a captain killed in this war, who, though a child, manfully contends against the pressure of want into which the family are brought by the sad event; encouraged by the cordial sympathy of the neighbors, and acting patiently on the motto: "Little by Little."

Mabel's Experience ; or, Seeking and Finding. 18mo 0 90

    A capital Scotch story that will delight all readers and do them good.

CARTERS' BOOKS FOR THE YOUNG.

The Straight Road the Shortest and the Surest. By A. L. O. E. 45

Paying Dear. By A. L. O. E.... .... 0 60

Esther Parsons. By A. L. O. E. 0 60

Christian Conquests. A series of Stories by A. L. O. E. 12 cuts..................................... 0 90

Try Again, and other Stories. By A. L. O. E. 12 engravings... 0 90

The Silver Casket; or, the Wiles of the World. By A. L. O. E. 8 illustrations........... 0 90

Stories of Jewish History. By A. L. O. E. 0 60

The Bags of Gold, and other Stories. By A. L. O. E. 6 cuts................................ 0 60

Falsely Accused, and other Stories. By A. L. O. E. 6 cuts................................ 0 60

The Sale of Crummie, and other Stories... 0 90

Maud Summers, the Sightless. 4 illus. 0 90

The Three Cripples. By the Rev. P. B. Power. 0 75

The Last Shilling. By the Rev. P. B. Power. 0 75

The Two Brothers and the Two Paths. By the Rev. P. B. Power... 0 75

CARTERS' BOOKS FOR THE YOUNG.

The Diamond Brooch, and other
Stories.. 0 60

The Buried Bible and other Stories. 0 60

Faithful and True. By the author of "Win and Wear," "Tony Starr's Legacy," etc. 16mo. 3 illus. 1 25

    A well-told story of Life on the Green Mountains—full of action and interest—fresh, and with an excellent moral to it. The main object of the book is to teach the importance of being "faithful and true," especially in the little things of every-day life.

The Safe Compass and how it
Points. By the Rev. Richard Newton, D.D. 6 illus.... 1 25

    Dr. Newton is one of the very best writers of juvenile religious literature in the land. He seems to have an inexhaustible fund of unexceptionable stories and illustrations, and knows just how and when to use them.

Claude, the Colporteur. By the author of "Mary Powell," etc. 16mo. 8 engravings............. 1 25

    A graphically told story of youthful labors, trials, and successes. It is a book that will be devoured with eagerness by the young reader.

The Post of Honor. A Story by the author of "Broad Shadows on Life's Pathway." 16mo............ 1 25

    A well-told story of Missionary Life, suffering and triumph—all founded on fact.

The Jewish Tabernacle and its Fur-
niture. By the Rev. Richard Newton, D.D. Illus...... 1 75

The Old Helmet. A tale by the author of "The Wide, Wide World." 2 vols.......................... $3 50

BOOKS FOR THE YOUNG,

PUBLISHED BY

ROBERT CARTER & BROS.,

530 BROADWAY, NEW YORK.

First Series, 90 cents each.

The Claremont Tales. By A. L. O. E......

Each tale illustrates one of the beatitudes, "Blessed are the poor in spirit," "Blessed are the meek," &c. These tales, while thus explaining and enforcing special Scripture truths, are ingeniously woven together, so as to give a connected and interesting story of Mrs. Claremont's children.

The Adopted Son, and other Tales. By A. L. O. E.....................

Three stories by this gifted lady—the first one shows what true bravery is; the second one, in a very attractive way, illustrates the Lord's Prayer; while the last one shows the advantages of industry and perseverance.

The Young Pilgrim. By A. L. O. E. 18mo.

The story of a boy, the reputed son of profligate parents, living in a family of professional beggars, but who turns out to be an earl's son, and finally succeeds to his title and estate. The conversion of this boy in the days of his humiliation, and his steadfastness to the truth after rising to sudden and enormous wealth, are well depicted.

The Giant Killer and Sequel. By A. L. O. E. 18mo......................

A tale of real life varied by a curious and successful mixture of allegory. The incidents of the story are those of a family living in a beautiful country home, the chapters of the allegory being read to them day by day, by the mother, with a view to the correction of their faults, such as sloth, selfishness, untruth, hate and pride.

CARTERS' BOOKS FOR THE YOUNG.

Flora ; or, Self-deception. By A. L. O. E.

A story of a young lady who was a member of the Church, and engaged in various active duties of benevolence, such as teaching in the Sabbath-school, visiting the sick, and the like, but who found, after the more serious duties of life began to crowd upon her, that she had deceived herself, and that she was only a formalist. A book for the older girls.

The Needle and the Rat. By A. L. O. E.

The Needle tells its own history, both how it was made and into whose hands it fell, embodying many pictures of life that are full of instruction—while the Rat's adventures are such as will interest all the children and do them good.

Eddie Ellerslie, and the Mine. By A. L. O. E. 18mo..

An admirable little book for young persons, in which truth is conveyed to the mind allegorically and in a very attractive and fascinating manner. The fair authoress has kept in view the motto, that "truth, like medicine, must be adapted to the weak and infantine."

Precepts in Practice. By A. L. O. E. 18mo.

Here are sixteen stories, every one based on some text in Proverbs, and presenting a clear exhibition of a great practical truth. Much skill is shown in developing in an easy and pleasant way, attractive to the young, great principles for the conduct of the life. If we may judge of it from our own impressions, this book will take hold of the reader's feelings, and excite more than common interest in these short and simple tales.

Idols in the Heart: a Tale. By A. L. O. E.

The story of a gay worldly family, living in wealth and fashion. The mother is dead. Into this family the father introduces a young wife and step-mother, who is a quiet but earnest Christian, and the chief drift of the story is to show how her religious character made itself felt in these circumstances.

Pride and his Prisoners. By A. L. O. E.

A story of social life, introducing a great variety of characters and incidents, the main object of all being to illustrate the different kinds of pride and the manner of deliverance from it.

The Christian's Mirror. By A. L. O. E.

Philias, a young minister—pastor of a large city church—falls asleep one Sabbath evening, after a hard day's service, and in his dream visits a great variety of different characters; while in his disembodied state he has access to them as he could not have otherwise. Thus their most hidden thoughts and motives are laid open, and thus, too, he is enabled to speak to them with a plainness which in other circumstances would not be endured.

The Shepherd of Bethlehem, King of Israel. By A. L. O. E.............

A poor curate, having received a fall and broken his leg, was confined for some weeks in humble lodgings. Being greatly disturbed by the noisy children of the house and neighborhood, instead of scolding and railing at them, he managed to allure them into his apartment and entertained them with stories of King David. The life and adventure of the Shepherd King of Israel are skillfully intermingled with the history of these children and neighbors, so as to make a story of remarkable interest.

The Poacher. By A. L. O. E.............

Two stories, one of a cripple, who, like most persons in his condition, was irritable, peevish and ill-natured, but who, under the teachings of the Spirit, became a living example of "love, joy, peace," &c.; and the other, the story of a young man who had been stolen in his infancy by an enemy of his father's, and bred to thieving and other wicked practices, but by a singular train of circumstances his parentage is discovered, and he is reclaimed to a virtuous and religious life.

The Lost Jewel. By A. L. O. E.............

A diamond of immense value, belonging to an English nobleman, is lost by his daughter while attending a ball, and passes through the hands of many persons who are ignorant of its value, each of whom parts with it for some trifling gratification. The object of the story is to teach that each of us is intrusted with a jewel far more precious than this glittering diamond, and that we are bartering our jewel, *the soul,* for the most trifling baubles.

Stories on the Parables. By A. L. O. E.

A series of twelve stories, each one illustrating one of our Lord's parables. They are written in the author's attractive style, and convey many important lessons of Scriptural truth.

CARTERS' BOOKS FOR THE YOUNG.

The Chief's Daughter. By A. L. O. E. ....

This little book also consists of two stories, the first one being a thrilling account of the first introduction of Christianity into Great Britain, and the second delineates the occupations and amusements of a little family of children during the absence of their mother.

Ned Manton. By A. L. O. E. ....

Two stories. The one shows the necessity of building our Christian profession on the true foundation, while the other illustrates in a pleasing light the Christian virtue of feeling for others.

War and Peace : a Story of the

Retreat from Cabul. By A. L. O. E.....................
This is an admirable story, founded on fact. It details the horrors of a winter's retreat over snow and ice of a small band of British soldiers, in which, though they were exposed to great privation and suffering, some of their number were yet enabled to experience that peace "that passeth understanding."

The Robbers' Cave: a Story of

Italy. By A. L. O. E. ....

The Crown of Success ; or, Four

Heads to Furnish. By A. L. O. E. ....
A sort of story allegory illustrative of the Child's studies, their difficulties and encouragements, in which Mr. Alphabet—the Ladder of Spelling—Grammar's Bazaar—the Carpet of History, and Mr. Chemistry play a conspicuous part.

The Rebel Reclaimed : a Tale. By

A. L. O. E. ....

Anna ; or, Passages from the Life

of a Daughter at Home......................
A story of a young lady, a professing Christian, whose religion was rather of a sentimental sort, always wishing to do some great good, but shrinking from the common duties that lay in her path. Through the influence of a cousin, she came to understand this matter better, gave up her self-indulgent habit, and became an active, useful Christian.

CARTERS' BOOKS FOR THE YOUNG.

Aunt Edith; or, Love to God the
Best Motive..

Aunt Edith is a maiden lady in Scotland of great excellence of character, to whom is providentially committed the training of two orphan families, one being that of a deceased sister, and the other that of a brother in India, who has lost his wife. The training of these families in truth and righteousness, obedience and kindness, order and neatness, is the staple of the book, which is wrought up with a great variety of pleasing incidents.

Mabel Grant: a Highland Story.
By Randall Ballantyne..................................

Life of Captain Bate. By the Rev. John Baillie...

The British army has given us such Christian heroes as Hedley Vicars and Havelock. These pages show how a *sailor* as well as soldier, can unite to personal valor the meek and quiet spirit of a disciple of Christ. Captain Bate fell in a forlorn hope at the storming of Canton in 1858. His journal shows that, amid the duties of his profession, he never forgot that he was a soldier of the Cross.

Life of St. Augustine. By the Rev. John Baillie..

The faith and patience of Monica, the mother of Augustine; the events of his wayward youth; the way in which the Lord led him, and the childlike beauty of his piety when converted, give to this little memoir a charm that will make it both popular and useful.

The Black Ship, and other Allegories and Parables...........................

This is an exquisitely beautiful little book. Its tales and parables are constructed with marvellous delicacy and skill—they are full of subtle and delicious fancy—they are rich in every line with deep and precious meaning.

Blind Lilias; or, Fellowship with God..

This is a simple but beautiful story of sanctified affliction. Little Lilias, with all the quick fancy and waywardness of the child, impressible, impulsive, and affectionate, becomes blind, and under this severe chastening her heart is prepared to receive the truth as it is in Jesus.

Blind Man's Holiday. A Series of Short
Stories. By the Author of "Sidney Grey."..............
  These stories are intended by the author to be read aloud to children of from six to eight years old, and are, therefore, written in language suited to their understanding, and devoted to subjects most likely to enlist their attention.

Blossoms of Childhood. By the Author
of the "Broken Bud."..............................

The Indian Tribes of Guiana.
By the Rev. W. H. Brett. Illustrated.................

Broad Shadows on Life's Path-
way: a Tale. By the Author of "Doing and Suffering," &c.
  Lucy, the heroine, is an English girl whose married life is passed in India, who there becomes a widow, and while yet a recent mourner, is overwhelmed by the horrors of the mutiny of 1857. Aided by a faithful servant, she escapes with life, though robbed of her beautiful babe under circumstances that lead her to believe in its murder. Returning to England, she devotes herself to benevolent enterprises, especially to the aid of the dressmakers of London, to whose peculiar temptations and perils a large part of the work is devoted. The book is truthful, delicate, and by no means morbid, and ends with the dispersion of the shadows and the happy restoration of the missing boy.

Brother and Sister; or, the Way
of Peace..

The Brother's Watchword............
  A story of a girl whose parents were dead, and who was left to the guidance of a brother, a clergyman, much older than herself. Through the influence of his wise counsels she escaped the snares of fashionable life which beset her, and became a decided and useful Christian in the midst of gay, worldly companions.

Bunyan's Pilgrim's Progress. 18mo.

CARTERS' BOOKS FOR THE YOUNG.

Clara Stanley; or, A Summer
among the Hills..........................

Little Crowns, and How to Win
Them. By the Rev. Jos. A. Collier ....
 This is a gem of a book. It is a series of familiar and well-conceived addresses to young readers on interesting stories from Bible history These discourses are not only instructive, but fascinating.

The Cottage and its Visitor. By the
Author of "Ministering Children."..................
 This little volume is intended especially to encourage and assist such as desire to benefit the poor but lack experience. It is mostly narrative, and has all the charm of the author's "Ministering Children."

Day-break; or, Truth Strug-
gling and Triumphant ....
 Little Maud Temperly has a bad temper to manage. She has many temptations, and at first but little help. Finally, through the instrumentality of a pious young lady who loves children, and is ever trying to do them good, she becomes a Christian. Thenceforth, "Right," which is still "struggling," is nevertheless "triumphant."

Days at Muirhead; or, How Little
Olive spent her Midsummer Holidays....................
 A story of a little girl, the daughter of a Liverpool clergyman, who went to spend her summer vacation with an uncle, also a clergyman, in a village in Scotland. The book gives the incidents of her midsummer holidays. It is a description of child life, as it may be supposed to exist in the family of a devout Scotch minister.

Days of Old. By the Author of "Ruth and Her
Friends..
 Three beautiful stories, illustrating the condition of Christianity in Great Britain in early times. The first story, "Wulfgar and the Earl," belongs to the time of Alfred the Great. The second, "Caradoc and Deva," belongs to the time of the Roman Conquest. The third, "Roland," is a tale of the Crusades.

www.ingramcontent.com/pod-product-compliance
Lightning Source LLC
Chambersburg PA
CBHW031418230426
43668CB00007B/352